Mass Media
in Greece

Mass Media in Greece

Power, Politics,
and Privatization

Thimios Zaharopoulos
and
Manny E. Paraschos

PRAEGER

Westport, Connecticut
London

Library of Congress Cataloging-in-Publication Data

Zaharopoulos, Thimios.
    Mass media in Greece : power, politics, and privatization /
Thimios Zaharopoulos and Manny E. Paraschos.
        p.   cm.
    Includes bibliographical references and index.
    ISBN 0-275-94106-X (alk. paper)
    1. Mass media—Greece.   I. Paraschos, Manny.   II. Title.
P92.G75Z34   1993
302.23'09495—dc20   92-18839

British Library Cataloguing in Publication Data is available.

Library of Congress Catalog Card Number: 92-18839
ISBN: 0-275-94106-X

First published in 1993

Praeger Publishers, 88 Post Road West, Westport, CT 06881
An imprint of Greenwood Publishing Group, Inc.

Printed in the United States of America

The paper used in this book complies with the
Permanent Paper Standard issued by the National
Information Standards Organization (Z39.48-1984).

10 9 8 7 6 5 4 3 2 1

This book is dedicated to

Angeliki and Dimitrios Zaharopoulos
for all their sacrifices

and

Janet, Sophia, and Alexi Paraschos
for their patience and understanding

Contents

Illustrations

TABLES

PHOTOS

Foreword

Today we see momentous changes in the world. Boundaries, allegiances, and political systems are in a state of unprecedented flux. Enemies have become allies; neighbors are now enemies. But in all this there is one thing that remained constant: a need to know —to know other cultures, other countries, other governments.

And the main institutionalized method of giving us such knowledge is the press—or the media systems of the world. We know that the quality of these media systems is uneven, that some are far more objective and thorough than others. But in even the best of circumstances we have gaps in our knowledge. The shift of focus of world attention has often confronted us with our own ignorance about a part of the world we thought we knew.

Students of the international press today are faced with a multitude of persistent and underlying questions that serve as a barrier to understanding. Not only are nations in disarray and even turmoil, and with them their media systems, but even in the rather stable nations are found basic issues and problems that cry out for explanation for the person seeking a real understanding of media.

Those of us hoping to plumb the essence of a national media system are concerned with fundamental questions: What are the philosophical traditions and underpinnings of the media system? What has been the media-government symbiosis of the country? What has been the effect of personalities (media leaders) on the media? How has public opinion affected the media—or has there been any real concern with public opinion? How has the dominant governmental philosophy or ideology impacted the media system? How has education—or, specifically journalism education—influenced the state of the media?

The above are but a few of the basic questions a student of the global media would like to have answered. Probably even more important are the crucial questions of press freedom and the concept of press responsibility to society prevailing in a country. Basic descriptive and statistical data are needed, to be sure, but the media student hopes to go beyond these ever-changing facts and to grapple with the more amorphous issues and concepts that significantly shape the outward appearance of the media system.

A constant need exists to increase information about countries whose past, present, and future are significant. We cannot really expect to keep up, but we are obligated to take advantage of good information, well-presented. How do we check the credibility of the information we get? Basically, we need to know something about the media system that provides it. And the only way to do this is to have the very best evaluation of a media system that we can obtain. Generally, we know little or nothing about the world media systems; and it is fortunate that there are scholars who are willing to do the hard work and insightful thinking required to give us the basic information and means of evaluation.

International interest in the media caught on back in the 1950s and 1960s with broad surveys of the world press, somewhat useful, but far too brief and superficial to be of much value so far as depth analysis is concerned. Then there came some regional media books, dealing with the press in such places as Latin America and the Middle East. These were followed, and in some cases simultaneously produced, by media studies of individual countries. Not many such books are as yet available, but slowly they are being published, supplementing the scattered data found in various academic journals.

Now, at long last, we have a study of the media in Greece. Thimios Zaharopoulos and Manny Paraschos have provided us in the following pages the fascinating story of the Hellenic press from its beginnings to its shaky present, leading into an uncertain future. This is not a happy story. In fact, it is the story of what can happen to a nation's media system if the progressive spirit and love of high standards are lost. It is also the story of a partisan press that is

concerned only with short-term political ends.

It is an especially interesting story for students of the world press for it shows that, because of the quirks of history and the inclinations of the nation's political elite, even a nation with an illustrious history and a rich cultural foundation can find its press system manifesting all the weaknesses normally found in the new, developing nations seeking a national identity since World War II.

Greece missed out on the Renaissance-inspired intellectual revolution in Europe. The spirit of freedom, the challenge of old ideas and conventions, the questioning of traditional governmental institutions, and the general intellectual restlessness that pervaded most of Europe into the nineteenth century held little interest for the Greeks. They were more concerned with parochial matters, many stemming from their unhappy sojourn in the alien world of the Ottoman Empire. Partisan politics held sway in Hellas, and short-sighted concerns of a nationalistic nature dominated the more intellectual and socially significant manifestations, muting them for a very long time.

A socially vibrant and progressive Greek press philosophy was stymied at the time that British and French journalism, for instance were developing a social conscience and a critical spirit which promised much-needed governmental change. Here were the Greeks, people with intellectual traditions that should have prepared them to be dominant among Renaissance Europeans, letting the winds of change pass them by as they wrestled with serious educational, economic, and political problems.

Such ideas as the importance of the masses, of public opinion, of pluralism of viewpoints, and the whole notion of the massification of communication—all of which led many Western European nations and America into the nineteenth century—were lost on Greece. The Hellenic concern with breaking the bonds of Ottoman influence, and with factional and other petty internal politics, provided Greece's leadership little time or inclination to deal with such issues as individual rights and intellectual freedom that were bounding about the continent.

Moderate and quality newspapers had rough-going in nineteenth century Greece; partisan and flamboyant papers garnered almost total audience attention. These newspapers set the stage during this critical period for the twentieth century press to follow; and the raucous, propagandistic organs that were generated then have left their mark on the modern-day Greek press. The media managers and the politicians had forged tight alliances, and the concept of objective, non-partisan news media was virtually unknown.

As the authors of *Mass Media in Greece* dramatically report, the Greek press had—and has—a negative societal impact on the life of the people, actually leading to a stultifying intellectual climate. The Cradle of Western Civilization had become almost impotent as a vital force for progress and innovative ideas, and this impotence was reflected in the country's press. It is true, of course, that such a situation exists today in many countries, but mainly they are "new countries" without the ancient cultural underpinnings of Greece.

Professors Zaharopoulos and Paraschos have provided the reader a balanced and insightful view of the Greek press, its history and current status. There are not too many bright spots in this view. In fact, the authors give considerable attention to the shadows that have engulfed Hellenic media development. They make it quite clear that the Greek media have not managed to play a constructive role in the nation's history—and especially has this been true in the post-World War II life of the country. My reading of the book even suggests that the role of the press there has been a retrogressive one. With a certain sadness the authors expose a lack of standards, consistency, style, and verification methods that contribute to a shallowness—even hollowness—of the Greek press. And this, coupled with the blind, unchecked, and cruel partisanship that guides most of the media, does little to make Greek journalism a role-model for any nation.

The authors talk of a "crisis" in Greek media. Old ideological foundations are changing, but have not really been replaced by new ones. Greeks seem to recognize, as the authors put it, that their social environment is "rotten," their political leaders are "dinosaurs," and their general media situation is "anarchical."

Not everything about the Greek press is bad, of course. The authors point to a few media personalities of high quality with professional standards, and to a few "relatively moderate" papers like *Eleftherotypia, Ta Nea, Kathimerini,* and *To Vima,* and to some electronic media capable of strengthening democratic institutions. But these are seen as exceptions and are not able to pull the Greek press out of its doldrums.

The authors, especially in the concluding chapter of this book, have done a real service for the reader by dealing with basic problems of the Greek press, explaining the many contradictions of Greek journalism, and highlighting what they see as the weak ethical base of the media system. Many readers will certainly find this the most interesting part of the book. It should be noted that one of the chief criticisms of the Hellenic press is that it has a patronizing attitude and a lack of respect for consumer. How often we in the United States hear this about our own press! The authors also point to the low esteem and credibility of the Greek press. Ditto for the U.S. press?

A partisan and polemic press always leads to a lack of confidence in the total information flow within a country. Add to this a kind of splashy superficiality, and credibility lessens even more. Unfortunately, the Greek press has found itself projecting such an image to its audiences for a very long time.

We should not be too hard on the Greek press, however, for the serious observer of the world press generally will find contradictions in the news columns, discrepancies in reporting among news agencies, slantings, exaggerations and exclusions, and opinion in news columns—and in editorials—that is shallow and uninformed. In one sense the Greek press is but a microcosm of the global media system.

The media picture in Greece is, like the media system of the world, rather dismal. But for Greece, as for the world, there is hope. For there is, in the midst of this desert of journalistic mediocrity prevailing almost everywhere, a small group of media that strives to rise above the hodgepodge journalistic formula. There are some few serious newspapers and broadcast units whose standards of editorial practice are conditioned more by an intellectual orientation and an idealistic vision than by a desire for partisan success or impressive profits.

What Greece obviously needs, and what every country needs, are more serious, public-spirited media which minimize gossip and other trivialities, and attempt to provide the citizenry a well-balanced diet of helpful, meaningful, and trustworthy information and interpretation.

I like what the French writer, Albert Camus, had to say about the characteristics of a socially sound and qualitative press system. He saw most newspapers as being too partisan, too popularized, insincere, unconcerned, and careless with the truth. He saw the press generally as being too self-centered, too careless with the truth, and seeking to please certain constituencies rather than to enlighten the whole audience.

Camus believed the task of a good journalist—a good press system—is to be a reliable historian, and to provide substantial news and insightful commentary and interpretation. Camus recommended that responsible press units make some sacrifices in profits and in readership in order to provide reflection and the scrupulous reporting necessary to keep high-level journalistic standards. A kind of virtuous journalism: that's what Camus demanded. And what did he mean by "virtue" as applied to journalism? Answer: Conciseness of expression, a feeling for form, a nonrigidity in style, incisive interpretation and piercing wit. Add to this a dedication to the truth, a love of authenticity, a great respect for freedom, and a willingness to accept responsibility for ones' actions.

From what the authors of *Mass Media in Greece* say about that media system in the following pages, perhaps Camus' formula, or one similar, would be helpful in salvaging what has become a very socially ineffective enterprise. There is the temptation to blame media deficiencies on the media managers of a country. Certainly they deserve much of the blame. But perhaps the audiences of the media, the consumers, should shoulder their responsibility for the kind of journalism they get.

A very important aspect of this book on the Greek media is the attention, especially in the conclusion, given to the media consumer. This is refreshing, for such an audience-acknowledgment is largely overlooked in journalism literature, especially in U.S.-published books dealing with media systems of other nations. What many of us would like to know is the extent to which the audiences have an impact on media performance, quality, and content. We often hear about media impact on audience members; perhaps we should know more about audience impact on media.

We are told that the press largely reflects the society in which it operates, and that it impacts the citizens' concerns and intellectual level. The press it is said, is an extension of the public it serves. This is obviously true to some extent, but should we not wonder if there are not public interests and concerns which are not reflected adequately in the press? Why cannot the public serve as "agenda-setters" for the press instead of the other way around? Perhaps journalism literature in the next decade will deal with this question.

The pages of this book that follow indicate that the Greek people have had little or no significant impact on their media. And this could be seen as meaning that Greeks deserve the kind of press they have had. But perhaps this is too harsh, for it is clear that in many nations the people actually do little to change the media, and generally accept the fare they are given. Acceptance, however, is not necessarily approval, and it may be worthwhile to devise new stratagems for public impact on the press.

Greek media, as the authors indicate, are at a crossroads today. Will the media remain stagnant, reflecting a stagnant society, or will they change to become a more progressive force in Greek society? The answer to these questions will not be given just by the press— but in a real sense, it must be provided by the Greek people themselves.

John C. Merrill
Emeritus Professor of Journalism,
University of Missouri-Columbia

Acknowledgments

For us this book represents "a dream come true." We have watched for more than twenty years from afar, but with great interest and love, the plight of the profession in our mother country. We have painstakingly gathered data from the dangerous time of the colonels to the exciting time of "allaghi." We have witnessed breakthroughs, innovations and professional disasters. And now we have the luxury to weave all these pieces of information into a book. It is a rare opportunity and we're honored to share in it. We only hope that the reader sees the positive as well as the negative aspects of what follows with the same sense that we do—that of hope for a better tomorrow.

Each of us would like to thank many people who had a hand in the completion of this book:

I would like to thank my wife Julia L. Crain for her understanding and help in editing much of this book; my sister Vaso Zaharopoulou-Yannakopoulou for helping me collect much of the information that went into this book; and my chair and colleagues in the Department of Communication at Pittsburg State University, especially Professor John Frair. Other people who helped me with this project include Shirley Purdy, Patricia Searle, Brian Webster, and Joe Wells.

Thimios Zaharopoulos
Pittsburg, Kansas, USA

I would like to thank my wife Janet Nyberg for her unparalleled knowledge of manuscript editing, her imaginative suggestions and endless encouragement; also my brother Akis Paraschos for his legal expertise and assistance in the law portion of the book. Finally, a simple but heartfelt "thank you" to my Greek journalist friends, who over the years served as my links with the profession and sources of inspiration, frustration, or depression.

Manny Paraschos
Maastricht, The Netherlands

Mass Media
in Greece

Introduction

Greece and Modern Greek Society

GREEK SOCIETY AND THE MASS MEDIA

Greece today finds itself in a critical transitional stage. It is attempting to move from a traditional, developing society to a more Western oriented, modern society. For most of the twentieth century, through changes in government, political allegiances, and orientation, Greece has tried to find a new role for itself—a role that would position the country differently within the European Community and among its Balkan and other Mediterranean neighbors. In addition, it has tried to find a role worthy of the Greek people's talents, one that goes beyond the country's traditional, but increasingly inadequate, identity as the birthplace of Western civilization.

This search has been affected by three elements directly related to Greece's geopolitical position—its domination by the interests of the Western nations as they emerged victorious after World War II, its membership in the European Community, and its role as an outlet to the Middle Eastern world and to Africa.

Greece has had a love/hate relationship with the United States since the days of the Truman Doctrine. During this period, the Greeks' initial affection for the United States was replaced by mistrust, as the political needs of the United States began to govern Greek foreign policy; the Greeks' attitude eventually became hostile, as they blamed the United States for its toleration, if not tacit support, of the colonels' 1967-1974 dictatorship, and for the continued lack of a solution to the Cyprus problem.

The European Community, through formal and informal pressures, has been trying to pull Greece into a development level comparable to that of the majority of the Community's members. In spite of efforts by a variety of conservative, liberal, and even bipartisan governmental structures, the results to date have been largely disappointing. So far the performance of neither the government nor the business sector is within the acceptable parameters of the EC.

Greece's role as a liaison to the Middle East has been a two-edged sword. Its importance as a NATO ally and trade conduit has increased, but the arrival of unchecked wealth from the Middle East or from Western institutions seeking to do business in the Middle East has upset the equilibrium of Greek society, and although it has made many people rich, it has made many more poor.

In the process, however, pushed or pulled, Greece has been able to take the first, crucial step toward that new role for which it has been searching—it has identified the reasons behind its lack of "modernization" and learned what it needs to do to join the majority of Western European nations and reach their standard of living. What Greece seems to be facing today and has been unable to do is to take the second step of this effort—it has not yet implemented the necessary changes.

In order to understand how Greece came to where it is today and why it is moving at the current speed toward its desired place in a "modern" world, one needs to understand the Greek institutions, especially those that affect the public focus and morale, such as the media. This book hopes to serve that purpose.

Unfortunately along this historical roller coaster ride, the Greek media have not played a catalytic role in the advancement of Greek society. Traditionally, the media's raison d'etre has been partisan goal advancement. Because the strategies of the Greek political environment have not changed much over the years, because of their partisanship, the Greek media always have had short-term and short-sighted goals. Routinely, they have been held hostage to personalities and practices that in Greece become updated and replenished with perilous irregularity. The continued polarization of

Greek society, the numerous elections held in the last few years, the seemingly unchanging set of political personalities, the financial instability of the country, and the recurring political and financial scandals are symptoms of a condition that would have been the natural and unanimous target of an uncontaminated media system. Not in Greece, however.

The chapters that follow will analyze the nature of Greek society and the role the media system has played in its evolution. In this way, the reader will have a better grasp of the dynamics that historically have woven the fabric of daily life in Greece and the institutions that have shaped its identity and eventually set its course.

THE DEVELOPMENT OF GREEK SOCIETY

Greece rests at the southeastern tip of Europe. It has an area of 131,944 kilometers and a population of about 10 million people, 3.5 million of whom reside in Athens, while the rest is scattered in smaller cities and towns, in over 2,000 villages, and on hundreds of islands. The sea and Greece's rugged terrain have played equally important roles in the lives of the Greek people since ancient times.

The history of the modern Greek state starts on March 25, 1821, when the banner of revolution was raised at a monastery in Peloponnesos, symbolizing the beginning of the struggle for independence from the Ottoman Empire. Most Western nations supported the Greek independence movement, and committees were set up everywhere to help the Greek people (Clogg, 1979, p. 54). Among the numerous contributions of foreigners and Greeks from the diaspora was the promotion of Greek independence through the press. Much of this work took place outside Greece, but some, like Lord Byron, went to Greece to fight for Greek independence by introducing letters and journalism inside the country.

The idea of the revolution itself was also imported from the diaspora. It was based on the desire for a new Hellenic state that would be a great successor to ancient Hellas. But when the War of Independence began, the majority of the people believed they were fighting as much for their Christian faith as for political freedom or the notion of a glorious new Greece (Frazee, 1977). This was the first sign of the schism between two approaches towards Greek modernization that would play a vital role throughout Greek societal development. One of these approaches was imported and Western oriented, while the other was local, centered around Greek culture as it has evolved through classical Greece, Christianity, and the Ottoman Empire. The Greek press has reflected this schism and has often played an advocacy role on one side of this debate or the other.

The main contradiction in the identity of Greece and its people is rooted in the perception of Greece as the birthplace of Western civilization and, simultaneously, as the representative of Eastern influence within the Byzantium. For example, P. J. Vatikiotis (1974, p. 1) defines Greece in a series of contradictions:

> Greece is a European country but it comprises a society that in perceptions, values, and social and cultural attitudes remains essentially Near Eastern and Ottoman. Yet it is not Muslim or Turkish. Nor it is Western, . . . it is a Balkan country, but not Slavic. . . . There are and have been many individual Greek democrats yet the country has hardly experienced any lengthy periods of political democracy. Similarly, there are many rich Greeks, but there is no great national wealth. . . . The Church . . . has on the whole commanded the loyalty of most Greeks. Yet there are few Greeks who are really devout Christians.

The Christian Orthodox faith became part of what came to be Greek culture and society. Even today, under the Constitution of 1975, there is no separation of church and state. Other strong characteristics of Greek culture include its **oral tradition, competition, patron-client relationships**, and **language**. All of these have greatly influenced the development of Greek society.

The modern Greek language is a strong identifier of Greek culture. However, by the time of the War of Independence, a gap had developed between the spoken (*demotiké*) and written (ancient *koiné*) language. As a true reflection of the aforementioned schism, Adamantios Korais, a revolutionary hero and Greek scholar from the diaspora, saw a way to unify the two and bring back the glory of ancient Greece. He developed *katharevousa* (pure), a synthetic language that was adopted as the official language of Greece. This eventually created the problem of diglossia, as two branches of the same language competed for recognition. Katharevousa was favored by the upper classes and the educated, while demotiké, a more analytic language, was spoken by the lower classes and the rural population.

However, in 1976 demotiké was declared the language of instruction (Voros 1978, p. 8). This not only provided a solution to a great social problem, but can also be seen as a reaction to the oppression of the right-wing military dictatorship (1967-1974) and its insistence on abolishing demotiké. While the press was first to adopt demotiké, even before 1976, language in Greece can still be recognized as a form of political identification.

Another element of Greek culture, clearly reminiscent of ancient Greece, is the oral tradition. D. Holden (1972) suggests that for the Greeks the substance of conversation (*kouvenda*) is less important than the style, as it is the process, not the achievement, of kouvenda that counts. Much of the public conversation takes place in the coffee shop, or *cafeneion.* The cafeneion is where men come to talk and transact business. They also come to read a newspaper or watch television, and then talk about its content (Zaharopoulos, 1985, p. 115).

Competition among the Greeks is a cultural characteristic directly flowing out of people's struggle for survival in an environment that is characterized by limited natural resources and rugged terrain. The resulting habit of internal conflict has often invited the intervention of outside powers. For example, not long after the War of Independence began, the Greeks were at odds with each other and only the intervention of Britain, France, and Russia kept the war from being won by the Ottoman Empire. The Great Powers imposed a foreign king on the Greeks to stabilize the young nation, and when this Bavarian king did not succeed, they imposed a Danish king.

The importation of political systems, such as royalty and a parliament, was accompanied by the importation of assorted cultural values. N. Mouzelis (1978, p. 140) states:

> The large-scale adoption of western institutions and civilization during and after the revolution of 1821 unavoidably clashed with a pre-existing institutional setting characterized by a pre-capitalist, underdeveloped economy, a patrimonial structure of political controls, and the anti-enlightenment, anti-western ideology of the Christian Orthodox Church.

But the drive to find a new golden age of Greece facilitated the "pushing aside of the endogenous culture." Mouzelis suggests that this culture "was seen as the shameful bastardized heritage of four centuries of Ottoman yoke. It was easy, therefore, to attack it and replace it, by another cultural tradition which, although dead, was really Greek" (p. 146).

The drive toward modernization started as soon as the new nation had secure borders. In 1833 there were 750,000 Greeks living within its borders, while more than a million others were still under Ottoman rule (Clogg, 1979, p. 70). From 1833 to 1837 Greece acquired a new administrative geography, a new legal system modelled after others in Europe, and founded the University of Athens.

From 1837 to 1864 Greece experienced the first example of army involvement in politics, the appearance of a new ambition, to recapture Constantinople, another intervention by Britain, and a new constitution allowing greater freedom of expression. At the end of the 1860s the population had risen to 1.1 million, mainly through expansion and through immigration to Greece. During this period and the years that followed, the Greek press, headed by 13 Athenian newspapers, was free but partisan, used by politicians to champion their views (Clogg, 1979, p. 80).

From 1864 until 1897 many positive developments took place, thanks to Charilaos Trikoupis. This prime minister helped develop a stronger economy, more railroad and telegraph lines, and an increase in the merchant marine fleet. He also strengthened educational requirements, built up the armed forces, and built the Corinth Canal. However, intermittent governments altered many of these accomplishments. In these critical times, journalists exercised heavy influence, so much so that eleven ministers and six prime ministers came from their ranks (Olson, 1966, p. 225).

Following an unsuccessful war with Turkey in 1897, Greece was forced to pay reparations. This, along with a fall in the world price of currants, then Greece's biggest export, brought bankruptcy to the country, which resulted in outside control of its economy. It also began a massive emigration from Greece. From 1890 to 1914, 350,000 Greeks emigrated, mostly to the United States (Clogg, 1979, p. 93).

Part of the problem was that the political modernization that took place in the nineteenth century was not followed by economic modernization or industrialization. As such, "Greece did not establish modern ideologies and organizations" (Legg, 1977, p. 285). This was also the root for the continued presence of two prominent features of modern Greece: patron-client relations among individuals, and foreign involvement in Greek affairs. According to K. R. Legg (p. 285), "patron-client relations flourish in environments perceived as hostile and threatening. . . . This insecurity reduces individual concern to the family and its survival."

Although scarce natural resources contributed to inner-family strength, they also fueled strong competition among families. This competition has taught the Greeks to distrust all those outside their particular in-groups. As J. K. Campbell (1964) indicates, families see their interests in opposition to those of other families. Furthermore, this competition extends to the realm of social prestige, and one method of achieving this is through social mobility; thus Greeks emphasize education and white-collar employment.

Patron-client relationships have also been one way of achieving social mobility. Although such relationships have existed since the Ottoman occupation, political modernization in the nineteenth century has enhanced political clientism. Legg (1977) states that the "government provided the single channel for mobility and the only source of income other than land" (p. 285). Individuals within various institutions maintained clients and thus kept their power bases, which included influence over segments of the press. Thus, the press always had an important role in the competition among various groups, and its partisan identifications were a natural outgrowth of political clientism. For both patrons and clients, the state existed for personal exploitation and manipulation. In effect, the social change that political modernization was to facilitate did not take place, because the existing patterns of interpersonal relations altered the imported political institutions (Legg, 1977, p. 288).

Approaches toward modernization were always a point of contention between the competing social groups and their foreign patrons. Furthermore, because of clientism, the competition filtered down to individuals. This competition was always present, not only because of the scarcity of natural resources, but also because of war, occupation, civil war, and dictatorships, which either were caused by or resulted in foreign involvement. In this environment the press, as well as every other social institution, became a tool of the competing forces in the struggle for survival and modernization.

Major attempts at modernization included those of Eleftherios Venizelos, who formed a government in 1910 and made numerous constitutional amendments and other social changes, including land reforms, the creation of the civil service, and the establishment of free and compulsory education. He also set minimum wages for women and children, legalized trade unions, and established a progressive income tax system.

Nevertheless, war was a constant reality. In the aftermath of the Balkan Wars (1912-1913), Greece enlarged in area by 70 percent and in population by 2 million (Clogg, 1979, p. 103). However, the domestic political turmoil brought renewed talk of capturing Constantinople (the Megali or Great Idea).

On the brink of World War I, a national schism developed between Venizelos and the king about which side of the war to support (Clogg, p. 106). Eventually, Venizelos won out and committed Greek troops to the Allied command. In exchange, Greece was allowed to send troops to Smyrna (in Turkey) to protect its large Greek population. Soon, inner squabbles brought back the king, who was not favored by the West, and the allies stopped supporting the Greek Asia Minor military campaign. Then, in 1922, Turkish forces launched a devastating counterattack, forcing the Greek forces to retreat (Clogg, 1979, p. 118). What followed is known in Greece as the Great Catastrophe; thousands of Greeks were slaughtered, and Greece was forced to leave Asia Minor completely.

The Great Catastrophe, resulted in tremendous psychological and physical shocks, with traces that remain in Greek society. The end of the Great Idea was signified by an agreement between Greece and Turkey, calling for an exchange of populations. This exchange made Greece a more homogeneous society, but filled it with a million poor refugees, who doubled the population of Athens. These immigrants were also instrumental in the creation of the Communist Party of Greece (KKE) (Clogg, 1979, p. 120).

After periodic rule by Venizelos and short-lived coups, the monarchy returned. As a result of strikes and the economic depression, the king brought to power Ioannis Metaxas, who slowly and dictatorially took control of the country under the pretext of fearing a communist takeover, and in 1936 set out to realize his dream of reshaping Greek society (Clogg, 1979, p. 134). However, this did not last very long.

During World War II, the Greek forces successfully defended the country from an Italian invasion, but they were unable to defend it against the Nazis. By April 1941 the Germans had total control of Greece; the Greek government fled to Egypt, while others began organizing a resistance network. The leftists formed the resistance group EAM/ELAS (National Liberation Front/National Liberation Army). A non-Communist resistance group, EDES (National Democratic Greek Union), also came into being later. Although EAM/ELAS controlled much of Greece, as Allied invasion time neared, the Allies forced the feuding EDES and EAM together. This lasted until soon after the government-in-exile, headed by George Papandreou, returned to Greece on October 18, 1944, when the guerillas refused to disband.

In 1946, after unsuccessful attempts at national reconciliation, elections were held without the participation of the Communist Party, and were followed by referendum that returned the king and atrocities committed by both sides (Clogg, 1979, p. 158). The most serious round of the civil war began, making Greece a battleground in the Cold War. Although EAM/ELAS did well initially, a series of world political events and massive aid from the United States helped the government win the war. Nevertheless, the war with Germany, the German occupation, the civil war, and famine had cost almost 2 million Greek lives.

The Truman Doctrine, which had helped the government win the civil war, also marked Greece's exit from British sphere of influence and entry into that of the United States, which "assumed control over virtually all major aspects of Greek public affairs" (Iatrides, 1977, p. 249). At this time, the United States appears to have discouraged industrialization, which contributed to keeping Greece locked as an underdeveloped nation (Tsoucalas, 1969; Wittner, 1982).

In 1951 Greece moved toward the Western alliance by becoming a member of NATO. Elections that year brought to power a conservative government, which drafted a new constitution in 1952 and provided relative stability and economic recovery over the next eleven years. However, in the late 1950s and early 1960s Greece was still economically underdeveloped. The conservative governments of those years, following Western approaches to development, attracted foreign investment for industrialization and also encouraged urbanization (Tsoucalas, 1969, p. 127).

Although some of this new urban population found work in the industries that foreign investment created, industrialization apparently did not absorb all available labor nor decrease external dependence. Furthermore, the economic modernization of Greece was in the form of tourism and shipping, which maintained dependence on foreign entities (Mouzelis, 1978, p. 29).

In 1963 a left-wing deputy, Gregoris Lambrakis, was murdered. Investigations showed that there were links between the right-wing assassins and highly-placed officials. Months later the prime minister, Constantine Karamanlis, resigned and fled to Paris. Generally, Karamanlis, like many other people in Greece, was disillusioned with the system. Elections were being rigged, large demonstrations were being held, patron-client relations were flourishing, and there was more interference in Greek politics by the United States and the monarchy.

In November 1963 the Center Union (CU) party, headed by George Papandreou, won the national elections by a small margin. Papandreou released political prisoners and called for new elections, in which the Center Union received 53 percent of the vote. The prime minister then made educational reforms, cut income taxes, and granted higher price supports for farmers. Meanwhile, his son Andreas was also involved in policy decisions as a cabinet minister, but the army and other right-wing groups accused Andreas of leading a group of leftist officers in preparations to "clean out" the army. At the same time, George Papandreou was trying to gain control of the Greek Central Intelligence Agency (KYP), and tried unsuccessfully to appoint new leaders to the armed forces.

After many attempts by the king to break up the CU, the right wing of CU split and formed a coalition government with support of the conservative opposition, the National Radical Union (ERE). There were large-scale demonstrations against this, and against the provision in the Constitution calling for "politically sound attitudes" on the part of government job applicants (Clogg, 1979, p. 185). This overall sociopolitical divisiveness was reflected in the press and its readers. In fact, political identification was directly related to the newspaper the particular citizen read.

The next election was scheduled for May 28, 1967. Meanwhile, the king and his top generals were planning to prevent Papandreou from taking over if he were elected, which seemed probable (Stern, 1977, p. 53), but their planned coup never materialized. Instead, on April 21, 1967, a group of junior officers launched a successful military coup. Martial law was proclaimed, civil rights were suspended, and many citizens were internally exiled. The powerful men of the junta were three colonels, who justified the coup by declaring that they acted to prevent a communist takeover.

Actually, throughout the history of modern Greece there have been few long periods of stable democracy, except between 1951 to 1963, and from 1974 to date. Two reasons for this stand out: the role of the army in politics, and foreign interference in the domestic political system. The role of the army, exemplifies a "weakness in the nation's civilian institutions as well as a peculiar perception of soldiers of their national role" (Vatikiotis, 1974, p. 25).

Like Metaxas, the colonels' junta, had as a goal the "discipline of the Greek people" and the creation of a "Helleno-Christian civilization." Although there was little opposition in the beginning, soon people started to resent the colonels. As the first signal of protest against the junta 700,000 people attended the funeral of George Papandreou in 1968. Outside Greece, prominent Greeks such as Melina Mercouri and Mikis Theodorakis were making the world aware of the ruthless activities of the Greek military police.

In November 1973, students occupied the Polytechnic School in Athens. When they started using a clandestine radio station inside the school to call on others to join them, junta strongman George Papadopoulos ordered troops and tanks to crush the students. Within days Papadopoulos was deposed in a bloodless coup by a new junta, which soon got into trouble over its support of a coup in Cyprus that was used as an excuse by Turkey to invade the island. As a result, the new junta was forced to invite civilians to take over the government (Clogg, 1979, p. 198).

On July 24, 1974, amidst unparalleled enthusiasm, Constantine Karamanlis arrived in Athens as the man picked to lead the country out of the crisis. Realizing that Greece was in no shape to fight a war with Turkey, he attempted instead to retain civilian control of the military and reinstate democratic institutions. Martial law was lifted, political prisoners freed, and junta appointees fired. Elections were called for November 1974. Before the elections, all political parties, including the Communist Party, which was now legal, were given access to the state-controlled electronic media, and for the first time Greek television was involved in an election campaign.

In the elections, Karamanlis' New Democracy Party (ND) won handily, and started the work of drafting a new constitution. Slowly inflation was curtailed, and the government began taking over banks and the only Greek airline. In the 1977 elections, ND received 42 percent of the vote, while Andreas Papandreou's Socialist Party (PASOK) became the official opposition, with 25 percent. On January 1, 1981, Greece became the tenth member of the Common Market and was well on its way to becoming a full-fledged member of a democratic Europe.

In 1981 PASOK won the elections on a platform of change (*alaghi*), becoming the first socialist party to govern the country. During the following eight years of PASOK rule, much emphasis was placed on strengthening the Greek welfare state. However, the economy never recovered. Furthermore, despite the many positive social changes that took place, the fundamental structure of Greek politics as well as societal divisions remained or intensified.

In 1989, elections brought an interim New Democracy-KKE coalition government to examine corruption charges against the Papandreou government, resulting from a banking scandal involving banker and publisher George Koskotas. Another election in 1989 brought another short-lived, non-partisan, national unity government, but again no party received an absolute majority. In November 1990, new elections brought New Democracy to power, under the leadership of Constantine Mitsotakis. This government is intent on privatizing industry and reducing the government's role in society, yet no major economic changes have taken hold. Greece continues to face grave economic difficulties, involving high inflation and skyrocketing trade and budget deficits.

It is reasonable to assume that Greece's slow (if any) achievement of Westernized modernization and industrialization is a result of various forces, which include cultural characteristics, a lack of natural resources, and the various cases of military, political, and economic domination. In describing Greece's economic, political, and cultural position, the concept of dependence is key. Greece is "a client in a world of indifferent patrons" (Legg, 1977, p. 293). Furthermore, because of Greece's geographical and economic position (e.g. as the gateway to the Middle East), a completely independent development approach that would do away with international clientism is impossible (Legg, 1977, p. 293). However, "Greece . . . belongs historically to a socioeconomic and cultural area very different from that of the West. . . . Greece can choose either a developmental strategy different from the Western one, or become what it is already in the process of becoming; an ugly caricature of the West" (Mouzelis, 1978, p. 152). The question, then, is whether Greece can eventually become independent or has to be a client to a larger patron such as the United States or the European Community (Papacosma, 1979).

N. Mouzelis (1978, p. 155) suggests that Greece find a new development approach, one that would make it independent. Although K. R. Legg (1977) does not advocate such an independent approach, he does agree that Greece is a special case, in that it is neither a modern nation, as are the industrially elite European nations, nor a third world, traditional nation. He believes Greece may hold a special place in a "transitional stage." He writes, "Transition is an elusive concept because countries such as Greece seem likely to remain in some unchartered area between tradition and modernity" (p. 296).

W. H. McNeil (1978) echoes that idea by stating that "the assumption that modernization is essentially identical world-wide seems partially false. . . . We ought to realize how new technical and market opportunities interacted with age-old traditional patterns of behavior (in Greece) to make a blend not duplicated elsewhere" (p. 251). It is very likely, then, that the Greek mass media have evolved out of that blend, and it has given them characteristics worth examining.

1

History of the Print Media

THE FIRST NEWSPAPERS

By the end of the eighteenth century the countries of central Europe had seen newspapers circulating for more than one hundred years. However, since Greece was marking its third century under Turkish rule, it should not be surprising that the first Greek newspapers were produced by the diaspora. Venice and Vienna, in particular, became centers of Greek migration and attracted merchants, teachers, priests, students, scientists, literary figures, and political idealists. Their keen interest in education and their passion for liberating their motherland helped spark their interest in mass communication and public opinion. Their choice of the printing press as a means of promoting their causes was one of the most significant developments in modern Greek history. It helped keep the spirit of the enslaved Greeks alive and solidified foreign public opinion in favor of Greek independence.

Although there are several historical references to it, the first Greek newspaper is said to have appeared in Vienna in 1784, but no physical evidence of it has been found. Said to have been published by George Bentoti from May through August of that year, the

newspaper was a weekly, but was banned after the Turkish government protested to Austrian authorities that it was causing unrest
among the subjugated Greeks on the mainland (Ipourgion, 1968).

However, what is generally recognized, and documented, as the
first Greek newspaper was *Ephimeris*, published beginning on
December 31, 1790, in Vienna by the brothers George and Poublios
Markidas-Pouliou. This twice-weekly, mostly four-page, two-col-
umn newspaper lasted eight years. It contained foreign news, mostly
about France and Greece, about matters of interest to Greek
merchants (like foreign currency availability), and also included
poetry and classified advertisements. *Ephimeris* also circulated in
underground in Greece, and it served as a vehicle for many of the
revolutionary poems of Rigas Feraios, the fiery Greek poet whose
writings were considered instrumental in inspiring the mainland
Greeks to revolt. His work finally brought about the imprisonment
of both himself and the publishers of *Ephimeris*.

Ermis o Logios was another early Greek newspaper, publishing
in Vienna from 1811 to 1821. It was successively edited by Anthimos
Gazis, Theoklitos Farmakidis, and Ioannis Kokkinakis, all well
known Greek intellectuals and educators. Published in the decade
preceding the Greek revolution against the Turks, the paper played
a dominant role in the preservation of Greek letters by regularly
printing articles on literature, science, the arts, and social life. The
paper is also known for having featured the writings on the Greek
language of the internationally known Greek educator Adamantios
Korais, mentioned in the introduction to this book as the developer
of katharevousa. *Ermis o Logios* ceased publication after it was
forced to publish the Patriarch's "aphorisms" of the leaders of the
then two-month-old Greek War of Independence (Mayer, 1957, p. 8-
9).

Dimitrios Alexandridis, a Vienna physician, published *Ellinikos
Tilegraphos*, the diaspora's longest publishing newspaper (1812-
1836), a twice-weekly that described itself as "literary as well as
financial." Other notable Greek newspapers of the time were *Kalliopi*
(1819-1821) of Vienna, *Athina* and *Mouseion* (1819) of Paris, and
especially *Melissa* (1819-1821) of Paris. *Kalliopi*, a conservative
publication, and *Melissa*, a liberal publication, specialized in erudite
political commentary and are credited with nurturing the ideological
schism that separated the revolutionary fighters soon after the
struggle started.

Korais had told the besieged Greeks to start up newspapers to disseminate news of "the sufferings which we undergo," because "through newspapers you can generate a general enthusiasm." He was so convinced of the power of the press to sway public opinion that he further advised them, "Write about your activities in newspapers that, if possible, are printed, or are even handwritten" (Koumarianou, 1991, p. 8).

Hand written indeed were the first three Greek mainland newspapers: the pro-revolution *Pseftofyllada tou Galaxidiou,* which was started in Galaxidi on March 27, 1821, and the similarly inclined *Aetoliki* and *Acheloos.* All three were calligraphically hand copied and distributed. The first Greek-mainland newspaper to actually be printed was *Salpinx Elliniki,* which appeared in Kalamata on August 1, 1821, and was published on equipment brought into the country by Dimitrios Ypsilantis, one of the two Ypsilantis brothers, both of whom had made their fortune in Russia and Romania and played important roles in the independence movement. The paper folded after three issues because of disagreements between Ypsilantis and the editor, Theoklitos Farmakidis. Early newspaper "centers" in the 1820s were the island of Hydra, home to *Ellinikos Kathreptis, Filos tou Nomou,* and *Geniki Ephimeris tis Ellados,* and Mesologgi, home to *Ellinika Chronika* and *Ellinikos Tilegraphos,* a newspaper that featured the works of Lord Byron (Ipourgion, 1968).

The first Athenian newspaper was *Ephimeris ton Athinon* (1824-1826). *Ephimeris tis Kyverniseos,* the oldest Greek newspaper still publishing, was founded in Nafplion, the first capital of modern Greece, in 1825, but moved to Athens and became the official mouthpiece of the government in 1834. Two additional newspapers of importance were the foreign language *Telegrafo Greco* and *Abeille Grecque,* both of which covered the developments of the Greek revolution but also focused on the issues of constitutional order, civics, and democratic institutions in the country's post-Ottoman era.

As Greece was being delivered from the trauma of 400 years of enslavement, it found itself a nation with no government machinery, no free institutions, no modern democratic traditions, and much illiteracy. As idealists, ideologues, opportunists, and revolutionary leaders attempted to join in democratic debate, their lack of experience turned the process into chaos. Ideological polarization, partisanship, and even violence erupted. Unfortunately, this era in Greek history decisively shaped the political process and institutional systems that were to follow. Since those uncertain post-revolution days, Greece has been following various versions of a loud, disorganized, and polarized political life, and the press has been one of the key contributors to the low quality of civic life in the country that once defined civic life for the rest of the world.

Opposition to the autocratic rule of Greece's first governor, Ioannis Capodistrias, who suspended the constitution in 1828, and controlled the press through a restrictive press law (2085/1831), gave birth to Greece's first official "opposition" paper, *O Appolon*, founded in Hydra in 1831. King Otto (1832-1862), Greece's first king, exhibited similar absolutist tendencies and was responsible for three laws in 1837 so restraining of the press that they were referred to as *typoktonoi* (press killers).

The mood of the time was reflected in the words of writer Alexander Soutsos, who wrote, "The press is free so long as you don't bother the authorities, the judges, our ministers and their friends. The press is free so long as you don't write" (Ipourgion, 1968, p. 11). With foreign influences dominating official decision making, royalists and democrats competing for the political platform, and native Greeks fighting those of the diaspora who had just returned, it soon became obvious that partisanship was the surest way for the press to become popular, and therefore powerful. The most notable papers in that spirit were an Alexandros Koumoundouros supporter, *Ethnikon Pnevma*, founded in 1866; an Epaminonda Deligiorgi supporter, *Ephimeris ton Sizitiseon*, founded in 1870; and two supporters of Charilaos Trikoupis, *Kairi*, founded in 1872, and *Proia*, founded in 1874. The most important of the satirical magazines of the time was George Souris's *O Romios* (1883), a liberal publication.

The first Greek daily was *Ephimeris*, founded in Athens by Dimitrios Koromilas in 1873. It originally was a densely written, four page publication with news from all of Greece and the world. This newspaper represented the first serious effort on the part of the press to reach a "mass" audience, and it offered news compartmentalization as well as regular features by specialized reporters. Its significance in Greek life was soon reflected by the staff it attracted. Some of the country's most active and eloquent intellectuals joined it, and the paper later claimed that its staff had produced six prime ministers and eleven cabinet ministers. Some of Greece's elite writers also worked in the paper—Kostis Palamas, Emmanuel

Roidis, Alexandros Papadiamantis, Timos Moraitinis, Babis Aninos, Aristotelis Kourtidis, Aristomenis Proveleggios, and Georgios Drosinis were some of the better known (Mayer, 1957, p. 129)

Another newspaper that played a key role in the public life of the country was *Akropolis*. The oldest Greek newspaper publishing until recently, *Akropolis* was founded in 1882 by Vlasios Gravriilidis, who along with Koromilas is considered to be one of the fathers of contemporary Greek journalism. Gavriilidis, was also an innovator, and his newspaper had an improved appearance, writing style, and reproduction. He introduced police reporting, investigative reporting, personality interviews, and assignments abroad. He brought the first Linotype machine to Greece, and his newspaper was the first to capitalize on advertising and job printing as important revenue sources.

A few years later, in 1889, Georgios Drosinis founded *Estia*, the second-oldest Greek daily still publishing today. *Estia* was started as a literary magazine but changed to a political daily five years later. The last major newspaper of the nineteenth century was *Embros*, founded by Dimitrios Kalapothakis in 1896. The paper survived many of the political upheavals of modern Greek politics by changing into a variety weekly. It finally closed in the mid-1980s.

Although the Athenian press has traditionally dominated the media of the country, provincial newspapers have often played important roles in communities they serve. Peloponnesos, as mentioned earlier, was the first part of mainland Greece to have newspapers. In addition to *Salpinx Elliniki* in Kalamata, notable nineteenth century newspapers, all issued in Patras, were *Kiryx* (1840), *Karteria* (1842), *Patrai* (1850), *Ergatis* (1882, one of the first labor newspapers in Greece), *Forologoumenos* (1891), and *Neologos* (1894).

In the Ionian Islands, in spite of strong press controls by the Venetians and the British, several newspapers flourished. *Spinthir* (1847) and *Rigas* (1850) on Zakynthos, *Fileleftheros* (1848) on Cephalonia, *Neolaia* (1849) and *Pegasus* (1873) on Lefkas, and *Filalithis* (1849) and *Patris* (1849) on Corfu were the most notable. The first newspaper of Thessaloniki was *Ermis* (1875), a biweekly, magazine-style newspaper that eventually became a daily called *Faros*. In Thessaly, prominent newspapers of the era were *Mikra Ephimeris* (1896) in Larissa, a Sunday newspaper that claimed on its masthead to be the "globe's smallest" because of its size (approximately 4.7 x 6.3 inches), and *Thessalia* (1880) in Volos.

THE TWENTIETH CENTURY

The dawn of the new century brought many innovations to the Greek press: better news organization, more newsworthy articles, better writing, and more illustrations. However, this soon meant higher prices. The original price of 10 lepta per copy had doubled by 1920, and quintupled by 1922. Through government involvement, the price per copy stabilized in 1925 to 1 drachma (100 lepta) (General Secretariat, 1988, p. 30).

Early into the twentieth century there appeared Greece's first evening papers, *Esperini* and *Astrapi*, both founded in Athens in 1901. Kostis Hairopoulos's *Chronos* (1903) would become the mouthpiece of the Athens Officers' Club and is said to have been instrumental in preparing the way for the short-lived 1909 officers mutiny. George Filaretos's *Rizospastis* (1908), a leftist paper, is publishing today as the organ of the Greek Communist Party. Other important papers also begun in this era: Spyros Nikolopoulos's *Ethnos* (1913), a newspaper that closed in the 1960s but has enjoyed a remarkable rebirth and is still publishing; *Politeia* (1916); *Eleftheros Typos* (1916), which closed in 1927 before reemerging in 1983; and *Athinaiki* (1919).

One of the most important journalistic voices in twentieth century Greece, was also founded at that time; *Kathimerini* was started by Georgios Vlachos in 1919. A political conservative, Vlachos instituted a more factual and less polemic style of writing than was usual then, and complemented that with his own articulate, sedate, but forceful editorials. Soon the paper and Vlachos had earned the respect of both friends and enemies, and to this day, although not its former self in either eloquence or stature, *Kathimerini* is considered an institution in Greek journalism. Considered one of the premier Greek journalists, Vlachos died in 1951, but his paper remained in the competent hands of his daughter, Helen Vlachos, until 1987.

Another journalistic institution in Greece, *To Vima*, was also founded during that period. It first was published as *Eleftheron Vima* by Dimitrios Lambrakis in 1922, and promoted itself as the newspaper that the new immigrants from Asia Minor could trust. The paper always has been a supporter of liberal political causes and with its sister-paper, *Ta Nea* (founded by Lambrakis in 1930), it reached its peak of popularity during George Papandreou's regime in the early 1960s and during the Andreas Papandreou regime in the 1980s. Although financial difficulties forced *To Vima* into weekly publication in 1982, it continues to be one of Greece's most respected publications. *Ta Nea* still has one of Greece's highest circulations and continues to be a respectable left-of-center newspaper. Both papers are still in the Lambrakis family, which owns Greece's largest media chain.

Aikaterini Vellidis's *Makedonia* was started as Thessaloniki's first morning daily in 1911 and still publishing today. Other notable publications in Thessaloniki were *Embros* (1913); *Eleftheria* (1913); *Fos* (1914), a paper that discontinued during the German occupation, and reappeared when it was over publishing until 1959; and *Ellinikos Vorras* (1935), a conservative morning paper that still publishes in Thessaloniki today.

The island of Crete gained its independence later than the mainland, and therefore its press did not start until 1901, with the publication of *Kyrikas ton Chanion.* This newspaper that soon listed as one of its contributors Eleftherios Venizelos, who later became one of the most important Greek political leaders of the twentieth century and who was once imprisoned for his anti-royalist columns.

During his reign (1936-1941), dictator Ioannis Metaxas ordered the complete control of all mass media, particularly through press law 1092/1938, to ensure their dedication to "nationalistic ends" (Anagnostopoulos, 1960). This resulted in a 40 percent drop in newspaper circulation and in the closing of several well-known papers.

Strict censorship was also maintained during the German occupation, which started in April 1941. The established press was told what to print, and many Greek journalists paid with their lives for refusing to criticize the Greek underground, as ordered by the Germans. Most of the mass information available to Greeks at the time was from Allied Forces radio broadcasts, the highlights of which were passed on by word of mouth, in cigarette packs, or through the underground press (Mayer, 1957, p. 320).

During the occupation the main purpose of the underground press was to keep up the spirit and will of the enslaved nation. Hundreds of publications of all political colorations in all major centers of the country appeared, closed, and reappeared. Most prominent among them were *Eleftheria*, founded by Panos Kokkas in Athens in 1944, which continued publication until the late 1960s; *Rizospastis*; and *Odigitis*, founded in Thessaly in 1943. The last two are still publishing as organs of Greece's Communist Party (KKE). During the German occupation, hundreds of Greek journalists were arrested, tortured, and executed for attempting to inform and uplift the spirit of their compatriots (Anagnostopoulos, 1960, pp. 301-302).

The middle and late 1940s saw the emergence of reckless partisanship, a development that fueled the flames of the bloody and divisive civil war, which pitted Greek Communists against Greek Nationalists for the right to govern the country after the German withdrawal in 1944. Because of the large number of political parties, this partisanship soon transformed the press into a plethora of small but weak newspapers. Notable papers reflecting the mood of the times were the rightist *Ethnikos Kyrix* (1945); the leftist *Avghi* (1952), which is still publishing as a supporter of the Greek Left (EAR), formerly a splinter group of the Greek Communist Party and now a member of the Coalition of the Left; and the leftist *Anexartitos Typos* (1958).

One major event of the era involved George Polk, a promising young CBS radio correspondent and protégé of Edward R. Murrow. Polk was assassinated in Thessaloniki in 1948, a few days before he was to conduct an exclusive and rare interview with a leader of the Communist guerrilla forces. Despite pressure from the United States and Britain for a just solution to the murder, Greek police investigations yielded the arrest and conviction of a Greek journalist, Gregori Staktopoulos, a disillusioned former Communist party member and *Makedonia* reporter who used to moonlight for the BBC. Staktopoulos allegedly confessed to the killing, but it soon became obvious that the evidence, the confession, and the trial were rigged against him, and he eventually served 12 years in prison out of an original life sentence. Since then several investigations, including one by Polk's colleagues in the United States, and hundreds of articles and books in Greece and elsewhere have offered various kinds and degrees of proof of Staktopoulos's innocence and the possible guilt of members of the then Greek authorities, who did not want the world, through Polk and CBS News, to have access to the other party of the war.(1)

By 1950 there were 60 dailies in the country, but only two had significant circulation outside their city of publication. Rural illiteracy, newsprint shortage, and poor transportation hindered the wider circulation of newspapers (Olson, 1965, p. 261). These were critical years in the development of the Greek press. A new constitution, drafted in 1952, declared the press free, but the communist newspapers remained banned. The civil war hysteria also resulted in police surveillance of journalists and the require-ment of a "certificate of loyalty" from many newspapers (Interna-tional Press Institute, 1955). In addition, many leftist newspapers were not fully distributed because distributors and buyers feared retaliation by the police.

After the 1950s produced a system of many, sensational, and financially weak newspapers that served as party mouthpieces, the 1960s consolidated press dependence on the parties and the govern-ment. The parties offered financial support and/or circulation assistance, and the government offered subsidies and protective legislation. The subsidies consisted mainly of government advertis-ing, newsprint import duty discounts, and postal rate breaks, while the protective legislation gave selected newspapers favorable meth-ods of newspaper distribution, duty-free newsprint consumption limits, page number controls, and so on. The government justified such controls as supportive of the weak newspapers and thus as a guarantee of press pluralism. In either case, this effectively meant that the press of Greece was a dependent press, becoming increas-ingly entrenched in and identified with the various political and economic power centers. It was also a press that had no inclination and made no serious effort to be independent or to set professional standards, such matters as objectivity, accuracy, writing and edit-ing, language, and ethics.

A veteran *Ta Nea* editor, Lykourgos Kominis (1985, p. 174) describes this "unacceptable" dependence this way:

> Almost all newspapers claim that they judge and criti-cize. "It's our role," they say, "to check the authority." But checking the authority with "Yes" cannot be done. "Yes, thank you for the information. I will check it out," perhaps might lead towards a better balanced relation-ship between these two paragons of public life. But the "Yes" is the rule. "Yes, I'll check it out" is the exception. "No" is almost nonexistent. The means the political

authority uses to "tie" journalism to its "chariot" are completely different from those used by the economic oligarchy. Not only is their "nature" different, but so is their philosophy. The most common way is through favors.

The 1960s also saw the creation of the first two important Greek newspaper chains: the Lambrakis chain, which included *To Vima*, *Ta Nea*, *Tachydromos*, *Economikos Tachydromos*, and *Omada*, and the Vlachos chain, which included the newspapers *Kathimerini* and *Mesimvrini*, and the magazines *Eikones* and *Eklogi.* The Greek newspapers of the 1960s were divided mainly into two camps: the political dailies, limited as they were by their political affiliations, and the sensational popular papers, which were preoccupied with crime, sex, gossip, accidents, and so on. Radio as a news medium was strictly auxiliary, for it was government owned and operated, and television was still in its planning stages.

During that politically explosive decade, serious journalism, within its own political parameters, of course, was practiced only by *To Vima*, *Kathimerini*, and *Avghi*, newspapers that represented different political camps (center, right, and left, respectively) and featured relatively low-key reporting, strong editorial voices, and thoughtful columnists. Their serious tone was also reflected in their grey appearance, lengthy stories, and lack of visuals (photographs, drawings, etc.). The circulation leaders of the time were the centrist *Ta Nea* and the rightist *Akropolis*.

The major innovation of the time, and a landmark in modern Greek journalism history, was the creation of *Mesimvrini*, founded on October 9, 1961, twenty days before the general elections. A revised version of the *London Daily Mail*, *Mesimvrini* was the brainchild of publisher Helen Vlachos and editor Panayiotis Lambrias. Its main innovations included (1) The "inverted pyramid" style of news writing, generally practiced by the major newspapers in other Western industrialized democracies; (2) a less partisan/political approach to news coverage, which included more balanced news reports, a serious effort to view the news from an objective and less political angle, more feature stories, and a non-hysterical editorial policy; (3) a bright, easy-to-read appearance, with larger typefaces, use of visuals, and a more open page design; and (4) use of the spoken language, demotiké. The paper revolutionized Greek journalism, tempted the reading audience, excited the profession, and scandalized the reigning conservative power elite. The latter, in fact, found *Mesimvrini*'s use of demotiké or *kathomiloumeni* intolerable for a member of the conservative press corps, which traditionally used katharevousa. The journalistic "shock" is best reflected by the newspaper's circulation history: first day, 100,000; second day, 9,000. However, from then until its closing at the start of the colonels' 1967 coup, the paper climbed daily on the circulation charts. The circulation of its last issue before the coup was 80,602 (Kominis, 1985, p. 206).

Despite *Mesimvrini*'s journalistic challenge, however, the vast majority of the Greek papers in the 1960s remained unchanged, chained to old practices and traditions. Truth and facts always had a partisan color and were met with appropriate mistrust, ridicule, or even litigation by the various governments in power. It had become a habit of the regime in power, for example, to prosecute a newspaper under "insulting the authorities" or "causing public alarm" laws. Several publications, from the leftist *Avghi* to the rightist *Vradyni*, were often fined by Athens courts.

One notorious case involved a December 1962 article in *Athinaiki* about Queen Frederika's mother, who allegedly lived in poverty in Germany, abandoned by her children. Charged with "slandering the Crown," a constitutionally prohibited offense, the paper's editor and publisher were sentenced to 15 months in prison and all unsold copies of the paper were confiscated. The trial of *Athinaiki* became front-page news for the rest of Athens' papers, which started publishing extra editions to cover it. In order to limit the political damage it was suffering, the conservative government then in power resurrected a 1945 decree that prohibited extra editions if they "caused anxiety and confusion in public opinion."

The *Athinaiki* case was symptomatic of the new attitude of the rightist government that vocal opposition was intolerable. This attitude was mainly in reaction to a dispute over the results of the 1961 election, won by the conservative National Radical Union (ERE) party of Karamanlis. George Papandreou, the leader of the narrowly defeated Center Union (CU) party, contested the results and took his case to the people. In the next six years, the political battles of the rightists, centrists, leftists, and the Royal Palace were fought mainly in the press and in the streets, and produced circulation records for most newspapers. They also elicited some of the most questionable journalistic practices, as publishers and some of their employees took a more open role in partisan politics.

With Papandreou on the offensive, Karamanlis began a haphazard and, as soon to be proven, costly anti-press policy. This lost him the active support of his party's most articulate proponent, Helen Vlachos and her papers *Kathimerini* and *Mesimvrini.* The rift surfaced through criticism of government policy, including the limitations on special editions, and Vlachos accused Karamanlis of becoming "increasingly sensitive to criticism" and even of becoming "sensitive to indifference." The disagreement grew considerably when Vlachos editorially led the fight in the "battle of the pages," a battle against the government's right to set limits on the maximum number of pages a newspaper can run in a week. The government argued that the regulation was necessary in order to protect the poorer, smaller publishers in their competition with the larger ones, a policy that guaranteed that even the least popular parties or leaders could maintain their mouthpieces.

The heated political climate and the increasing polarization of press and readers led, at the end of 1963, to accusations that the Karamanlis government had secretly funneled money to friendly publishers for their continued support. The scandal, known as *ta mystika kondylia* (the secret funds), was to have been investigated by both the Union of Journalists of Athens Dailies (ESIEA) and the newly elected government of George Papandreou, but nothing was officially proven or officially announced about the case.

The great circulation gains, due almost exclusively to the political controversies of the time, made many publishers prosperous but did not necessarily help the reporters, who in the fall of 1964 went on strike demanding better wages. Since 1960, they argued, circulation had increased by 40 percent and advertising revenue by almost 80 percent, while their salaries had remained virtually the same. It took two mediation courts and almost one year for the issue to be resolved, with the second mediation court granting most of the strikers' demands.

The political temperature rose again in the summer of 1965, when the ASPIDA case, allegedly involving partisan paramilitary activity by junior officers ideologically sympathetic to the premier's son, Andreas, brought George Papandreou in direct confrontation with King Constantine. This caused the premier's resignation and signaled the beginning of a series of unprecedented royal involvements in the affairs of state that eventually paved the way for the 1967 military coup. The rightists supported the king's position against the centrists—a rift that the press cultivated to the extreme. Interest in this conflict yielded yet more circulation gains and also deepened the involvement of newspapers in politics. It was characteristic of the times that five of the twelve civilians mentioned in the final government report on ASPIDA were connected with the press (Rousseas, 1967). Although a few junior officers were convicted of engaging in paramilitary activities in the ASPIDA case, no involvement by Andreas Papandreou was proven, and the case is generally accepted as being manufactured by the rightists.

Testimony about some publishers' active involvement in party affairs is given by Andreas Papandreou (1970) in his *Democracy at Gunpoint*, in which he often refers to the machinations of his in-house political foe, publisher Christos Lambrakis of *To Vima* and *Ta Nea*. In fact, Papandreou and several prominent chroniclers of the era often mention the involvement in party affairs of such publishers as *Eleftheria*'s Kokkas, *Athinaiki*'s Yannis Papageorgiou, and *Makedonia*'s Vellidis. Probably most notorious of the issues they refer to is that of the 1965 "Lambrakis plan," that would have reduced the King-Center Union confrontation by naming as premier one of the conservative CU members such as Stephanos Stefanopoulos, to replace George Papandreou and minimize the ascending power of Andreas Papandreou. As the plan was being materialized, Andreas Papandreou's supporters burned copies of *Ta Nea* and *To Vima* in front of the newspapers' offices.

As the feud climaxed in August 1965, the centrist paper *Ethnos* ran a story that the CIA was involved in the fatal grenade explosion during the commemorative services held at the Gorgopotamos Bridge, in central Greece, in November 1964, accompanied by a copy of a U.S. embassy letter to the Pentagon, which the article said was proof. The services had been severely criticized by leftists, and the rightist press had promoted the idea that the communists must have planted the grenade.

The most important pre-junta news media event was one that shocked both the journalistic and political circles of Greece. It was allegedly orchestrated by Kokkas in *Eleftheria*, the January 1, 1967, front page of which featured an article and commentary on the alleged "minutes" of a December 20, 1966, meeting between, among others, representatives of the Monarchy, represented by the King's political adviser Dimitrios Bitsios; ERE, represented by its leader Panayotis Kanellopoulos and *Kathimerini-Mesimvrini* publisher Helen Vlachos; and, publisher Lambrakis, allegedly representing George Papandreou and the CU's conservative wing. The story, *To Mnimonion tis Synomosias* (The Memorandum of the Conspiracy), as the headline presented it, was allegedly based on Kanellopoulos' handwritten notes. At this meeting, according to *Eleftheria*, there was unanimous agreement that ERE would withdraw support from the government of the CU's deserter deputies (*apostates*), led by Stefanopoulos, in return for the creation of a mutually acceptable transitional government, and elections within six months.

These revelations, which Kokkas never proved in court after he was sued by Kanellopoulos and Vlachos, led to a public schism between father and son Papandreou, although in the interest of party unity the latter voted in Parliament to support his father's recommendation of a transitional government and elections. These elections, which in all likelihood would have resulted in a CU victory, were superseded by the military coup of April 21, 1967 (Papandreou, 1970, pp. 201-203; Rousseas, 1967, p. 45).

THE 1967 COUP AND THE POST-JUNTA PRESS

The dictators were draconian on press issues. "We prohibit any announcement, publication of information, or comment that, in any manner, opposes directly or indirectly the regime," was their first order. For two days there were no newspapers, and only scattered news reports came over Greek radio. Foreign newscasts became the main source of news for the newly isolated Greeks. On Sunday, April 23, only three of the thirteen Athenian political dailies appeared: *Akropolis, To Vima,* and *Eleftheros Kosmos.* The latter ended up being the regime's great supporter and apologist. *Avghi* and *Dimokratiki Allaghi,* the leftist morning and afternoon dailies, respectively, were banned, and their offices and files confiscated. *Eleftheria* did not publish because Kokkas had gone into hiding, and to pretest the coup, *Kathimerini* and *Mesimvrini* were instructed by Vlachos not to publish. Full censorship was imposed; foreign correspondents had their calls interrupted; foreign publications were admitted only with articles cut out; Mikis Theodorakis's music was banned; and tourists were prevented from taking pictures unflattering to the military. Many journalists, including Lambrakis and the leftist Leonidas Kyrkos (*Avghi*), were arrested. Vlachos was also arrested in the fall of 1967 for smuggling out of the country several letters to prominent world leaders and to international press organizations asking them to keep "harassing the colonels." Later in the year she escaped to London from where she served as one of the regime's most prominent critics.

The Censorship Service was established as part of the Ministry to the Premiership, which was headed by Colonel Papadopoulos. Its guidelines (especially Decree No. 19603/C) included a long list of forbidden items, including the use of demotiké, offensive remarks about the regime, and historical references to the Communist Party. The regime's philosophy of the press, articulated on several occasions by Papadopoulos, was that the press that had the obligation to help in national development and to be socially responsible by covering the affairs of state positively. "We have not banned freedom of the press," he said in a speech to ESIEA, "because, allow me to say, the press before April 21, (1967) was not a press" (Papadopoulos, 1968, p. 43). After six months the censorship was relaxed, by which time newspaper circulation was down to less than half its pre-junta level. However, throughout its stay in power the regime kept harassing and imprisoning journalists, especially those of the center and left.

The only newspaper that was not subject to prior censorship in 1968 was *Eleftheros Kosmos.* However, its circulation started declining despite the fact that people bought it just for "show." Helen Vlachos (1972, p. 64) wrote that *Eleftheros Kosmos* was "a safe bit of printed paper to tuck into your pocket when visiting government offices, police stations or friends in prison." However, other newspapers, which found ways to oppose the junta, primarily through international news, saw their circulation rise. Nevertheless, the junta punished those papers by placing an import duty on newsprint that went up as circulation increased (Vlachos, 1972, p. 69).

In order to better police the profession, in August 1969, Papadopoulos, now premier, issued a press code, which was promptly rejected by ESIEA (1969). The outcry against the proposed legislation was so universal that even *Eleftheros Kosmos*, the regime's mouthpiece, refused to discuss it. On October 3 the government announced that censorship was ended and that an amended version of the press code would go into effect on January 1, 1970. In the next four years, however, many journalists suffered under the grip of this regime, and this contributed greatly to the general atrophy of the profession, while the government-owned media—radio and especially television—received preferential treatment and witnessed unprecedented growth. In fact, the colonels had so much affection for television that they regularly bought state-of-the-art equipment the staff of the television stations did not know how to use, and therefore, it was left in boxes for years.

The end of the dictatorship in 1974 found Greeks slowly shifting their political allegiance to the left, a shift that culminated in the election of Andreas Papandreou's PASOK party to power in 1981 and its re-election in 1985. It also found Greek journalists ready to return to their pre-junta practices. But although the political climate was warming up and circulation quickly returned to almost 1965-1967 levels, times had changed. One major difference was the ubiquitous presence of television, which started absorbing some of the advertising money and offered Greek media consumers a visual approach to news and entertainment to which they had not been exposed previously. Several newspaper journalists left their print jobs for television, while others combined careers in both. Another difference was caused by the technological revolution, which allowed most papers to modernize their appearance and their efficiency in news gathering and processing. Technology was also the main force behind the eventual "liberation" from government control of the electronic media in the late 1980s. Privatization and commercialization followed; their impact is still unclear.

One final difference concerns the attitude of the publishers, who by and large seem to have shifted their energies away from direct involvement in political decision making to addressing more traditional professional issues, such as product improvement, media marketing, and diversification. The most important journalistic event of the immediate post-junta era was the creation of *Eleftherotypia*, a newspaper that owes its existence mainly to the April 1975 reporters' strike (over salaries, benefits, and working conditions), which left Greece without newspapers for more than two weeks. To fill the vacuum, the strikers joined temporarily to produce *Adesmefti Gnomi*, a newspaper that eventually brought together the talent and the financing that resulted in *Eleftherotypia* in July 1975.

Eleftherotypia's major innovation was that owners Christos Tegopoulos and Christos Siamantas agreed to share its profits with the staff and allow a staff-management governing board to make all personnel decisions. The guiding force behind this unusual effort was Alexandros Filippopoulos, a veteran journalist, prolific talent scout, and former editor of *Apoyevmatini*. The paper's left-of-center political line, which matched the public mood of the time, and *Eleftherotypia*'s "reporters' newspaper" logo made it a hit. Unfortunately, *Eleftherotypia*'s revolutionary governance concept, its self-styled "journalistic expedition to rehabilitate the Greek press," never fully materialized, and Filippopoulos himself was dismissed within a year. The newspaper, however, continues to be one of Greece's best and most popular dailies.

Filippopoulos, himself, was destined to leave his mark on Greek journalism. After his departure from *Eleftherotypia*, he joined the business empire of George Bobolas who was the major stockholder of the *Great Soviet Encyclopedia* in Greece. Filippopoulos edited the encyclopedia and gathered a talented staff. From this position, with Bobolas' funding, he launched *Ethnos* in 1981, the first successful Greek tabloid, with a journalistic style (in language, writing, design, visuals, and use of color) that revolutionized the Greek press. The paper's aggressive style of reporting, its strong pro-PASOK, pro-Soviet and anti-American stands, and its publisher's association with the Soviet encyclopedia caused members of the Western and rightist Greek press to speculate that the paper was a Moscow-funded instrument of Soviet propaganda. In fact, Paul Anastasi, an Athens correspondent for *The New York Times* and *The London Daily Telegraph*, in 1983 wrote *Take the Nation* (Ethnos) *in Your Hands*, which charged that *Ethnos* was a KGB "disinformation" organ ("Greece's disinformation daily," 1983). The book was highly litigated, and both sides won in various stages of appeal. The final outcome, one year later, was a nebulous decision that allowed both sides to claim victory. *Ethnos* also introduced Greek readers to the game of bingo, which brought suits from competing publishers and was declared illegal (as unfair competition) in May 1986. With or without bingo, *Ethnos* remained the best selling Greek newspaper for most of the 1980s.

The turn of the public mood to the parties of the left encouraged the creation of additional newspapers of that ideology, while right-wing *Eleftheros Kosmos* closed down in 1982. Two of the most important papers that started publishing at this time are *Avriani*, founded in 1979, which practices an extremely sensational, personal, pro-Papandreou kind of journalism, and *Eleftheros Typos*, founded in 1983, which started as a PASOK supporter but changed to PASOK critic a year later. These two newspapers challenged the Greek newspaper establishment by charging half as much as the others.

One interesting development of the post-junta period has been the demise of the morning press, to the benefit of the evening newspapers. Today there are three times as many evening as morning newspapers, a complete reversal of the situation in the 1960s. The reasons are several. Because of rules covering distribution deadlines and labor work hours, afternoon papers have more time to prepare their product, and they can circulate to all parts of the country almost as early as the morning papers. Afternoon papers in Athens, for example, are on the newsstands at 10:30 a.m. Another reason is the entry of the evening papers to the Sunday edition market. Traditionally Sunday editions were the exclusive turf of the morning papers and their biggest source of advertising revenue. With the evening papers publishing on Sunday, under a slightly different title, morning papers found their resources severely curtailed, something that made product improvement and competition very difficult. The most important victim was *To Vima*, which had to discontinue daily publication and became a Sunday-only newspaper.

Another possible reason for the demise of most morning newspapers may be that their Greek readers do not have the luxury of having their newspaper delivered to them. Christos Bousbourelis, a former editor of *To Vima*, attributes the low morning circulation to past political experience, as quoted by M. Garoufali (1982, p. 2):

> Traditionally people bought the morning paper at the neighborhood kiosk. In the post civil war period the political police would make the kiosk vendors report the names of those buying communist or other non-conservative papers. Out of fear, people quit buying at the kiosk and started buying the afternoon papers in the center of the city where they would not be checked. Then the dictatorship came and the afternoon paper there remained a habit.

The problems of the morning dailies were symptomatic of a larger malaise among Greek papers, which were trying to survive and succeed in an environment of evolving competitive forces, and changing consumer needs and behavior. Late in 1982, PASOK undertook a study of press finances and found that all the major dailies except for *Ethnos* and *Ta Nea* were losing money. In order to promote press pluralism, the government decided to help the ailing print media by easing the terms of their 1.7 billion drachmas ($17 million) in renovation loans and by forcing government-owned television to cut its advertising by 30 percent.

The most notorious chapter of the Greek press history of the 1980s, belongs to George Koskotas, a young Greek-American entrepreneur who managed to move from bank teller to bank owner and publishing tycoon in five years. His financial prowess and personal dynamism soon netted him ownership of *Kathimerini, Vradyni,* and scores of other successful popular magazines, as well as lesser newspapers, a radio station, and a soccer team. He even imported the latest computer technology, which he used to publish *24 Ores*, a *USA Today* clone with a nameplate so blatantly similar to that of the latter that the Gannett company, which publishes *USA Today,* sued him.

Unlike traditional publishing giants in Greece, Koskotas maintained friendships that transcend political party allegiances, and his popularity seemed to be universal. His empire crumbled in 1988, after rival newspapers exposed dark elements of his rise to financial power. Later he was charged with embezzling his bank's (Bank of Crete) money. He escaped to the United States where he was arrested and later extradited to Greece. The parts of his media empire were bought by others or closed.

Investigations into Koskotas's dealings, and into his popularity even among his political foes, led to coconspiracy and embezzlement charges against Andreas Papandreou and several of his political operatives and other government members in power during the Koskotas reign. Although Koskotas testified that he had created his media empire at the strong urging of Papandreou in order to help promote PASOK, Papandreou was exonerated and his subordinates were convicted of relatively minor charges. Koskotas's testimony was repeatedly discredited, and he was even reprimanded for lack of credibility by the presiding judge.

Meanwhile, the Bank of Crete, now under government supervision, is still in the courts trying to take back control of GRAMMI, Koskotas's media company. However, it is still not fully known how GRAMMI's publications were transferred to others while Koskotas was fleeing from Greece. Koskotas's own trial, which is to take place late in 1992, may clear up some of these questions.

NOTE

1. Significant recent books about the Polk case have been written by G. Staktopoulos, *Ipothesi Polk* [The Polk Case], Athens: Gnosi, 1984; K. Marton, *The Polk Conspiracy*, New York: Farrar, Straus & Giroux, 1990; and E. Keeley, *The Salonica Bay Murder*, Princeton, N.J.: Princeton University Press, 1989.

2

History of Broadcasting

EARLY DEVELOPMENTS

In Greece, as in many other countries, radio broadcasting started in the early 1920s. But while by 1923 there were over 500 radio stations in the United States, Greece was still just beginning to experiment. On March 1, 1922, when Greece was heavily involved in the Asia Minor military campaign, Costas Petropoulos, a professor of physics at the University of Athens, demonstrated a complete radio receiving set to the Society of Physics Sciences.

A year later the first broadcasting experiment in Greece took place, at the Votanikos station of the Ministry of the Navy's Radio Electric Service in Athens, using a 200-watt transmitter. These first experiments lasted only a few weeks and were conducted with imported equipment made by a Swedish company, Swensa Radio Aktiebolaget ("Radiofonia," 1956, p. 572).

During the next two years, more experimental transmissions took place in Athens, at the Megaris School. This was the first school in Greece to offer courses in radio and electronics engineering. Amateur radio operators experimented with a transmitter that had only "one oscillator and five triodic tubes with parallel connection between them . . . and a carbon microphone" ("Radiofonia," 1956, p. 572). These broadcasts, assisted by the newly formed Union of Greek Amateur Wireless Operators, were advertised in the press, and as a result, people began building or buying their own sets so they could receive these and foreign radio signals.

The Ministry of the Navy, which regulated broadcasting between 1921 and 1926, demanded a license fee of 500 drachmas, which was equivalent to about $100, to be paid by the owner of each receiving set. In addition, installation of an outside antenna was prohibited, and only one antenna inside each house was permitted. From these it appears that the government wanted to discourage broadcasting until it had a firm control of it. In fact, people residing in Northern Greece were not permitted to own a receiver until 1928 ("Radiofonia," 1956, p. 572).

In 1926 the Ministry of Posts Telegraph and Telephone (PTT) established the Radio Electric Service to take over regulatory control of broadcasting. The PTT would later make periodic broadcasts from the port city of Piraeus for the Coast Guard, and would broadcast church services for hospital patients (Emery, 1969, p. 282).

The first broadcasting station with regular programs was set up in Thessaloniki in 1928 by Christos Tsingiridis, who while living in Germany for several years, had studied radio electronics at the University of Stuttgart. Upon his return to Greece, Tsingiridis had brought with him the equipment needed to construct his transmitter. He operated his station from studios he built on the grounds of the Thessaloniki International Trade Fair. His station had a 4.5-kilowatt transmitter and operated on a medium-wave frequency of 218.5 kilohertz, using an antenna 45 meters long (Keshishoglou, 1962, p. 20). The station's early programs included music, news, interviews, lectures by professors, and occasional editorials by Tsingiridis himself. At this early stage, he had to operate using his own funds, and it was not until many years later that he started making a profit from an increasing amount of advertising.

In 1929 the Venizelos government began making some efforts to expand radio broadcasting. It started the process by taking bids for the installation of a transmitter to serve the entire country. The lowest bid came from Heraclis Dimitriadis, who proposed to install and operate a 12-kilowatt Marconi transmitter and charge each radio set owner 1 drachma per day. This agreement collapsed, however, when conflicts arose between Dimitriadis and the government. A similar agreement in 1930 with Emmanuel Marcoglou was later declared invalid by the government (Hatzidoulis, 1988, May 27).

Nevertheless, experimental broadcasting by the Friends of the Wireless Club (FWC), created in 1927 continued to take place for a few more years (Triantafillopoulos, 1987). The FWC held a seminar on radio technology in 1930 that included a broadcast of the keynote address by the Minister of Transportation (Hatzidoulis, 1988, June 1). However, there were only a few thousand radio receivers in Greece at the time, tuned to the above stations and to Greek language programming from Italy. The cost of a receiver was around 8,000 drachmas, which was prohibitive for the average citizen (Hatzidoulis, 1988, May 23).

In 1936 the authoritarian government of Prime Minister Metaxas decided to build its own radio broadcasting system. For Metaxas, a Greek broadcasting system was not only a matter of national pride, but also a means to "educate" Greek society. His strong fondness for the German Third Reich resulted in a heavy German involvement in the Greek economy. In line with this, in 1936 the government awarded a contract to the German company Telefunken to build a medium-wave 100-watt transmitter in Thessaloniki, a short-wave, 5-kilowatt transmitter on the island of Kerkyra (Corfu), and a short-wave, 20-kilowatt transmitter in Athens. This contract was soon voided, but was replaced by a new contract under which Telefunken would install one short-wave, 15-kilowatt transmitter at Liossia, 7 kilometers outside Athens (Keshishoglou, 1962, p. 18).

On March 25, 1938, Greece became one of the last European countries to establish a national radio station, as King George II inaugurated the first national broadcasting station in Greece. Regular programming, consisting of music by the station's symphony orchestra, choirs, news, and classical music, did not start until May 21, 1938 (Hatzidoulis, 1988, May 21). In 1938 the government established the Radio Broadcasting Service to operate all state broadcasting, and placed it under the political supervision of the Ministry of the Press and Tourism. However, the technical aspects of radio broadcasting would be controlled by the Ministry of Transportation and Communications.

Months later, another contract was signed with Telefunken to increase the power of the national station from 15 to 70 kilowatts, but the Italian invasion of Greece postponed the plan. During the first stages of World War II, the two existing stations carried news from the front and helped boost the morale of the soldiers and the public (Keshishoglou, 1962, p. 21).

During the German occupation (1941-1944), further expansion of radio broadcasting was halted. The occupying forces abolished the Ministry of the Press and Tourism and formed the Hellenic Broadcasting Society (AERE) to be in charge of broadcasting. At the same time a censorship committee, working out of the German Embassy, supervised special propaganda broadcasts ("Radiofonia," 1956, p. 572). The occupying forces also ordered all owners of radio receivers in and around Athens to register their sets with them. The sets were then sealed to receive only the national station in Athens, which the German forces controlled. Other radio sets around the country were confiscated, and people were repeatedly ordered to turn their radios in or face life imprisonment and even death (Keshishoglou, 1962, p. 22). This was done to isolate the Greek people from the rest of the world, but many Greeks kept their radios hidden—some even buried them in their backyard—and many frequently listened to the BBC's Greek broadcast "Edo Londinon" (This is London) (Bays, 1988).

The Germans wanted to use the two radio stations in Greece for propaganda and to entertain their troops. They were perfectly capable of operating the German-constructed station in Athens, but the Tsingiridis station in Thessaloniki had been constructed by Tsingiridis himself, and it resembled chaos (Keshishoglou, 1962, p. 24). As a result, the Germans were forced to draft Tsingiridis to operate the station for them. Tsingiridis was constantly sabotaging German transmissions by pretending equipment breakdowns and often shutting down the station for supposedly needed repairs. Seeing this, the Germans imprisoned Tsingiridis and tried to operate the station themselves. Unable to do so, they again brought him back, placed one of their engineers with him to learn how to operate the station, and also filmed every move Tsingiridis made inside the station. Aware of this, Tsingiridis constantly made irrelevant connections, and the Germans never did become able to operate the station. Finally, they allowed Tsingiridis to run the station even though he continued to shut it down for "necessary repairs." The German forces eventually built their own 20-kilowatt station in Thessaloniki (Keshishoglou, 1962, p. 25).

While departing from Greece on October 12, 1944, the German forces tried to destroy the national station with time bombs, but their plans were discovered by radio technicians and the Greek resistance, and the bombs were deactivated. On October 20, two days after the national government returned from exile, the station resumed regular operations ("Radiofonia," 1956, p. 572). However, the Germans managed to destroy most of the Tsingiridis station, and they took back their own station's equipment. Tsingiridis put his station back on the air in September 1945 (Keshishoglou, 1962, p. 26).

During the 1940s the national radio station in Athens operated under censorship rules and broadcast mostly in the evenings. Its programming consisted of news, children's programs, classical and contemporary Greek and foreign music, plays, and church services, as well as educational programs directed at women, farmers, and other social groups (Kotsaki, 1988).

BROADCASTING AFTER WORLD WAR II

Along with other major reorganizations, the Greek government in 1945 decided to reorganize and expand radio broadcasting. Law 1775/1945 established the Hellenic Radio Foundation (EIR), with an executive committee appointed by the government. EIR was responsible to the Ministry to the Premiership. The foundation acquired the titles to all the radio stations previously owned and operated by AERE and was granted monopoly over broadcasting in Greece. Actually there was only one station with regular programming owned by the state, as the other station was owned by Tsingiridis. EIR attempted to force Tsingiridis to broadcast the national signal, and when he refused they closed down his station ("Radiofonikos stathmos," 1945). It seems the government wanted total control of this important tool because it could play a role in the outcome of the ensuing civil war.

EIR then proceeded to build its own station in Thessaloniki, which was completed in 1947. This station had very low power, and its signal could only be received in and around Thessaloniki. Thus, in 1947, when Tsingiridis died, EIR was in charge of only two stations in Greece, with three studios at Zappeion, in central Athens, operating with old and sparse equipment. Since the stations carried no advertising, they were financed through license fees from an estimated 40,000 radio receivers (UNESCO, 1947, p. 123). In 1948, as the financial situation was improving, a short-wave, 7.5-kilowatt transmitter was installed in Athens and $50,000 worth of receiving equipment and spare parts were imported (Keshishoglou, 1962, p. 29).

In the late 1940s the building of radio stations started to accelerate. Stations were built not only by EIR but also by private interests and the armed forces. The armed forces station was started as a pirate station by soldiers for their own entertainment during the civil war (McDonald, 1983, p. 164). Other armed forces stations were constructed with U.S. Pentagon assistance in 1949, when law 968/ 1949 established the Central Radio Station for the armed forces. By the end of 1949 five such radio stations were being operated by the Army Geographical Service (McDonald, 1983, p. 164). Armed forces stations were established to "enlighten" the people of Northern Greece about the dangers of communism during and immediately after the civil war. The United States, which had taken a major role in this conflict, helped the Greek government by building two radio stations that would be transmitting Voice of America (VOA) programs part of the day and Greek government programming the rest of the day ("New U.S. radio," 1949). The stations remained and expanded even after such an immediate danger no longer existed. In 1951 law 1663/1951 legally authorized the operation of military broadcasting stations. It stated:

> The National Defense shall be authorized to install and operate stations for sound broadcasting, television or other applications of radio, or call stations, for the purpose of informing, instructing, entertaining and generally raising the educational level of the Armed Forces, and in wartime, of strengthening the morale of the nation at war, due respect being paid to the obligations assumed in the international sphere with regard to power and wavelength (Emery, 1969, p. 284).

The armed forces stations directed their broadcasts not only toward the armed forces but also toward the general public. Their programs were financed through army funds and revenue from broadcast advertising. U.S. support for the military stations' activities was further reinforced through donations of radio receivers to villages so that villagers could be "furnished with arguments to combat the incitive propaganda of communist agents, and in the northern border areas to contest the broadcast information offered across the Iron Curtain by the Soviet controlled radio" (Sadgwick, 1953).

Because the armed forces stations were gaining popularity, EIR established a new service in 1952 called the Second Program, to provide a type of service similar to that of the armed forces stations. The Second Program carried commercials and more popular music programming, as opposed to the original station's (First Program) more serious orientation. The First Program carried news, information, education, and fine arts programming, but no commercials. Nevertheless, all stations from 1946 to 1953, whether military or civilian, were under strict preventive censorship, exercised by the government through law 818/1946 (McDonald, 1983, p. 162).

Following the end of the civil war, private radio stations began to appear. The first such station went on the air in 1950 and was operated by the University of Athens. This station did not last very long, but other private stations were established in 1952. EIR did not encourage the creation of such stations, but they did not try to stop them either, evidently because most of them had low power and were away from Athens. These stations were also financed through advertising (Keshishoglou, 1962, p. 39).

Following the approval of the 1952 constitution, parliament passed law 2312/1953, which established a more detailed framework within EIR, once again granting it monopoly over broadcasting, although military stations were unaffected. While programming and regulation were under the control of the Minister to the Premiership, and technical operations were under the control of the Ministry of Transportation and Communications, EIR, as a public service agency, was granted administrative and financial autonomy. This model that remained in effect for several years, and some of its elements are still in effect today.

Article II of the new law gave EIR the right to "maintain and exploit all technical means for the broadcasting of both domestic and foreign programs." Article III created a nine-member administrative council to establish EIR policies and oversee its operations. The members of that council included government officials and some private citizens, appointed by the Minister to the Premiership. The director-general of EIR was appointed by the cabinet upon the recommendation of the Minister to the Premiership (Emery, 1969, p.

284). Between 1945 and 1965 there were 22 directors-general of EIR (McDonald, 1983, p. 162).

In September 1954 EIR established the Third Program, patterned after the BBC's Third Programme, placing more emphasis on classical music but operating only a few hours each day. The political stability and economic recovery of the 1950s and early 1960s, which enabled Greece to grow economically, politically, and culturally, also increased the number of radio stations. By 1961 there were five private and twelve EIR stations, and also twelve armed forces radio stations, operating mostly in Northern Greece. The armed forces stations had less power and covered much less territory than the national stations (Keshishoglou, 1961, p. 39).

TELEVISION AND FM RADIO

Television and FM radio were late arriving in Greece. Private interests were experimenting with television in 1953, but the government was not yet involved. In the late 1950s the government was to use $15 million in war reparations from Italy to build a 17-station television network, but in view of the country's critical financial needs and heavy damages resulting from earthquakes, it decided against such a plan at the time (Emery, 1969, p. 290).

In 1960 at the Thessaloniki International Trade Fair, the first public television experiments were conducted by the Public Power Company, but they only lasted the duration of the fair (Dinopoulos, 1987, p. 16). In 1964 a private company called Television of Northern Greece was given permission to broadcast events of the Thessaloniki International Trade Fair to the about 5,000 television sets in existence at the time (Gemelos, 1972, p. 75). In June 1965 the first television station began operating experimentally for two hours each day in Athens, under the auspices of EIR ("First Greek TV," 1965). At the same time the armed forces started their own television experiments, in Athens. The armed forces seemed to have greater success than EIR, because they were able to utilize army film crews and other army facilities (Dinopoulos, 1987, p. 17).

By 1966, although there was still no regular FM radio broadcasting, the experimental television broadcasts continued. That year a three-day symposium was held in Athens to discuss the issue of television in Greece, while the public anxiously awaited Greek television programs. The few people who had television sets at this time were only able to pick up experimental broadcasts and Italian television (Dizard, 1966, p. 73). The delay in the arrival of television was partly from the government indecision on the issue and from difficulty in coming to satisfactory terms with international bidders to build a television system, and partly from opposition by domestic newspapers and cinema theater owners (Gemelos, 1972, p. 74). There also can be no doubt that the political unrest in the mid 1960s had an adverse effect on the development of television. The caretaker governments did not have the strength or willingness to promote such a development because of the more important political and economic decisions facing them at the time.

The first official television broadcast by EIR took place on February 23, 1966, for two hours in Athens, consisting mainly of news and of travelogues acquired from various embassies (Dinopoulos, 1987, p. 17). The objective of these broadcasts was to train people in this new field, to see how they could adapt television to Greece, and to organize a structure for the administration of a television system.

Meanwhile, Greek Armed Forces Radio expanded its television broadcasts to three nights per week, starting at 9 p.m. each evening after EIR television went off the air (McDonald, 1983, p. 167). The armed forces were given technical assistance for their television station by the U.S. government. This station inaugurated the practice of selling time to producers, who broadcast various programs that included commercials. This station's first commercially sponsored program was "Mission Impossible," sponsored by liquor vendors. The advertising agencies jumped at a chance to sponsor television programs, as they had done with radio years before ("Greek armed forces TV," 1967). EIR began to allow similar sponsorships in 1971.

When the military took over the government in 1967, one of the first buildings to be seized was the EIR building. On April 21, 1967, at 6 a.m., an official decree was broadcast over the radio stating that the Armed Forces had taken over the government of the country (Schwab and Frangos, 1973, p. 13). During the first few days the junta used the facilities of the armed forces stations and forced EIR to also carry that signal (McDonald, 1983, p. 164). According to Helen Vlachos (1972, p. 59) the new radio administrators were "speaking in harsh new military tones, and issuing a stream of orders followed by threats and very few explanations."

The junta realized the medium's excellent propaganda potential and started the development of a more extensive television system to help gain popular support. This was similar to what the Metaxas dictatorship had done with radio in the 1930s. Nevertheless, in the 1960s Greece and Turkey were the only countries on the European continent without a nationwide television network. However, Eurovision provided Greek television with major world events, such as the first moon walk, certain international soccer games, and the IXth European Games, which Greek television originated from Athens with the help of the Office de Radiffusion Television Franchaise. Regular nightly programming was started, first by the armed forces channel in November 1968, while EIR regular nightly programming started in April 1969 (McDonald, 1983, p. 170). In 1970 a new satellite earth station was built at Thermopylea, which finally brought Greece closer to the rest of the world.

The building of a nationwide television system in Greece started in 1971, when the European subsidiary of Northrop Corporation undertook the installation of a $12.5 million radio and television network that would link the whole country for the first time, and also would enable Greece to beam radio signals outside the country. This network consisted of seventeen transmitters, which would broadcast television and two FM programs, one stereo ("New radio TV network," 1971).

In 1968 the military junta created the Armed Forces Information Service (YENED) to take over Armed Forces broadcasting and to provide "national, moral, and social education" to the armed forces and the public. In 1970 law 745/1970 replaced EIR with the Hellenic Radio-Television Foundation (EIRT). The junta continued to control all broadcasting in Greece by stacking EIRT's five-member board with generals (McDonald, 1983, p. 172). The junta had as a goal the re-education of the Greek public, and toward that goal it controlled all Greek mass media, including the few private radio stations in operation. Most broadcasts at the time consisted of either propaganda or popular commercial programming. There was also cultural censorship, some of which had started even before 1967, and continued until 1981. The music of Mikis Theodorakis continued to be banned from the radio until the military junta fell in 1974.

At this time YENED was the more popular and more profitable television station, and it stayed that way until 1973. EIRT television, which always had budget deficits, ran more informative programs than YENED. Starting in 1968 most of EIRT's income was generated through a special fee on residential electricity bills (Doulkeri and Dimitras, 1986, p. 139).

BROADCASTING UNDER DEMOCRATIC RULE

In 1974 civilian rule was once again restored. Parliament approved a new constitution, which took effect in 1975. Article 15 of the Constitution deals with cinema, music, and broadcasting. Although the conservative party, New Democracy, which was responsible for drafting the Constitution, regarded the censorship that had been exercised under the junta as undesirable, it was not willing to grant broadcasting the freedom afforded to print media. Thus, Section 2 of Article 15 states:

> Radio and television shall be under the immediate control of the state and shall aim at the objective transmission, on equal terms, of information and news reports as well as works of literature and art; the qualitative level of programs shall be assured in consideration of their social mission and the cultural development of the country.

Based on the above article of the 1975 Constitution, a new broadcasting law was enacted by the conservative-controlled parliament, practically restructuring Greek broadcasting. Law 230/1975, which took effect on April 1, 1975, established Hellenic Radio Television (ERT), to replace EIRT as the legal entity for broadcasting. ERT became a public corporation, governed by a board of directors appointed by the cabinet. This board was comprised of 20 people, all from high offices in government, banking, and education, who were to be "selected on the basis of their good standing and prestige and in a position . . . to contribute . . . to the attainment of the objectives of ERT" ("Greek radio-TV law," 1976). The head of the board of directors would be the governor of the Bank of Greece. The powers of the board of directors, however, were mainly advisory, and the board rarely met.

The administrative council of ERT had more power to actively take part in day-to-day operations than the board of directors. The council was to be comprised of seven members, appointed for three years by the Council of Ministers (the cabinet). The purpose of the administrative council was to "supervise and control ERT services," to draw up budgets and plans for the development of ERT, and to "express its opinion on the overall policy."

However, the true supervisory authority of ERT, according to this law, rested in the Ministry to the Premiership. Specifically, the deputy minister appointed the director-general of ERT as the head of the daily operations, assisted by two assistant directors, also appointed by the cabinet. As such, the legal and operational structure of ERT, even as a public corporation, was heavily controlled by the government.

According to law 230/1975 and all subsequent broadcast laws, the purpose of ERT is to provide "information, education, and recreation for the Greek people (through) the organization, operation and development of radio and television" (Article 1). In addition, Article 3 of the same act states that "ERT programs must be imbued with democratic spirit, awareness of cultural responsibility, humanitarianism and objectivity, and must take into account the local situation." Finally, law 230/1975 (Article 4, paragraph 1) went on to state: "The transmission of sound or pictures of any kind by radio or television by any natural person or legal entity other than ERT and the Armed Forces Information Service shall be prohibited" ("Greek radio-TV law," 1976). This paragraph brought an end to any legal private broadcasting in Greece.

Law 230/1975 further indicated a desire to take away the broadcasting privilege of the armed forces. Article 4, paragraph 4, stated that two years after April 1976 the "Armed Forces Information Service shall be amalgamated with ERT, if the necessary economic, technical and organizational conditions prevail." This "if," however, delayed the implementation of this law.

Color television arrived in Greece in 1979, as the Karamanlis government selected the French SECAM system ("Color TV arrives," 1979). This was another example of the head of the government turning to a foreign power, to which he was loyal, for new technology. In 1979 some television programs were broadcast in color, but it took another year until all programs were in color.

The legal structure of ERT was one of the targets of the opposition socialist party, PASOK, before it came to power in 1981. PASOK promised to change this structure because it was used to promote only the party in power, especially before elections (McDonald, 1983,

p. 205). Following the elections of 1981, however, PASOK did not make ERT more independent of the government, although it did make more air time available to other parties represented in parliament.

In 1982, PASOK followed through with the intention of the 1976 law to do away with broadcasting by the armed forces. The new law, 1288/1982, transformed YENED into ERT-2, and ERT into ERT-1. ERT-1 remained a public corporation owned by the state, governed, theoretically, by a board of directors. ERT-2, on the other hand, became a public service of the Ministry of the Premiership and was governed by a general council of five members appointed by the Minister to the Premiership. The president of the council was the director of all ERT-2 services. Thus, the party in power controlled ERT-2, because most of its important decision makers were appointed by it.

In fact, there was practically no difference in the control of ERT-1 and ERT-2, because the Deputy Minister to the Premiership was in charge of both. Not only were the top administrative positions filled by the government, but also all non-permanent positions, although permanent civil service employees were somewhat safe in any government change. Usually, however, the government appointed the heads of ERT-1 and ERT-2, who even approved the actors and actresses in various programs, keeping in mind their political affiliations. In the way it handled broadcasting, PASOK did not appear to be much different, from New Democracy.

It seems that no party has willing to part with radio and television, although during the 1985 election campaign New Democracy promised, if elected, to allow private broadcasting within the confines of the Constitution. PASOK responded that if this happened, broadcasting would be in the hands of foreign and domestic capitalist interests. Nevertheless, PASOK did promise to create a single, more efficient broadcasting entity.

PASOK was indeed reelected in 1987, and another new legal structure for broadcasting was approved by parliament. After much discussion, the new broadcast law (1730/1987) took effect in October 1987. The major change brought about by this law was that now one company, Hellenic Radio-Television S.A., (ERT), has complete control of state broadcasting. The new company has five divisions, of which the major three are Hellenic Television 1 (ET-1), formerly ERT-1; Hellenic Television 2 (ET-2), formerly ERT-2; and

Hellenic Radio (ERA), made up of the three ERT-1 radio services
(ERA-1, ERA-2, ERA-3), ERT-2 radio (ERA-4), and the Voice of
Greece short-wave radio service (ERA-5). In addition, ERT S. A. was
to establish an Audiovisual Media Institute and a Production and
Marketing company, something not yet accomplished.

Nevertheless, the major importance of this law is that despite its
initial opposition, the government included in the law a provision
allowing establishment of private radio stations. However, in
actuality private broadcasting in Greece was already a reality, as
1987 completely opened Pandora's box called *eleftheri radiofonia*
(free radio).

3

Privatization of the Broadcast Media

FREE RADIO

The idea of non-state radio had been around in Greece long before the 1980s. Free radio or eleftheri radiofonia, as non-state radio came to be called, had been practiced heavily since the 1950s by radio pirates, who risked heavy penalties by broadcasting a few hours each day from their homes. Although most were broadcasting on AM, the first FM radio pirate went on the air in 1957 (Roumeliotis, 1991, p. 253). Law 1244/1972, enacted by the military junta in 1972, provided serious measures against pirates, including fines, confiscation of equipment, and imprisonment (Balis and Kapsis, 1986, p. 11).

The radio pirates varied, but they all had in common a love for music and for the thrill of interacting with an appreciative audience. As an example, in 1987 "Yannis," a radio pirate, built a 30-watt FM transmitter in his home. He operated twice a week, four hours each time, transmitting after midnight so as not to interfere with national radio stations. He broadcast mainly Anglo-American music and would often accept requests. Like most radio pirates, he used a code number (952) for identification purposes. He did not accept advertising and did not like pirates who did. Pirate radio was his hobby.

For most pirates, radio was an expensive hobby however. Pirate 397, for example, had operating costs of 20,000 drachmas ($108)* per week, but was rewarded by an average of 200 nightly phone calls from listeners (Balis and Kapsis, 1986, p. 13). Furthermore, this hobby had dangers. Yannis, for example, had been found out twice by the police and had gotten away with warnings. It did not matter much to him whether amateur stations were legalized, because he was sure he would continue to operate no matter what. This was not to be, however, because Yannis was caught by the police for a third time, and all his equipment was confiscated (Chakos, 1987).

In 1986 the special telecommunications control office of the Ministry of Transportation and Communications (MTC) apprehended 500 pirates in Athens, but only prosecuted those who carried advertising (Hasapopoulos, 1986). This, however, did not stop an estimated 1,000 other radio pirates from operating, in Athens alone (Balis and Kapsis, 1986, p. 13).

Another pirate station was Star Radio, which went from just another pirate number on the air (772), to a licensed station. Beginning as a pirate station, 772 soon joined forces with other pirates and friends, and the operation slowly enlarged to the point of operating daily, from 8 p.m. to 2 a.m. Star Radio's formula was simple: the announcers talked about things that interested them and their listeners, who were in their late teens and early twenties. The announcers played primarily foreign music, read poetry and letters on the air, and took requests. Gradually they created a fan club, a program guide, and car stickers, and they held underground meetings with some of their dedicated listeners.

This station changed names four times before it settled on Star Radio. The programming evolved as some group members went away to college, while others had to join the army. Most of the 17 young people involved in 1987 were attending the University of Athens. Each would have his or her own show on the air, playing personal records or albums donated by two record companies. The station was located in a small room in a house 15 miles from the center of Athens (Margiori, 1987).

---

*An average exchange rate of 185 drachmas per $1 has been used for the period 1985-1992, throughout this book.

The free radio movement in Greece was greatly influenced by related efforts in other countries, such as free radio in France and pirate radio in England (Boyd, 1986). In France, demands for free radio (*radio-libres*) were made from 1977 until 1981, when the state radio monopoly was lifted (McCain and Lowe, 1990, p. 92). Similarly, citizens' groups in Greece seriously began to demand the right to operate radio stations with such notable illegal stations as Anti-Lalos, which broadcast openly for 24 hours in 1983, and Kanali 15, which covered the national elections in 1985. Both, however, were closed down by the police. Groups such as Kanali 15 defined free radio as the ability to practice broadcasting just as the Constitution had intended, for quality, objectivity, and cultural growth. They defined free radio primarily as "citizens' radio" (Koundouros, 1987).

However, what gave impetus to the development of Greek free radio was pressure by opposition political parties, which wanted a piece of the airwaves. Many politicians simply wanted their voices to be heard, since state radio was primarily the voice of the ruling party. During the 1986 municipal elections, six mayoral candidates from Greece's largest cities, coming primarily from the conservative opposition, made free radio part of their political platforms. Their demands were not so much in support of the rights of amateur radio broadcasters as in support of a breakdown of the government's monopoly over the airwaves, especially concerning news and public affairs programming. The eventual victory, in Greece's three largest cities, of the opposition New Democracy (ND) party candidates, who had all pledged to build radio stations, put pressure on the government to act.

In November 1986 Prime Minister Andreas Papandreou's son, George, then Deputy Minister of Culture, spoke out in favor of free radio, which he defined as opening up the airwaves to young people, radio amateurs, and political party youth groups. He declared that "conditions for the permission of free radio in our country are ripe as never before" (Tolios, 1986, p. 25). He further stated that free radio should begin with the legalization of amateur radio, but that he could envision municipal radio stations and eventually a medium "without limits," including "political radio" (Tolios, 1986, p. 25). This announcement, created controversy within the governing socialist party, PASOK, as some top party members did not want to give up control of the broadcast media. The controversy was put to rest in December 1986, as Andreas Papandreou announced his support for the creation of a parliamentary committee to examine the issue and come up with recommendations on the "boundaries of free radio." He defined free radio as Greek citizens having the right to operate local radio stations (Fatsis, 1986).

The idea of abolishing the state radio monopoly had come up in 1982 and again in 1985, when some within PASOK proposed a law that would allow local governments to establish municipal radio stations (Pretenteris, 1986). At this time PASOK party members were in control of local governments in most large cities. However, following the 1986 municipal elections, in which New Democracy mayoral candidates won in several major cities, PASOK shelved the idea until George A. Papandreou took his public stand a few months later.

Municipal radio was not a new idea in Greece. Private, nonprofit stations, under the protection of their local governments, were operational in three cities beginning in 1960. These stations, in Amaliada, Ierapetra, and Mesologgi, were allowed to operate because they had tremendous public support and because they cooperated with ERT. In another case, following the merger of ERT-1 and YENED in 1982, a former YENED radio station in the northern Greek city of Kozani was, to a great degree, taken over by local social groups while maintaining its affiliation with ERT-2 (Petropoulou, 1986). Furthermore, in 1980, 65 city mayors and village presidents throughout the country demanded that ERT provide a short, regularly scheduled program devoted to local governments. Such a program started on ERT-1 radio in 1982.

The next step in the development of municipal radio took place in 1984, when the Central Union of Greek Municipalities and Villages (KEDKE) made its first proposal for local radio stations. One of the architects of that proposal was the leftist parties, mayoral candidate for Athens in 1986, Theodoros Katrivanos, who declared that, if elected, he would establish an Athenian municipal radio station. The New Democracy candidate in that same election, and the eventual winner, Miltiadis Evert, adopted that proposal, and thus pressure on the central government intensified.

Even after the prime minister's announcement, the new mayor of Athens insisted that if a legal structure for free radio was not created by the end of March 1987, he would proceed with his plans to build a municipal radio station, even if that meant violating the current law. The government responded that if a legal structure was not ready by then, it would still find a way to accommodate the mayor ("Ekviasmos," 1987).

Nevertheless, not all parties agreed with the way the state radio monopoly should be lifted. PASOK was itself divided as to how far this process should go. Many within the party simply wanted to legalize the traditional radio pirates/amateurs, without allowing them to broadcast news or public affairs programs. Others wanted to allow provincial radio stations to operate under the provincial governors, whom the governing party had appointed, but not under the elected local mayors, many of whom were affiliated with the opposition. New Democracy, on the other hand, was in favor of private broadcasting, while the Coalition of the Left was opposed to private radio, believing that it would lead to private television controlled by foreign interests. The Coalition was in favor of nonprofit, amateur radio stations, and believed that the answer to the problem was for the government to allow the state media to function more democratically ("Ti tha giny," 1986).

Meanwhile, cities throughout Greece started planning to build radio stations, but Athens was the first on the air. On May 31, 1987, municipal station Athens 98.4 FM began broadcasting without a license, initially operating 12 hours a day. Just two days before, the government had issued a ministerial decision (14631/22/2691/29-5-87) allowing the establishment of municipal radio stations.

The inauguration of Athens 98.4 was the first important challenge to the state's broadcasting monopoly. This station was constructed at a cost of about 100 million drachmas ($545,000), initially employing 85 people, most hired on a one-month contract (Kanelli, 1987). Yannis Tzannetakos, a lawyer and former leftist leader of the Association of University Students, was hired as its first manager. Surprisingly, most of the people hired were not followers of New Democracy, and this in itself was a major change, and caused much discontent within the ranks of New Democracy (Papachristos, 1987). It was very unusual for a politician not to stock a government enterprise with members of his own party.

The station's programming was mostly live, consisting of music, news, talk, and commercials. In some people's view, however, not much had changed politically. The station was another example of authoritarian rule, except that this time it took place at the local level. This was reinforced by the absence of the opposition city council members from the station's inauguration ("Radio apo ta idia," 1987). Although it had an ethics and standards committee made up of journalists from various political viewpoints, the committee was seen by many as a goodwill gesture by the mayor and not something that was likely to last.

The second municipal station, Kanali 1, was put on the air on June 26, 1987, in the city of Piraeus, Greece's third-largest city and the port of Athens, by another opposition (ND) mayor. This station sought a more local orientation than the Athens station, and many of its employees considered Athens 98.4 much like state radio (Cowell, 1987).

This was followed by station FM-100 in Thessaloniki, Greece's second-largest city, in September 1987. Soon KEDKE proposed again that local stations be established as public corporations in most Greek provinces, and operated jointly by provincial cities and towns (Lionarakis, 1988, p. 139). The work of establishing such provincial stations would be done by the Hellenic Corporation for Local Development and Local Government (EETAA), which started training managers for the proposed stations. The first such station went on the air in July, 1990, in Agrinio. Radio Station of Etoloakarnania Province, as it is called, is a joint corporation of several municipalities and private interests (Roumeliotis, 1990, July).

Meanwhile, municipalities around the country were experimenting with radio transmissions. Before the end of 1988 the first joint effort came from eight Athenian suburbs, which established Diavlos 10 in a working-class region of Athens. By March 1989 there were 13 municipal stations throughout the country, and their number would continue to grow rapidly (Roumeliotis, 1989, March).

Meanwhile, although PASOK was forced to abolish the state broadcasting monopoly, it was determined to keep the new stations in check. The government often attempted to keep the mayors within the bounds of the law by trying, in some cases successfully, to demolish the illegal transmission towers of the municipal stations in Athens and Thessaloniki. The mayors fought back, with party loyalists guarding the transmission tower sites.

However, the first examples of municipal radio were not what many had envisioned free radio would be. As columnist Petros Efthimiou (1987) stated, "Free radio is a chance for a change in (people's) mentality and practices," but unfortunately, municipal radio only perpetuated the old mentality. It was politicians' radio, not public or nonpartisan radio. Furthermore, even the managers of the first two municipal stations had doubts about municipal radio. Tzannetakos said that free radio should be much more than municipal radio, while the manager of the Pireaus station, Kanali 1, said he did not believe in municipal radio, because "people don't want to listen to small-town problems" (Papaspyrou, 1987, p. 69).

At this early stage of free radio, many problems arose, ranging from inexperience on the part of the radio announcers to questions about the role and identity of free radio. There were such questions as, Should private radio stations be allowed to exist? What happens to radio amateurs? Should non-state broadcasters be allowed to broadcast news? And if yes, under what conditions? Where will money for these stations come from? And finally, what is the political nature of these stations going to be, keeping in mind that politicians were instrumental in the stations' establishment?

Some of the above questions were answered by the new broadcasting law, 1730/1987. Although ERT was given monopoly over broadcasting, Article 2, Paragraph 4 of this law stated that the Minister to the Premiership could grant licenses for the creation and operation of FM radio stations for local coverage. Such licenses could be given to local government, individuals, and corporations, but no individual or corporation could have more than one license, nor could there be private radio networks or chain broadcasting.

This law further created a commission to supervise license proceedings. The Local Radio Commission was made up of the following people: The president of the Council of State (the Constitutional Court), the president of the Civil Law (Supreme) Court, the president of the executive council of the Union of Journalists of Athens Dailies (ESIEA), and two faculty members from Greek universities, all appointed for three-year terms.

The law further established that details on private radio were to come later, via a presidential decree (Helliniki Eteria, 1988, p. 245). This decree (25/1988) was published in the *Government Gazette* in January 1988 (FEK 10A/15-1-88), and it outlined details for the establishment of radio stations. It allowed establishment of FM stations by entities as set forth by law 1730/1987, between 87.5 and 107.7 megahertz, with a license required. Also, it set out the parameters for such operations.

These stations have as a goal the objective and on equal

terms transmission of information and news as well as
products of speech and the arts, while upholding the
qualitative standards of the broadcasts which are imposed by the (broadcaster's) social mission and the
cultural development of the country (Article 1, Paragraph
2).

Municipal stations were to be supervised by an executive council
representing all parties within each city council. The decree also
established technical standards and set maximum amounts of time
to be used for advertising. It gave priority for two-year renewable
radio licenses to local governments, press groups, and radio amateurs (in that order). Its most controversial provision, however, was
the requirement that most stations have an ethics and standards
committee, primarily made up of journalists (Article 15).

The above restrictions reflected the uncertainty political leaders
had about a truly free radio. PASOK generally held that all new
stations were politically opposing it. New Democracy did not support
free radio unconditionally, but only in the ways it could help ND as
a party or hurt the government. For example, even some members
of New Democracy did not want private stations to broadcast news.
Finally, the Coalition of the Left was in a true predicament. On one
hand it did not support private broadcasting, but on the other, it saw
it as possibly the only way for media democratization.

Most broadcasters were opposed to the presidential decree,
many because it imposed limitations on news coverage, and many
because they did not want any restrictions at all. Furthermore, while
some declared that the standards imposed on local stations were
harsher than those applicable to state radio, in terms of news and
political reportage, others opposed them because they forced municipal stations to take into account all the parties represented in
local councils.

There was criticism of the new guidelines for coverage of political
campaigns, which were seen as not allowing true democratic dialogue. Finally, there was criticism of the requirement that journalists make up the ethics committees, because newspapers were not
required to have similar committees, and because this excluded
other media experts (Koundouros, 1987).

A major problem with the law and the decrees was in what they
left out. They dealt with political broadcasting, which was dear to the

party in power, but did not deal with such important questions as the number frequencies that were available. This was not helped by the fact that the parliamentary committee charged with establishing criteria for private radio did not do much more than debate the issue (Stafyla, 1987).

Nevertheless, the first radio station licenses were approved in May 1988. There were 29 licenses granted, most of them to municipalities and publishing companies (Roumeliotis, 1988, May 10). The commission never announced the criteria used in allocating these licenses, and did not tie the licenses to specific frequencies. As the first private station, Top FM of the Lambrakis Press Organization, went on the air in May 1988, it became clear that radio amateurs were not being served. However, a few former pirates were recruited as program producers by municipal and private stations.

Many broadcasters in Athens continued to pirate the airwaves and face difficulties with the law. Provincial pirates fared better; many of them were granted licenses, and they eventually took up 40 percent of the total provincial listening audience, leaving 60 percent for state radio (Roumeliotis, 1988, Oct. 17). Besides traditional pirates, other individuals or companies were also broadcasting without a license.

Under the new status quo, the number of radio stations exploded. Many stations in Athens and Thessaloniki began operating on a 24-hour basis, resulting in increased competition for audiences and radio personalities. By the end of 1988 there were 22 licensed radio stations in Thessaloniki besides the four ERA radio services, and possibly up to 100 pirates sharing the airwaves (Roumeliotis, 1988, Oct. 31). In Athens, at the same time, there were 52 fully licensed or license-applied-for stations and up to 20 more unlicensed stations, in addition to some 60 other applicants waiting to get the remaining frequencies. With another set of license applications approved in early 1989 (Roumeliotis, 1989, February), more than 200 licenses had been approved for the whole country. However, it was hard to know the exact number of stations operating, as some were operating without a license, while others with a license were not yet on the air. In May 1989 the Local Radio Commission granted 22 more licenses, but it allocated only 16 frequencies and ordered that some stations share frequencies (Roumeliotis, 1989, May).

Such action by the Local Radio Commission, and the lack of well-made plans in general, resulted in additional problems. There were pirate stations using licensed frequencies, stations illegally using relay transmitters or second frequencies, stations broadcasting with greater power than allowed, stations building transmitters in unauthorized areas, and city mayors operating more than one station without a license. For example, besides FM-100, the mayor of Thessaloniki, Sotiris Kouvelas, built two more stations in that city, FM-101, a youth-oriented station carrying primarily foreign music, and FM-100.5, a fine arts station.

These problems forced many station owners in 1989 to unite under a Continuous Committee for Local Radio (DETORS). But the owners were not very cohesive, as some had conflicting political philosophies. Indeed, some of the greatest problems of free radio were political. Although the major municipal stations would allow all parties to be heard, for which some mayors were criticized by their own parties for not being partisan enough, most municipal stations were kept under the direct control by the mayor. Despite this, among the different stations, many more political voices were being heard. The private radio stations also tended to promote a healthier discussion of political ideas through their news and public affairs programs, particularly interview programs, which often made news themselves as they provided a forum for many politicians and public opinion leaders to voice their concerns.

In this new situation, state radio did not remain unaffected. In Thessaloniki, where FM-100, came to attract 50 percent of the listening audience, the central government decided to fight by joining the trend. It built a new radio station, 102 FM Stereo, along the lines of free radio but with greater emphasis on Greek music. Furthermore, three of the four national radio services increased their percentage of live programming, which initially had averaged less than 25 percent, while the Fourth Program completely changed its format, targeting younger audiences. One of its most innovative changes was to turn over the airwaves to radio pirates for one hour each night. The ERA stations also decreased their amounts of Greek folk and traditional music in order to compete with the more Anglo-American sound of the private stations. Furthermore, ERT constructed another new regional FM station, Aegean Radio, on the island of Lesvos. At the same time, many state radio stations that had been broadcasting for years on AM started transmitting on FM as well.

However, financial problems started taking their toll on the new stations. Although Athens 98.4 had managed to generate a profit of 105 million drachmas ($567,000) within the first seven months by becoming the most popular station in Athens (Neofotistos, 1988), soon there were so many new stations that radio advertising expenditures, initially only 6 percent of total, were divided up (Chalkou, 1990). In 1989, radio's share of total advertising expenditures increased to 7.3 percent, but this was still not enough.

Financial difficulties especially hurt stations operated jointly by smaller municipalities around Athens, resulting in the first strike by non-state radio station employees (Roumeliotis, 1989, January), while at other stations employees were not being paid regularly. In addition, music licensing groups threatened legal action because the stations were not paying music royalties.

Financial problems also resulted in greater competition among the stations for revenue-producing popular programming and radio personalities, especially in Athens. Both private and municipal stations depended on their popular programming to gain huge audiences so they could generate profits and political support, respectively. During the first two years, numerous on-air personalities, as well as station managers, switched stations, either for more money or because of programming or political differences. In this environment, free radio came to mean live radio; promotions such as contests, giveaways, and bingo; and primarily Anglo-American music.

Foreign music, however, had made its appearance in Greece long before the advent of free radio. Besides pirate stations, most of which transmitted foreign music, state radio had also historically provided a good amount of foreign music. At just about any time of the day, listeners in Greece could find foreign popular music on some station. The Second and Fourth Programs provided the most foreign music at the national level. These two services broadcast foreign music intermittently throughout the day and had specific programs during the week that played foreign music exclusively. The Second Program broadcast foreign music exclusively during 26 percent of its total programming hours, while 14 percent consisted of a mixture of Greek and foreign music (Tsampras, 1985, Apr. 6). The Fourth Program broadcast foreign music exclusively during 10 percent of its total hours, while 23 percent consisted of a mixture of Greek and foreign music (Tsampras, 1985, Apr. 27).

In general, Greek state radio was already providing the greatest variety of programming radio could possibly offer, given the number of stations and number of program services involved. ERT radio services had traditionally packaged programming in blocks. These were prerecorded, either by members of its permanent staff or by independent producers. A public affairs program, such as "Selides," targeting women, was produced with the help of four people. It provided information about fashion and medical issues and included interviews and topics considered of interest to women, interspersed with musical breaks (strictly Greek music), and no commercials except at the end (Macridis, 1987).

An example of a different type of program was "Liga Loya Mes Ti Nychta," which was broadcast once a week. It was produced and announced by a young woman who chose a theme for her show (e.g. rhythm and blues), used her own records, wrote text to discuss between songs, and recorded the show with the help of one of ERA's engineers. The half-hour show was produced free of charge (Vlavianos, 1987). A similar program on a private or municipal station would be live, could include a contest, and would be interrupted by commercials.

Most new radio stations did not narrowcast throughout the day, as do U.S. radio stations, but filled one-to three-hour blocks with specific programs. For example, the Pireaus municipal station had ten zone-producers, each responsible for three-hour programming blocks. Because these new stations came on the air almost at once, many producers/performers either came from state radio or were former radio pirates (Papandonakou, 1987).

These former pirates were strictly disc jockeys; spinning records that were often connected with a common theme. One such popular program was "Black Velvet," consisting strictly of black or soul music, which started on the Athens municipal station but after a year jumped over to a private station. Most new radio stations allocated about 30 percent of their programming to news, public affairs (discussion), and sports, and the rest to music. The music portion had a distinctly American influence. Besides black or soul music, the stations carried shows with heavy metal, jazz, 1960s rock, rock concerts, American and European top-40, and some even carried American country music.

The weekly ratings for radio stations became important and controversial, as they often showed contradictory results. According to these ratings, the most popular stations in Athens in the late

1980s were Athens 98.4, and the private stations Sky, Top FM, and Antenna. They all played Greek and Anglo-American music along with their sports, news, and public affairs programs. Another popular station was Jeronymo Groovy, a former pirate station that had been on the air since 1966.

The disappointed George A. Papandreou often criticized the existing free radio. He was particularly upset that amateurs did not get many of the allocated licenses, and at the programming offered by private stations. He once said that one could not tell from the sound of Athens stations "whether they broadcast from Athens, Xanthi, or Italy" (Roumeliotis, 1988, November).

As the first two years of free radio came to an end, the competing centers of power in Greek radio were the government-run radio services (ERA), the municipal radio stations, and the private, press-owned radio stations. At the same time, radio amateurs, the only true practitioners of free radio, were fighting to be allowed to participate. The continuous development of private radio stations without much supervision by the state had led to freedom on the air waves but also to tremendous technical, political, and financial problems. Despite all the problems, however, free radio, as a movement, was popular. It sparked political and philosophical debates, and it was widely discussed in the media. Although many felt that this chaotic state of Greek radio was a temporary situation, the Greeks have a saying that "nothing is more permanent than the provisional." Meanwhile, the privatization of radio whet the people's appetite for greater choices in television programming as well.

PRIVATE TELEVISION

Initially, the alternative to the two Greek television channels was the videocassette recorder (VCR). From 1982 to 1987 there was a 900 percent increase in the number of VCRs in Greece, as more than 40 percent of Greek households acquired one. By 1987 over 2,000 video clubs had opened throughout the country (Kayos, 1987). This demand for videotape rentals resulted not only in the creation of a Greek video production industry, but also in heavy videotape piracy. It was estimated that in 1988 video piracy was a 6 billion drachma ($32.5 million) business (Bakoyannopoulou, 1988). At this time there were over 200 legitimate video production companies in operation, while the number of video clubs had increased to 2,500 (Kanelli, 1988).

However, satellite television soon became the newest alternative to ERT programming and videotape rentals, causing a 30 percent drop in video rentals and the closing of many small video clubs (Kanelli, 1988). As soon as political parties realized the benefits that could result from the public's dissatisfaction with ERT television, they started examining ways to take advantage of the situation. In October 1987 the mayor of Pireaus, Andreas Andrianopoulos, set up a satellite dish in a city square to demonstrate satellite television to his city's residents.

In November 1987, not more than six months after the introduction of municipal radio in Thessaloniki, mayor Sotiris Kouvelas announced his intention to construct a municipal television channel that also would retransmit satellite channels. Kouvelas said that the prime minister should not be the only one receiving satellite channels, referring to Andreas Papandreou's use of a satellite dish antenna ("Dimotiko kanali," 1987).

Nevertheless, PASOK had always refused to allow the introduction of satellite television. It even refused to join an EEC satellite project, Europa, because it feared "cultural invasion and technological dependence" ("Olympus," 1984). In fact, in 1987 more than 200 people or groups in Greece, including political leaders and foreign cultural institutes, had satellite dishes, even though at the time, they were not thought to be legal (Roussis, 1987). It was not until 1988 that the government issued guidelines allowing satellite reception (Makris, 1988).

Satellite reception was introduced on a wide scale in Athens in 1987, as a way to encourage residents of the historic Plaka area to give up their individual antennas. The government wanted to restore the traditional look of Plaka; to accomplish this, the whole area was wired to a central antenna, and the residents were offered four satellite channels besides the Greek stations. Similarly, in 1983 some residents of the northern Greek cities of Komotini and Xanthi replaced their own television antennas with cable, made available to them so their respective towns could become more aesthetically pleasing (Kazakopoulos, 1987).

In January 1988 the mayor of Thessaloniki went ahead with his plans, and started terrestrial transmission of satellite channels RTL, TV Cinq, Super Channel, Sky, and RAI-Uno. This action led to long court litigation, because ERT had exclusive rights to broadcasting in Greece. The constitutional Supreme Court (Council of State) eventually ruled in favor of ERT (Venizelos, 1989, p. 31). Satellite stations initially became very popular, causing video rentals in the city to decline sharply (Apostolou, 1988). The government, meanwhile, sent police forces to demolish the mayor's transmission tower, but city residents stood in their way.

A few months later the mayor of Athens issued a new ultimatum; if the central government did not make satellite programming available to Athenians by Christmas 1988, he would. Soon afterward the government announced that it would make satellite channels available on Greek terrestrial television frequencies in ten cities, including Thessaloniki. It started negotiations with the satellite channels to get their permission for terrestrial transmission, something that the mayor of Thessaloniki had not done.

In October 1988 the first six such channels were transmitted in Athens. They were SAT-1 (German), Super Channel (British), CNN (American), TV-5 (French), RAI-Due (Italian), and Horizon (Soviet). Despite initial problems with reception, the public was happy to have more television program choices. This resulted in a frenzy to obtain the "best and most expensive" television antennas for the best possible reception of the satellite channels, though most Greeks do not adequately understand a foreign language (Koray, 1988). The government was thus able to take the initiative away from the opposition, while occupying valuable frequencies with these channels and thus making it difficult for the opposition to establish television channels of its own.

Private television, however, was still seen by many as unattainable. The prime minister maintained that television was different from radio, and that at most the only change likely to take place would be a third ERT channel with the participation of private interests (Yobazolias, 1987). Nevertheless, television privatization in Europe, and domestic developments, increased support for the establishment of private channels. The political opposition maintained its attack on the government's monopoly of television, primarily because of what it called unfair treatment on television news. In Athens the mayor established a videotape service, sold or distributed via video clubs, to transmit weekly programs, such as "alternative" news, music/variety shows, and documentaries (Neofotistos, 1988).

At the same time, advertising agencies insisted that ERT was not satisfying the demand for programming or advertising time, and they demanded that private television be allowed (Papaioannou, 1988). There were even cases of television pirates, one of whom showed soft-porn films on an ET-2 frequency after that channel went off the air (Hasapopoulos, 1986).

Meanwhile, the mayors of Thessaloniki and Pireaus announced that they would start municipal television stations in their respective cities. Both mayors began with experimental transmissions, but ERT responded by taking them to court for violating its monopoly over broadcasting, and by announcing plans to build stations in Crete and Patras. ERT also offered the city of Pireaus more news coverage of its municipal affairs, and offered a weekly information program to the Local Government Association (Protogyrou and Petroutsou, 1989, January).

In December 1988 in the Thessaloniki area, in anticipation of a new station to be built by the mayor, the government's third channel, ET-3, went on the air, but with very limited programming. Nevertheless, Thessaloniki's municipal station, TV-100, went on the air in January 1989, as the mayor again thumbed his nose at ERT and the government ("ERT: O Kouvelas," 1989).

Unlike the mayor of Thessaloniki, the mayor of Pireaus actually applied for permission to use a television frequency. However, not receiving an answer from the government, and realizing that frequencies were quickly being taken up by satellite channels, he soon took over a television frequency for his station TV Plus. This station was to be a cooperative effort with a private company and would introduce subscription television to Greece. It would operate six hours a day for its subscribers, while the rest of the day it would serve as the municipal free television channel for Pireaus (Fitras, 1988).

This station went on the air as a municipal channel on December 30, 1988, but did not last more than a week. ERT responded not only by bringing lawsuits and trying to demolish the mayor's transmitters, but also by placing Super Channel on the TV Plus frequency. When Super Channel objected to being retransmitted without receiving royalties, ERT placed ET-3 on that frequency instead, thus making it available in the Athens area.

The ET-3 programming consisted of old ERT programs, as well as news, sports, and public affairs programs from Northern Greece. The creation of ET-3 was something that officials from Northern Greece had long demanded. The TV-100 programming lasted from

6 p.m. to midnight each day and consisted of news (in opposition to ERT news), cheap movies, Greek video movies, sports, city council meetings, and some programming taken from the satellite channels (Protogyrou and Petroutsou, 1989, March). The ERT stations in Crete and Patras, however, only broadcast regional news segments for the ET-1 national news.

Meanwhile, in March 1989, the PASOK government announced its willingness to allow a third national channel, operated by private interests. At the same time, the mayor of Athens was negotiating with the Union of Owners of Athens Dailies (EIIEA) to establish a joint television venture. Problems in uniting all the publishers did not allow this to materialize, but it became the spark for further developments, as PASOK entered into secret negotiations with some of the publishers for a third national television channel (Protogyrou, 1989). However, it seemed that PASOK was reluctant to proceed before the scheduled June 1989 elections, or possibly was trying to force publishers to give it favorable campaign coverage (Pretenteris, 1989). Either way, nothing happened before the elections.

Following the elections, New Democracy and the Coalition of the Left formed an interim government, to investigate alleged PASOK scandals and to prepare for new elections. A month later the interim government announced that it would grant a television station license to each of two groups of newspaper owners and publishers. The Vardinoyannis family of *Mesimvrini*, George Bobolas of *Ethnos*, Christos Tegopoulos of *Eleftherotypia*, Christos Lambrakis of *To Vima* and *Ta Nea*, and the Alafouzos family of *Kathimerini*, would operate Mega Channel. The other license went to publishers Aris Voudouris of *Eleftheros Typos*, Panos Karayannis of *Apoyevmatini*, Christos Kalogritsas of leftist *Proti*, Makis and George Kouris of *Avriani*, and Minos Kyriakou, a shipowner who wanted his own channel but had been turned down by the government. The second group would operate Nea Tileorasi. However, this group's plans for a television station did not materialize, even though it was granted a temporary license (#210/2-Dec. 2, 1989).

However, the publishers of the pro-PASOK *Avriani* put their own station on the air, while Kyriakou also made plans to establish a station. It seemed that private television would be introduced to Greece in the same way private radio had before. According to Pretenteris (1989), "in an atmosphere of general (public) approval and political party bickering, in line with the best traditions of the

Greek nation, the first step in the establishment of private TV in Greece took place" (p. 8).

In September 1989, as the country was preparing for yet new elections, the cabinet voted to give Teletypos, Inc., a license to operate Mega Channel on Channel 7 in Athens, as approved by the Ministry of Transportation and Communications. Mega Channel went on the air on November 20, 1989, with a temporary license (#19710/2-Aug. 28, 1989), while *Avriani's* Kanali 29 also went on the air, without a license, to represent the pro-PASOK, anti-government line. Similarly, the Thessaloniki suburb of Kalamaria, governed by pro-PASOK officials, established its own station, Argo-TV in opposition to TV-100.

By the end of 1989 there were several television stations on the air, including TV Plus, which restarted its operation in August 1989. Kyriakou's Antenna TV, went on the air on December 31, 1989, with the conservative government's support. Of all the television stations, only Mega had been granted a (temporary) license. Meanwhile, the new elections, in November 1989, once again failed to produce a clear majority, and a non-partisan government was formed until the next elections. However, before these elections the government had been able to enact a new television law establishing the framework for the operation of private television stations, thus raising people's hopes for a workable approach to the airwaves.

4

Print Media Today

NEWSPAPERS

The New Challengers

As the decade of the 1990s started, the Greek print media were faced with the biggest challenges since the end of the 1967-1974 military dictatorship. These challengers were (1) the new competitive forces in the electronic media (on the political and economic fronts) and (2) the need to harness efficiently the publishing tools offered by new technologies. For newspapers, these challenges required reconsideration of traditional publishing goals and marketing strategies. For magazines, they required the discovery of new and specialized audiences.

The presence of the newly deregulated and privatized electronic media manifested itself in different ways. Many and diverse stations appeared in all parts of Greece, especially in the major urban centers. Several print media veterans joined these media and started new professional careers as broadcast "stars." The energy, visual and aural qualities, and immediacy of the new media soon undermined the importance of the print media, which had long-been the informants and entertainers of the Greek public. Some old-fashioned publishers expected these effects to be minimal, but in fact the competition caused an erosion of audience attention that transcended even the traditional party loyalty that normally drives Greek newspapers.

One aspect of the competition that was particularly painful to the print media was the wave of "press review" programs, on both radio and television, which detailed descriptions of articles, news treatments, and even verbatim readings of stories from the day's newspapers. In early 1991, the Athens journalists' and publishers' unions asked the stations to limit their newspaper story descriptions, but their complaint went unanswered (Papachristos, 1991, Nov. 3).

The Erosion Begins

The trend of weakening circulations started in the late 1980s but continued into the 1990s. Well known dailies were forced to close during that time. These included *Akropolis*, modern Greece's oldest; *Vradyni; Proti; Alithia*; and, in the fall of 1991, *Epikairotita. Exormisi* became a weekly. There was an attempt to revive *Vradyni* under the name of *Nea* (new) *Vradyni*, but the new name was legally challenged by the paper's previous owners. The paper finally appeared with the name *Vradyni Kairi* (Evening Times), but closed on November 2, 1990, after only 11 issues (Papachristos, 1991, Nov. 3; 1991, Nov. 11). The newspapers that survived had lost approximately 15 percent of their circulation between 1986 and 1990. More specifically, in 1986 dailies were selling an average of 1.3 million copies per day, while in 1990 they were selling only 1.1 million; weekly papers were selling 870,000 copies in 1986 and 742,000 in 1990; and Sunday papers (extensions of the dailies) were selling 566,000 in 1986 and 450,000 in 1990.

Circulations deteriorated further in 1991. During the first half of the year, as the print and electronic media competition peaked, national newspapers lost approximately 11 percent of their circulation; it went from a daily average of 795,328 in January to 711,008 in June. The four morning dailies collectively lost about 16 percent of their circulation, as they went from 73,203 to 61,616 average copies daily. The 12 evening dailies collectively lost about 10 percent of their circulation during the same months, as they went from 722,125 average daily circulation in January to 649,392 in June ("Kyklofories," 1991).

A second reason for the decline of newspaper readership is also related to competition from the electronic media. The established press was unable to fully appreciate the many dimensions of the reader confidence crisis or to devise ways to solve it. During 1990 and 1991 these new competitive forces raised media consumption issues that went beyond the traditional political/partisan menu of media activities. The new issues included selection of news and entertainment content, style of presentation (from graphics and color to language), ease of access to specialized content (compartmentalization), utility of information to the consumer, and media credibility in exchange for reader loyalty. These issues became the new battlefields on which newspaper publishers, editors, and reporters in Greece found themselves, probably for the first time.

Traditionalist publishers, spoiled by the partisan successes of their past, thought they would wait this crisis out, too, while many journalists simply were not up to the task that modification would require. A former newspaper editor and media critic, Lykourgos Kominis (1991), has directly attributed the decline of the daily press to the inadequacy of the country's journalists, who continue to enter the profession "without breadth of knowledge, without the proper preparation, and without the foundation that is necessary for the job" (p. 40).

Another reason for the general newspaper malaise is the period of relative moderation in the country's politics. Circulation increases in Greece have traditionally been tied to political unrest. In fact, the media watchdog weekly *Pontiki* reports the circulation figures of the daily newspapers next to the headline of their lead stories, as if the figures and headlines were directly and causatively related. Kominis (1991, p. 41) wrote that the reason circulation changes are such a direct result of the political climate is that the largest portion of newspapers readers comes from "the fanatic, partisan elements of the reading public." The "most faithful readers," according to Kominis, "are the fanatic supporters of the parties."

Lack of an adequate number of such "fanatics" was given as the main reason for the failure of *Anagnostis*, an interesting, "new breed" kind of newspaper that started in May 1991. *Anagnostis* was a moderately conservative publication with subdued but clean design and toned-down headlines. The paper sold more than 50,000 copies its first day but went down to 2,000-3,000 average daily circulation in a few weeks. When it closed in July 1991, its last editorial decried the "end of an effort that found no (reader) response." The editorial concluded, "We tried to stress ethical and correct behavior and a subdued tone, but apparently the time for this (kind of journalism) has not come" ("Proto," 1991).

The change in the national political mood, however, did play a significant role, shifting readers from loudly partisan newspapers to more moderate ones. When a conservative government ruled Greece, in the fall of 1991, the national circulation leadership went from the unabashed rightist *Eleftheros Typos* (about 145,000 copies daily), which had held it for over a year, to the centrist *Ta Nea* (152,000). Declining circulation figures also were instrumental in forcing the evening *Avriani* and morning *Logos* to combine their struggling Sunday editions in November 1991. The resulting publication did not seem to attract any new readers.

Paradoxically, in spite of the obvious pattern in readership declines, newspaper income from advertising and circulation more than doubled between 1986 and 1990, from $124.4 million to $253.3 million. Advertising income alone almost quadrupled, rising from $22.8 million in 1986 to $80.8 million in 1990. Although the percentage of the newspapers' income from sales dropped, from approximately 82 percent in 1986 to approximately 69 percent in 1990, actual income from sales increased from $101.6 million in 1986 to $172.5 million in 1990 ("132 kathimerines," 1991). Approximately 25 percent of the money spent in advertising in Greece went to the publications of the Lambrakis Press Organization (*Ta Nea, To Vima, Economikos Tachydromos, Tachydromos, Pantheon, Marie Claire, RAM,* and *Archeologia*) (Papachristos, 1991, Dec. 15). There are only a few publishing success stories like this. The majority of the mainline Greek newspapers lose money or break even.

Although high inflation rates accounted for these increases in newspaper income from advertising, the percentage of advertising money spent on newspaper and magazine advertising actually shrank. Of total advertising expenditures in Greece in 1989 ($312 million), radio and television (mostly government operated) received 48 percent, while newspapers and magazines received 44 percent. In 1990, of the total amount ($422 million), 49 percent went to radio and television (now mostly private) and 44 percent to newspapers and magazines. It was the beginning of a consistent pattern. In 1991, of the total spent ($551 million), 54 percent went to television (alone), and 40 percent to newspapers and magazines ("Diafimisi '90," 1991; "Diafimisi '91," 1992).

An additional problem of the Greek press is the antiquated press distibution system. It is made up of about 12,000 points of sales, thus resulting in newspaper copy return rates of 40 percent ("Pou ofilete," 1992).

The profits of some publishers, the political ambitions of some businessmen, the changing political mood, and the new publishing technologies inspired several industrialists and journalists to combine efforts and enter the newspaper publishing field, in spite of the difficult prospects of marketability. Therefore, during the late 1980s and early 1990s, as new publications replaced failed ones, the number of daily and weekly newspapers held relatively steady.

Official statistics reported by the International Federation of Newspaper Publishers showed that in 1990 Greece had 132 dailies and 115 weeklies. There were 129 dailies in 1986-1987, and 133 in 1988-1989. There were 114 weeklies in 1986-1987, and 116 in 1988-1989 ("132 kathimerines," 1991).

More than 25 percent of Greece's general circulation, political dailies are published in Athens and have a national circulation. Approximately 20 of the daily newspapers are specialized sports and financial dailies. Athens alone has four financial dailies (*Imerisia, Kerdos, Express,* and *Nafteboriki*) and three sports dailies (*Phos, Echo,* and *Filathlos*). About 100 dailies are published in provincial centers, such as Thessaloniki, Patras, Kalamata, Volos, Larissa, Chania, Zakynthos, and Corfu. Thessaloniki, as the second largest city in Greece, has by far the most active newspaper life outside Athens. Its flagship newspaper, *Makedonia,* just celebrated its eighty-first anniversary, and it and *Ellinikos Vorras* are large enough to have sizeable bureaus in Athens. Although the former is a centrist and the latter rightist, they both have reputations of activist but not excessive journalistic behavior. *Thessaloniki* is the third major newspaper in that city.

With some exceptions, which vary with the times and the national political fever, most of Greece's major dailies are partisan in content, tabloid in size, sensational in appearance, and low in credibility. Perhaps this may explain why Greece has one of the lowest newspaper readership rates in Europe, 121 copies sold per

1,000 inhabitants; the rate in Switzerland is 387; in Belgium, 224; in the Scandinavian countries, 474; and in the United States, 267. Since March 1990 most newspapers were sold for 100 drachmas (approximately $.55). However, many Sunday editions raised their price to 150 drachmas in the Spring of 1992, and in July 1992 many daily papers also went to 150 drachmas except the following: *Logos,* 50 drachmas (from 80); *Avriani* and *Niki,* 80 drachmas (from 70); *Eleftheros* remained at 50 drachmas; and *Rizospastis, Eleftheros Typos, Apoyevmatini, Mesimvrini, Eleftheri Ora,* and *Estia* remained at 100 drachmas (see Tables 4.1 and 4.2).

Table 4.1
National (Athenian) Daily Newspapers

Newspapers	Circulation*	Position/Affiliation	Publication
Ta Nea	144,000	Center-Left/Pasok	Afternoon
Eleftheros Typos	140,000	Rightist/ND	Afternoon
Eleftherotypia	99,000	Center-Left/ Independent	Afternoon
Ethnos	72,000	Leftist /Independent	Afternoon
Apoyevmatini	62,000	Rightist/ND	Afternoon
Avriani	35,000	Leftist/Pasok	Afternoon
Niki	24,000	Leftist/Pasok	Afternoon
Mesimvrini	15,000	Rightist/ND	Afternoon
Eleftheros	9,500	Extreme Rightist	Afternoon
Estia	5,000	Rightist/Independent	Afternoon
Eleftheri Ora	1,700	Rightist/Royalist	Afternoon
Kathimerini	31,000	Rightist/Independent	Morning
Rizospastis	18,500	Communist/KKE	Morning
Avghi	2,700	Leftist/Coalition	Morning
O Logos	2,500	Leftist/Pasok	Morning

Source: Pontiki (1992), July 2, p. 34.
Note: *Average nationwide daily circulation for April 1992.

Table 4.2
National (Athenian) Sunday Newspapers

Newspapers	Circulation*	Position/Affiliation
To Vima	179,700	Center-Left/Independent
Eleftherotypia	155,000	Center-Left/Independent
Eleftheros Typos	131,800	Rightist/New Democracy
Ethnos	90,000	Leftist/Independent
Kathimerini	74,500	Rightist/Independent
Apoyevmatini	74,000	Rightist/New Democracy
Logos-Avriani	46,500	Leftist/Pasok
Rizospastis	32,000	Communist/KKE organ
Niki	20,000	Leftist/Pasok
Exormisi	6,400	Leftist/Pasok organ
Avghi	4,500	Leftist/Coalition
Eleftheri Ora	3,100	Rightist/Royalist
Epoche	2,450	Communist
Ellinikos Kosmos	2,000	Extreme Rightist/EPEN

Source: Pontiki ,1992, July 2, p. 34.
Note: *Average nationwide circulation for April 1992.

In 1992, the dominant Greek newspapers, those usually referred to as "the Greek press," are the Athens four morning and eleven evening dailies (see Photo 1). They are best identified through their general political inclinations, and most belong or support a faction of the party to which they normally lean. Although rightist newspapers are in the plurality, the most popular are the ones that are centrist or left-of-center.

Government Pressures and Publishers' Wars Revisited

In addition to the problems brought on by competition from the electronic media, since 1990 Greek newspapers have faced legal and

The major Athenian and national newspapers

political pressures from the government and have been involved in several wars among publishers. The most significant government pressure resulted from the passage in 1990 of an anti-terrorism law, which allows, in the name of "the social and public good," for the prosecution of newspapers that choose to publish declarations of terrorist groups. The law was passed after November 17, a terrorist organization with a 16-year history of political assassination and sabotage, in 1989 killed the prominent Greek publisher Pavlos Bacoyannis, who was the son-in-law of Prime Minister Constantine Mitsotakis. The Mitsotakis government, with a governing majority in parliament of one, the smallest in modern Greek history, passed the law after long and acrimonious discussion, both in parliament and on the front pages.

The general opposition to the law by the journalistic community in Greece was forcefully demonstrated in the first implementation of *tromonomos* (terror law), as the law was euphemistically known. In June, 1991, *Eleftherotypia*'s veteran managing editor, Seraphim Fyntanidis, a prominent and widely respected Greek journalist, tested the authorities by publishing the complete text of a declaration by November 17. He was prosecuted and imprisonment, followed by those of the editors of *Niki, Ethnos, Avriani, Pontiki, 48 Ores* (a twice-weekly), and *Logos* of Athens and, a few weeks later, of *Imerisios Kyrix* of Larissa, all of whom published the declaration fully or partially. The editors were convicted in September, 1991, and initially refused to appeal on the grounds that the law was unconstitutional. They served their sentences amid major anti-government protests from Greek and international journalism and human rights associations. Most continued to run their newspapers by telephone from their prison cells, until their respective organizations paid the alternative fines and the editors were released.

Soon after his election in 1989, Prime Minister Mitsotakis, who often took pride in his "lifetime in politics as well as journalism," told the ESIEA that he was "dedicated to the principle that press freedom is the oxygen of democracy" and that "a 'bad press' is preferable to a 'muzzled press'" ("Tromokratia," 1991). However, two years later, when he and his ruling New Democracy were battered in the front pages and the in opinion polls, his view of the press was different. By the middle of 1991 a campaign to intimidate the press seemed to have started. At the end of June, as the Greek economy failed to respond favorably to his corrective measures, the prime minister

summoned the publishers to admonish them about the negative
reviews given to his economic policy by their publications ("Na
grafete," 1991).

Particularly unacceptable to the prime minister seemed to be the
criticism by *Kathimerini*, a newspaper usually positively inclined
toward Mitsotakis's party. In 1991 the newspaper was sued (and
later convicted, under "insulting the authorities" legislation) for
"insulting" the prime minister, and later in the year its managing
editor was dismissed on the grounds that he contributed articles to
another newspaper, the media watchdog *Pontiki*. Many of his
colleagues thought he had been dismissed for political reasons and
related to the prime minister's criticism of the paper. Also in 1991,
the government began to prosecute *Kathimerini*'s owner Aristidis
Alafouzos, who is also a shipowner, on sea pollution charges and on
charges that his radio station, Sky, was illegally expanding its
transmitter site (Kyrtsos, 1992). Government critics said that since
these irregularities are relatively common in Greece, the Alafouzos
prosecutions seemed selective and politically motivated (Papachristos, 1991, Mar. 3). Government actions on a variety of charges
against journalists, media, or media owners, some seemingly unre-
lated to press performance, appeared to signal the start of a
systematic campaign of intimidation against media critical of the
government.

A sensitive issue for Greek journalism saw the light of publicity
in September and October of 1991 through the pages of *Eleftheros
Typos*, which accused *Ethnos* of employing journalists who were also
on the government payroll ("Tromokratia," 1991; "Pelorio thema,"
1991; "Parte thesi," 1991). This delicate issue goes back to the 1960s,
when for the first time governments in power officially admitted
hiring working newspaper journalists to also work in the public
relations or press offices of various government ministries or agencies. Because at the time Greek journalists were receiving notoriously poor pay, working part time for government press offices was
accepted as a necessary evil.

In 1991, Prime Minister Mitsotakis confirmed that journalists
who were working full time for newspapers were also part-time
employees of the government's General Secretariat of Press and
Information. He promised to give their names to the newspaper
publishers later in 1991, but never delivered on his promise.
Furthermore, several of his ministers, on separate occasions, said

that they saw nothing wrong with the practice. The president of ESIEA, Dimitris Mathiopoulos, said, "I don't know of journalists being bribed. On the contrary, I know of journalists who are hard working, and it is natural for them to receive compensation wherever they happen to offer their services" ("Parte thesi," 1991).

As the discussion evolved through the pages of the daily press many opinions were presented but no clear consensus emerged. Veteran editor Christos Pasalaris said that "certainly a journalist can work in the press office of a legal party" but "cannot favor or ignore a party" in the news. Former *Ta Nea* editor Yannis Kapsis, a distinguished journalist who also served as deputy minister of foreign affairs of the Papandreou government in the 1980s, said that he came from "the old generation of journalists that believed and believes that any other compensation of journalists beyond that of their newspaper is incompatible with the ethics of the profession." Angelos Stangos, the respected former managing editor of *Kathimerini*, echoed the same sentiments and repeated the call of many journalists that ESIEA start an investigation immediately, to clear the air "for the good of all of us" ("Parte thesi," 1991).

As a new political reality emerged after the end of the dictatorship in 1974 and the Papandreou wave of change swept the Greek political and media scene in the 1980s, nontraditional publishers, such as industrialists, entered the journalism field. At times these nonpublishing interests flexed their publishing muscles. In 1991 the Greek reading public watched *Epikairotita*, which had the same owner, Socratis Kokkalis, as the telecommunications company Intracom, question the validity and fairness of Greek government contracts with Avin Oil, owned by the Vardinoyannis family, owner of *Mesimvrini*, and part owner of Mega Channel. *Avriani* and *Eleftheros Typos* attacked the propriety of some government telecommunication contracts with Kokkalis's Intracom; *Mesimvrini*, Vardinoyannis, and the government all issued statements denouncing the accusations and declaring nothing improper in the agreements ("Polemos petrelaion," 1991; "Kokkalis," 1991; "Vgikan," 1991).

Another newspaper war involving the owners of some of the most prominent newspapers commenced in early 1991, with an editorial in liberal *Eleftherotypia*, written by its publisher, Tegopoulos, questioning some of the business transactions (shipping, Sky radio) of Alafouzos, owner of the progressive conservative *Kathimerini*. Prime

Minister Mitsotakis, who as a conservative had enjoyed *Kathimerini*'s
support, exacerbated the problems of Alafouzos by suggesting, in a
television interview, that an investigation start into the case of an
Alafouzos' ship caught with illegal cargo, and into the ownership Sky.
Many said that the prime minister's attitude toward *Kathimerini* had
changed because the newspaper was beginning to show support for
the more centrist wing of Mitsotakis's party, ND, and to question his
fiscal policies.

Fueling the speculation that the prime minister's public disagreement with *Kathimerini* was politically motivated was the reaction of Dimitrios Rizos, editor and publisher of the pro-Mitsotakis
Eleftheros Typos, who soon joined the fray with similar articles
critical of *Kathimerini*, until he was told by three ND ministers, who
serve on the board of directors of the *Eleftheros Typos*' parent
(Voudouris) Press Foundation, to not undermine the political clout
of a newspaper of the same political coloration because "it would hurt
the party." Business transactions seemed to be the reason behind
later attacks by Rizos on Tegopoulos holdings and on *Eleftherotypia*'s
political leanings (Papachristos, 1991, Mar. 17; 1991, Apr. 7).

Controversial changes, which also seemed politically inspired
took place within the management ranks of the most prominent
communist daily, *Rizospastis*. These changes began in March 1991
with the resignation of the paper's editor and many staffers, and they
ended in the fall. Disgruntled employees said that their troubles
(mainly reassignments) were caused not by their performance but by
the political changes taking place within the Communist Party as it
was struggling to find its identity after the collapse of Moscow as its
ideological center. The paper's publisher, in a letter to ESIEA and
other related unions defending the changes, detailed the history of
the conflict and outlined the peculiar difficulties for a communist
newspaper in dealing with the rights and responsibilities of employees who do not wish to obey the operational guidelines, in this
instance the political direction, of the newspaper ("Nea Dianomi,"
1991; Papachristos, 1991, Mar. 31; 1991a, Apr. 14; "Politiki grammi,"
1991).   In the meantime, after KKE split and pulled out of the
Coalition of the Left, *Avghi* has been expressing the Coalition's
political views, although it is not necessarily that party's press organ.
However, given the inability of the Coalition of the Left to financially
support this low circulation, but well-respected daily, its chances for
survival are reportedly limited (Kontoyannis, 1992).

MAGAZINES

Statistical yearbooks often list Greece as having almost 57,000 periodicals, about half (28,000) in Athens. Children's periodicals are the most numerous type with more than 10,000 titles, again, half of them headquartered in Athens. Although these figures may be exaggerated because they include newsletters, company magazines, etc., there is little doubt that the Greek magazine market today is saturated. This and the relentless competition from private television have put the Greek magazine market in a critical condition.

Until the 1980s, the traditional Greek magazine was of poor quality in content, appearance, and reproduction. Often it imitated foreign magazines and even copied articles and pictures from them.

The ideological, political, and economic changes of the 1980s, however, ushered in a new era in magazine publishing. New ideas, some from abroad and some strictly domestic; new publishers; and new technologies considerably elevated the level of the Greek magazine—in many cases, to the European standard. Today the Athens kiosks offer a cornucopia of magazines of every quality, size, color, interest, and price (see Photo 2).

The end of the 1980s marked a milestone in the life of the Greek magazine; it was when publishers recognized that the road to success was through specialized magazine, and not general magazine, and through monthly rather than weekly publications. From 1989 to 1990 the top general interest, variety magazines in Greece, *Tachydromos*, *Eikones*, and *Ena*, lost about 24 percent of their average circulation and about five percent of their share in advertising. At the same time, significant gains were posted by specialized magazines, especially television, women's, children's, computer, automotive, consumer, and music magazines. Television program magazines, for example, gained 47 percent in average circulation; financial magazines gained 54 percent; and automotive magazines gained 57 percent (Vlastari, 1991).

Television program guides, which cover a wide variety of topics, all related to television entertainment, are by far the most popular Greek magazines. In a volatile market, the average circulation of these magazines at the top of the circulation chart in 1991 had more than twice the average circulation of the second tier of competitors. There were four major such magazines with high circulation (see Table 4.3), while two more (*Tilecontrol*, *TV Zapping*) were introduced

An Athens Kiosk, selling magazines

Table 4.3
Major Magazines

Magazines	Circulation	Publication	Content
7 Meres TV	250,000	weekly	television
Tiletheatis	200,000	weekly	television
Tilerama	195,000	weekly	television
Auto Motor	80,000	monthly	automotive
4 Trochoi	78,000	monthly	automotive
Klik	72,000	monthly	urban
Eine	60,000	weekly	variety
Kai	54,000	weekly	variety
Eikones	53,000	weekly	variety
Marie Claire	51,000	monthly	youth
Radiotileorasi	50,000	weekly	television
Elle	48,000	monthly	women's
Car & Driver	48,000	monthly	automotive
Tachydromos	47,000	weekly	general
Gynaika	46,000	monthly	women's
Playboy	42,000	monthly	men's
Pantheon	35,000	weekly	variety
ENA	32,000	weekly	general
Domino	25,000	weekly	variety

Sources: Chalkou, M. (1990); *Epikinonia, 5* (1991), p. 41; *Pontiki*, (1992, April 16), p. 2; Papachristos, (1992, May 24).

in March 1992. These last two TV program guides are interesting in that the publisher of the first already publishes one major television program guide, while the second is a joint venture, the first of its kind, between major newspaper publishers, Bobolas and Lambrakis ("Selida tou typou," 1992, Jan. 18). Although the competition among all these television magazines has intensified, their circulation has reached unimaginable heights as it is aided by free gifts, quizzes, drawings and other promotions. As a result, although the low-circulation television program guide, *TV Programma,* closed down in 1992, most others gained in circulation by an average of 10 percent. Furthermore, the two new magazines, *Tilecontrol* and *TV Zapping,* have a circulation close to 100,000 each (Papachristos, 1992, April 12).

Television program guides also have been increasing their share of the advertising expenditures devoted to magazines. That share is now over 12 percent, while automotive magazines hold 11 percent of the advertising expenditures going to magazines, and home and decoration magazines as a group take up about six percent of such advertising expenditures. On the other hand, general interest or variety magazines are losing advertising; having gone from 34 percent to 21 percent of periodical advertising expenditures in just two years (Papachristos, 1992, May 24).

The most popular foreign magazines are the German *Auto Motor und Sport* (average circulation 80,000), and the American *Playboy* (42,000) and *Penthouse* (20,000). Most of the Greek magazines are monthly and cost between 100 and 500 drachmas ($.55-$2.70) ("Periodikos typos," 1991).

About 37 percent of Greeks may be considered regular magazine readers. Most of them (57 percent) are women; most are between 12 and 34 years of age; most have a secondary or higher education; and most live in the two urban areas of Athens and Thessaloniki ("Anagnosimotita," 1990). Whereas men are the primary consumers of newspapers by a margin of about 61 to 39 percent ("Esis ke e E," 1992), women are the primary consumers of most magazines, including television program guides, although a few magazines mainly reach a male audience, including *Playboy, Penthouse, Status,* and *Max.*

Magazine publishers translated the demographic lessons of the 1980s into new, dynamic, focused, colorful, well reproduced, specialized publications. By studying the interests of consumers, for example, *Tachydromos* was able to reverse its decline and produce a magazine that is relevant in content; captivating, bold, and easy to follow in format; and colorful and glossy in reproduction. News personalities, serious and playful features, gossip, and consumer news dominate its content. Color photographs of all sizes embellish its appearance. A new arrival, *Klik,* founded in 1987, has captured the imagination of young Greeks through boldly and colorfully written articles on AIDS, Madonna, music, sports, pop art, film, and the active lifestyles of the 1980s and 1990s.

Of special note are the women's and feminist magazines in Greece, a type that goes back to the eighteenth century. Such magazines made their first appearance in Constantinople in 1845. Today's women's magazine market consists of publications that address women of various intellectual and economic backgrounds. Best examples of this market are the popular *Gynaika* and *Pantheon* and the specialized *Synchroni Gynaika, Agonas tis Gynaikas, Isotita kai Fylo,* and *Dini* (Doulkeri, 1990, pp. 77-86).

Specialization has meant the birth of magazines on cooking, computers, family life, consumer issues, finance, restaurants, politics and ideas, science, entertainment, hobbies, sex, arts, history, and so on. The current Greek magazine market is as active and diverse as the markets of most of Europe. However, Greece's general financial malaise of the early 1990s has brought on a dangerously keen competition for readers and advertisers. This drastically reduced the number of those who read more than one periodical and has nurtured a cannibalistic mentality in the industry. Sales promotions and other marketing gimmicks followed. Even respectable *Eikones* found it necessary to imitate the practices of the television magazines and in the spring of 1992, it often appeared in plastic sacks containing gifts (maps, handkerchiefs, etc.).

Amidst this competition, one of the world's largest magazine publishers, Hachette, has entered the Greek market. It recently bought the publishing company Evropaikes Ekdoses (European Publications), which is publishing *Playboy, Max, Car & Driver, Avantage, Elle, Elle-Decor,* and *Kai,* and more recently came out with a weekly tabloid *Loipon* ("Evropaikes," 1992).

THE ATHENS NEWS AGENCY

The Athens News Agency (ANA) is the main wire service of most Greek news media, especially of the provincial press. It is a semi-governmental agency; its editor is appointed by the government and serves under the Minister to the Premiership. The editor hires the staff, supervises the financial and technological aspects of the service, and controls its daily news product.

ANA employs about 250 reporters, translators, technicians, and administrators in Greece and in several foreign countries, including the United States, Belgium, United Kingdom, Germany, and Turkey. Its services include full international news coverage, one part of it in English, and a special section of only Greek news, that goes to Greek and Cypriot papers and also many expatriate Greek organizations. A 16-page bulletin in English and French is distributed daily to foreign government agencies, ministries, diplomatic services, and tourist information services. Because of its service nature, ANA is not a profitable agency and depends on substantial annual subsidies (more than 1 billion drachmas) for its survival ("Athinaiko Praktoreio Eidiseon," 1990; "Chrima me to tsouvali," 1991).

ANA was conceived in 1901, when the Greek government appointed the editor of the Athens French daily *Messager d'Athenes* to negotiate an agreement with the French news agency Havas for a telegraphic service to Athens newspapers. Four years later ANA was born, but it did not really become a productive operation until it was reorganized and modernized by the Venizelos government in 1931 (General Secretariat, 1988, p. 42).

In November 1991 the Greek government formed the country's second news agency, in reaction to the news that the Yugoslavian region of Macedonia had declared its independence and was preparing for its own diplomatic and media activity abroad. The new agency is the Macedonian News Agency (MNA), headquartered in Thessaloniki. MNA quickly reached cooperation agreements with most of the major international news agencies, but during its first year managed to carry news primarily related to the debate surrounding the recognition of Yugoslavian "Macedonia."

5

Press Issues

LEGAL ISSUES

After the fall of the military regime in 1974, the democratically elected Greek parliament put on the top of its agenda the creation of a new constitution. The center-right coalition that governed Greece then passed, over the strong objections of PASOK, the leftist opposition, a constitution that is not much different from the 1952 document it replaced. In fact, Article 14, specifically dealing with press freedom, is almost an exact copy of Article 14 of the 1952 constitution, something that the PASOK representatives said did not meet the demands or conditions of a modern democratic state. Although the article contains provisions similar to those of the constitutions of most countries, it does allow for considerable limits on the press (*To Syntagma tis Elladas*, 1990, pp. 47-48). Specifically, Article 14 states:

1. Every person may express and propagate his thoughts orally, in writing or through the press in compliance with the laws of the state.
2. The press is free. Censorship and all other preventive

measures are prohibited.

3. The seizure of newspapers and other publications before or after circulation is prohibited. Seizure by order of the public prosecutor shall be allowed exceptionally after circulation and in case of:

    a. an offense against the Christian or any other known religion;

    b. an insult against the person of the President of the republic.

    c. a publication which discloses information on the composition, equipment and set-up of the armed forces or the fortifications of the country, or which aims at the violent overthrow of the regime or is directed against the territorial integrity of the state.

    d. an obscene article obviously offensive to public decency, in the cases stipulated by law.

4. In all the cases specified in the preceding paragraph, the public prosecutor must, within 24 hours of the seizure, submit the case to the judicial council which, within another 24 hours, must rule whether the seizure is to be maintained or lifted; otherwise it shall be lifted ipso jure. An appeal and a recourse to the Supreme Court may be launched by the publisher of the newspaper or other printed matter seized and by the public prosecutor.

5. The manner in which full retraction shall be made in cases of inaccurate publications shall be determined by law.

6. After at least three convictions within five years for punishable acts defined under paragraph 3, the court shall order the definite ban or temporary suspension of publication of the printed matter and, in severe cases, shall prohibit the convicted person from practicing the profession of journalist as specified by law. The ban or suspension of publication shall be effective as of the date the court order becomes irrevocable.

7. Press offenses shall be subject to immediate court hearing and shall be tried as provided by law.

8. The conditions and qualifications requisite of the profession of journalist may be specified by law.

9. The law may require that the means of financing newspapers and periodicals should be disclosed.

However, Article 15 does not extend similar protection to other media:

1. The protective provisions for the press in the preceding article shall not be applicable to films, sound recordings, radio, television and any other similar medium for the transmission of speech or images.
2. Radio and television are under the immediate control of the state and shall aim at the objective transmission, on equal terms, of information and news reports as well as works of literature and art; the quality of programs shall be assured in consideration of their social mission and the cultural development of the country.

Most media and legal scholars consider Article 15 unfairly restrictive and, as a University of Athens professor Panayotis Pavlopoulos (1991) calls it, "especially invasive" as compared with the relatively generous protections provided to the printed press by Article 14.

Other complementary constitutional provisions are Article 4, which guarantees citizens "equality before the law"; Article 5, which protects the "free development of the personality of the citizen"; and Article 25, which addresses the government's responsibility to protect the "human rights of the individual."

The 1975 Constitution guarantees the right to publish and disseminate ideas; this is an improvement over its 1952 predecessor, which only guaranteed "the right to publish." The most common legal test for the press in the immediate post-junta period had to do with dissemination of information. A particular target was the distributors of leftist publications such as *Rizospastis* and *Odigitis*, who were routinely harassed by overzealous prosecutors of the then conservative government, invoking laws passed by previous dictatorial regimes. Laws used in these prosecutions were those dealing with the newspaper circulation system and had originally been designed to ensure equal treatment of all publications. Defining the "distributor," however, resulted in many legal and physical confrontations between the government and the distributors (Paraschos, 1983).

Today in Greece, as in most of the West, the most common legal problem the press faces is litigation on the grounds of defamation (libel and slander). Articles 361-372 of the Penal Code offer several definitions of defamation, such as "insulting the honor of a person in word or action or in any other way," "slandering the reputation of a person," "disseminating in any way through a third party information that injures someone's honor," or "simple malicious insult to the memory of the dead." Maximum punishment in most instances is incarceration of up to two years, except in cases of malicious defamation ("the information is false and the accused knew it was false"), in which case the incarceration is increased by at least three months. When the insulting information refers to a "public servant" and deals with the performance of his or her work, the law also allows the employing public agency also to file suit against the originator of the information, thus enlarging the legal case against the defendant.

Civil defamation of the honor or the reputation of a person, entitles the plaintiff to recover property losses and moral injury monetary rewards of no less than 300,000 drachmas if the defendant is an Athens or Thessaloniki publication, and of no less than 50,000 drachmas if the offending publication is published anywhere else in Greece. Truth is a defense against defamation suits (Article 362). Criticism of "scientific, artistic, or professional works," criticism "included in a document of public authority on issues of its jurisdiction," and criticism expressed in demonstrations for "the exercise of legal authority" are not illegal (Article 367).

Hundreds of journalists, publishers, and media owners have been prosecuted under these statutes since the fall of the junta, but relatively few have gone to jail or actually had to pay fines. One catch in the law is that unless there is a final decision (through all appeals) on the case within 18 months of first litigation, the charge is dismissed. It is estimated that 90 percent of defamation cases are settled out of court or automatically dismissed.

One piece of legislation that is also at the center of the Greek journalists' legal problems is article 181 the Penal Code, which deals with "insulting the authorities through the press," which in effect makes it easier for a public servant (e.g. a policeman) to sue and win against a news medium. This article says that "whoever publicly insults a public authority or the Parliament-recognized leader of a political party" may be incarcerated for a maximum of three years. The person who publicly insults or defaces "an emblem or symbol of the country or the President of the Republic" faces a maximum incarceration of two years. It is significant to note that in the spring of 1991 the Ministry of Justice proposed an important revision of

Article 181 that eliminated the public prosecutor's right to initiate the legal proceedings, a right that had made it possible for politically motivated prosecutors to act on their own. Although the same revision added the "judicial authorities" to the class of individuals worthy of the law's protection against "insulting the authorities" legislation, the proposed originator of a suit against a news medium under the revised article can only be the aggrieved party. The same requirement was also proposed for Article 198 of the Penal Code, which deals with "blaspheme;" only an "offended party" may sue, not the public prosecutor operating independently. The changes had received widespread approval and were expected to be approved by the parliament in 1992 (Mandrou, 1991, July 21).

Article 181 has been a target of severe criticism over the years. A university of Athens professor, Nikos Androulakis (1978), in an eloquent representation of this criticism, focused on two key instances of "vagueness" in Article 181. First, he pointed out that in terms of the "object of the insult," it is unclear whether the law aims at protecting the position (the office in government) or the person who occupies it. Second, he objected to the description of an "insult," which is so broad that it inevitably results in "criminalization of political disagreement." However, in early 1992 the (civil) Supreme Court (Arios Pagos) ruled that the Penal Code's provision dealing with "insulting the authorities through the press," is intended to protect the office or position and not the person occupying it ("Arios Pagos," 1992).

Perhaps the most unusual legal obstacle for the Greek press can be found in the Article 191 of the Penal Code, which deals with "dissemination of false and alarming news." Though rarely used since, during the military regime it was a common weapon of prosecutors who wanted to silence the opposition. The article imposes a minimum three-month incarceration and a fine on anyone who "disseminates false information or rumors able to bring alarm and fear to the citizens or to shake public trust" in the national currency, the armed forces, or the nation's international relations.

Greece's obscenity laws reflect the country's rather puritanical and simplistic legal view of pornography, in spite of the licentious appearance of most magazine covers and movie advertisements. Legislative Order 5060/1931 says obscenity is anything that "according to public sentiment insults decency." Publication, distribution, and possession of such material is illegal. Since 1990 the law has rarely been used in litigation. What is used more often, in a "creative" extension to the press, is Article 353, which prohibits causing a "scandal through obscene acts" and punishes "anyone who knowingly insults the morals of another performing an obscene act in his presence" with incarceration of up to two years.

News-source confidentiality has never had legal viability in Greece, and in fact, Press Law (1092/1938) specifically makes it illegal for a journalist to keep sources confidential if the sources are members of the military community. This provision, along with the Espionage Act (Obligatory Law 375/1936), which explicitly forbids "publication of any military information without prior written approval of the appropriate military authority," make it extremely difficult for Greek media to write with impunity on any issue related to national defense. What makes this situation even more troublesome are laws that penalize persons who "knowingly cancel the prosecution" of criminals (Penal Code, Article 231), or those who fail to report criminal acts in a "timely fashion to the authorities" (Penal Code, Article 232).

In 1992, two journalists are being prosecuted for such "crimes." One, Georgia Kontrarou, for reporting on closed legal proceedings, and another, Nicoletta Tsitsanoudi, for "protecting a criminal," because she refuses to reveal her source for a report on a series of crimes in central Greece ("Diokete dimosiographos," 1992).

Probably the most notorious recent law affecting Greek journalists today is the anti-terrorism law that became effective January 1, 1991. This new law allows a Supreme Court prosecutor to prohibit publication of statements by terrorist organizations. Although not widely litigated, the law gained its "fame" because it was inspired by the 1989 assassination Pavlos Bacoyannis, and because its first major test involved seven of Greece's best known editors.

In particular, Article 6 of the "Law for the protection of society from organized crime," states that "the prosecutor may forbid the publication, through the press and the media of mass communication, of announcements, declarations and any kind of statements made by the organizations or teams described in Article 1 or their members." Violators may be penalized by a minimum incarceration of three-months and a 5 to 50 million drachmas fine. Radio and television stations face the additional penalty of being closed down for up to six months.

As we saw in Chapter 4, the case was started in June 1991, when

Eleftherotypia printed (on its front page) a declaration by November 17, the country's long lasting and best known terrorist organization. In an editorial on the day of publication, *Eleftherotypia* said it was publishing the note because "we believe that the reading public, all the Greek citizens, have a right to be informed of, even if they completely disagree with, the actions and thinking of an organization that for 16 years now remains unstopped by the police of all the governments that have ruled." In a few hours the public prosecutor had arrested the newspaper's editor, for violating Article 6 of Law 1916/1990. His arrest was followed by arrests of other editors who also printed the declaration, all or in part, a few days later ("Agria epithesi," 1991).

In the months that followed many and intense discussions took place in the parliament, on the front pages, on the airwaves, in international journalistic organizations and forums, and within government and opposition circles, in an effort to end the impasse between the government-inspired prosecutors and the majority of Greek journalists, but to no avail. The case received so much worldwide publicity that it was mentioned in the U.S. Department of State Annual Report on Human Rights as an example of a limit to press freedom.

Nevertheless, the government continues to send mixed signals with regards to the enforcement of this law. On one hand the editor and the publisher of Larissa's *Imerisios Kyrix* were given a 5-month jail term for printing a November 17 declaration. On the other, the public prosecutor did not act when *Eleftherotypia* and *To Vima* published another November 17 declaration on May 9 and 10, 1992, respectively. After a more recent attack, in July 1992, November 17 sent its declaration to a radio station, which made it public immediately, before the public prosecutor issued his restraining order. However, two newspapers that published follow-up declarations are being prosecuted.

Depending on the political mood of the country or the region, the laws that deal with "the public incitement to the commission of crime" (Penal Code, Articles 184 and 186) and "the public praise of a crime" (Penal Code, Article 185) are applied to the press. Penalties for these crimes range from three months to three years incarceration.

Other notable cases in 1990 and 1991 involved the newspapers *48 Ores* and *Ethnos*, which were prosecuted for "insulting the judiciary"; *Kathimerini* and Sky Radio, which were accused of "insulting the prime minister"; and *Pontiki*, which was accused under a 1931 law (5060/1931) of printing an obscene cartoon on its front page ("Dimosiografika," 1991).

The mere existence of the "insulting the authorities" law, the prosecutorial capriciousness inherent in the "false and alarming news" legislation, and the defamation law provision that allows the government to join a suit brought by one of its employees against the media, show that in Greece there exists a pro-government environment with regard to the press. This press-restrictive climate is also reflected by the fact that in praxis judges have meted out considerably harsher sentences in those defamation cases where the allegedly defamed party was a public servant in the performance of his or her job.

This plethora of legal weapons available against the Greek media, and the political or partisan ways they are used by government prosecutors and private individuals, result annually in hundreds of frivolous suits, almost all of which result in dismissal or out-of-court settlements. This seems to have numbed the media's fear of prosecution and to have eroded the fabric of press-government relations. So instead of the "chilling effect" on the media such a legal environment might be expected to have created, the exact opposite seems to have occurred—a complete disregard of common journalistic restraint. The unchecked rudeness and sensational play of half-truths that scream from the front pages of most Greek newspapers is a product of this fruitless cycle of legal gymnastics.

OPERATIONAL ISSUES

A visitor in Greece will need only the merest smattering of Greek to discover that the newspapers prominently displayed by the corner kiosks as well as the radio and television stations broadcasting into the nation's living rooms have deep ideological differences and different media philosophies. The resulting conceptual and visual asymmetry can be viewed as a triumph of political pluralism, a disaster of partisan misinformation, or something in between. In any case, unless one is experienced in dealing with this kind of media and can mentally accommodate this kind of journalism, the result will probably be disorientation, resentment, or rejection (see Photos 3-5).

Comparing the afternoon headlines

Afternoon newspapers at an Athens Kiosk

Foreign publications at an Athens Kiosk

The vast majority of Greek print and broadcast media are unabashedly partisan, sensational, and political. Story selection and play differ so widely from paper to paper and station to station that members of the audience often have to expose themselves to more than one medium in order to have a complete picture of reality. It is not unusual, for example, to see headlines in the same day's newspapers describing the same event as both a "national success" and a "national catastrophe," as the two extremist newspapers *Eleftheros Typos* ("Ethniki epitychia," 1992) on the right and *Avriani* ("Katastrofi ya tin Ellada," 1992) on the left, did in covering the meeting of the Greek and Turkish prime ministers in February 1992 (see Table 5.1 for coverage of President Bush's visit to Greece in 1991).

Furthermore, since street sales continue to account for the largest portion of their income, newspapers frequently utilize 72 pt. and even larger type headlines and contain language that is provocative, crude, and full of innuendo. Color is used in distracting abundance.

With few exceptions, news writing is obtrusively partisan, colorful, excessive, at times crass or patronizing, and often laced with adjectives that in most Western media would be considered incompatible with fairness. In most cases there is no visible effort to show impartiality in the news accounts, and opinion-loaded language is used freely in relating the day's events.

Although Greek newspapers often "talk" to their readers through the use of personal pronouns, etc., no systematic effort seems to be made to offer a summary lead or a connection with yesterday's version of a story, or to double-check quotes, or to match figures in charts and text. There seems to be no evidence of a disciplined, "stylebook" kind of writing and the consistency that it requires. Language types range from the formal, precise, old-fashioned katharevousa to "gutter." Editorial and, especially, column writing, both very popular with newspaper readers, follow even fewer rules, and the style often is strictly personal, even in spelling preferences and grammar usage.

Table 5.1
Major Newspaper Headlines on Bush's 1991 Visit to Greece

Newspaper/Party Affiliation	Headline
RIGHTIST	
Eleftheros Typos/ND	Solutions for Everything, Promises Bush
Kathimerini/Independent	In View of Final Solutions, for Cyprus and the Aegean
Apoyevmatini/ND	National Success, The Cyprus Issue is solved
Mesimvrini/ND	Warm Phil-Hellenism But No Promises
Eleftheri Ora/Royalist	The Plantation Owner Arrived Yesterday
LEFTIST	
O Logos/PASOK	Frigid Bush: Cyprus is not Kuwait, said the Caesar
Avriani/PASOK	He Divides the Aegean in Three
Niki/PASOK	They are Selling Aegean-Cyprus
Ta Nea/Independent	He Cut Athens in Two: Fires, violence and arrests
Ethnos/Independent	What the Three Discussed
Eleftherotypia/Independent	Bitter (world) Order, Bush on Cyprus and the Aegean
Avghi/Coalition	Bush: No Commitments, on Cyprus and Greek-Turkish (relations)
Rizospastis/KKE	Bush: "I Feel At Home"

Greek newspaper design aims mainly at attracting the eye, and not at serving the reader. Most national dailies are tabloid size. The small types and cluttered layouts allow many stories to be used. In many instances, the photographs are badly composed and cropped, and the persons shown in them identified improperly, if at all. The increased utilization of graphics has had a positive effect, but the copy and the graphic often do not exactly match.

Probably the biggest problem with the Greek news media is a serious lack of cross-checking, source verification, and information attribution. The unusual self-righteous, partisan slant and the absence of a systemic requirement or tradition of sound editorial practices often appear as a conscious effort to ignore all the potential "other sides" to a story. Such at times is the magnitude of abuse of professional standards that on May 5, 1992, in the midst of a heated international debate on the impact on Greece of a potential world recognition of the former Yugoslavian republic of Macedonia, ESIEA took the rare step of making the following announcement:

> The Executive Council of ESIEA regrets some instances of inexact reporting and unjustified editorializing on events that deal with national issues.
> With this in mind, the EC of ESIEA cautions that sloppy news gathering and presentation injure our national interests and at the same time show irresponsibility in the exercise of the profession.
> These occurrences are foreign not only to journalistic principles but also to the traditions and ethics of the journalistic world of Greece.

Kathimerini, To Vima, Ta Nea, and *Eleftherotypia* are the only publications that seem to have developed, in varying degrees, a consistency of style and a respect for the reader, the news, and the crafting of the story. These four newspapers do exhibit the shortcomings listed previously, but with a refreshing irregularity.

The relatively new trend of less ideological and more profit-motivated businessmen-turned-publishers, and the recent competition given Greek newspapers by the electronic media seem to have forced the newspapers, probably for the first time, to go beyond satisfying the partisan instincts of their readers and look for new ways to attract and keep them. The first such sign appeared at the end of 1991, when *Ta Nea*, *Eleftherotypia*, and *Ethnos* started the trend of compartmentalization, providing their readers with the first pull-out news and feature sections. Sports, health, business/money, life-style, arts/culture, entertainment, women, and television seemed to be the consensus topics of the three papers. In addition, some newspapers such as Monday's *Ethnos* and *Kyriakatiki* (Sunday) *Eleftherotypia* carry magazine inserts.

Outside the newsroom, most media people are actively involved in syndicalist affairs. On the forefront of most professional battles is the Union of Journalists of Athens Dailies (ESIEA), an organization that was founded in 1914 with the purpose of safeguarding "press freedom" and of protecting, among others, the "ethical, economic, professional, and insurance" interests of its members (Kominis, 1990). ESIEA, which is also open to broadcast members, has a sister organization in Thessaloniki for the journalists of Macedonia and Thrace (ESIEMT). The union's pension and health insurance plans have long been a source of pride for its members.

Although ESIEA's membership admission policies are often "bent," membership is closely supervised and generally sought after by professionals. Membership alone can result in easier access to sources, political or not. For example, in Greece in the fall of 1991 a French actor, Alain Delon, refused to talk to one of ERT-1's star anchors because she was not registered as a journalist and his contract forbade him from speaking to media people who were not "official" journalists. Also respected is ESIEA's disciplinary council, which evaluates professional conduct. In 1992 the Athens News Agency editor was expelled from the union for "vengeful dismissal of colleagues."

Probably ESIEA's most visible work is in negotiating with the Union of Owners of Athens Dailies (EIIEA). In December 1991, for example, it managed to obtain a 16 percent pay raise for its members. ESIEA is also a vocal supporter of press freedom legislation, but generally represents the older, more conservative journalists.

Since the 1980s membership in EIIEA has changed considerably. Several traditional and long-time publishers were replaced by industrialists and businessmen, who saw the possibility for profit in the print and the emerging broadcast media and the opportunity to exert unobtrusive pressure on the government to promote their other business interests. Thus individuals connected with the oil, steel, book publishing, telecommunications, and shipping industries purchased full or partial interest in newspapers and broadcasting stations. Due to the complexity of these purchase transactions, it is often not clear exactly who owns what, a practice that is permissible for certain companies under Greek law.

Publishing successful newspapers and magazines can be very profitable. Greek law allows publishers to exempt from taxation 4 percent of their gross revenues. For certain publishing firms, even this small percentage amounts to millions of dollars (Kyriazidis, 1990).

One of the big issues for publishers in the last few decades has been the government's interference with setting the per copy sale price of a newspaper, with the maximum number of pages a newspaper is allowed to print per week, and with the distribution system of newspapers. The government's original reason for interfering in these matters was to ensure pluralism by protecting the small publisher. This practice, which is still carried on today through law 1072/1988, allows the evening dailies to hit the stands as early as 10:30 a.m., which undermines considerably the circulation of the morning papers ("Nomoi," 1988). Perhaps this is why 11 of Greece's top 15 dailies are evening newspapers.

Unfortunately, the noble cause of protecting the small publisher has been corrupted, and over the years many of these measures have been enforced with partisan yardsticks and generally have undermined the capitalist nature of the publishing business. In particular, the issue of government involvement in setting the number of printed pages has a long and controversial history. Since Greece imports almost all of its newsprint, the government originally thought that the press would benefit from a duty-free newsprint importation license, if some rules were adopted to ensure an equitable distribution of the imported newsprint among large and small publishers. This, of course, was disadvantageous to the large publishers, whose growth could be manipulated based on their partisan performances. Furthermore, most Greek press laws have, as part of their punitive provision, the cancellation of the publisher's duty-free newsprint importation license. For a small publisher that could be devastating.

Technologically, most large publishing houses have state-of-the-art editorial and photocomposition facilities and presses. It is estimated that between 1975 and 1990, 50 percent of the back shop employees of newspapers lost their jobs due to technological improvements ("Afxanonte," 1991). The country's largest chain, in circulation, income, and prestige is the Lambrakis Press Organization, which publishes *To Vima, Ta Nea, Tachydromos, Economikos Tachydromos, Marie Claire, Archeologia, Pantheon, RAM* (computers), and *Diakopes* (tourism). The Lambrakis Press Organization (DOL) also owns a travel agency.

Job placement in print and broadcast journalism in Greece has changed little in the last two decades. Good writing skills and personal or familial contacts have traditionally been the major prerequisites for entering the profession. Because of the lack of formal journalism education, the people who enter the profession are either high school graduates or graduates of universities with degrees in law, literature, political science, or economics.

Upon entering the profession, the aspiring journalist would soon find a male-dominated world from top to bottom. The retirement from *Kathimerini*'s helm by Helen Vlachos (who ended her journalistic career on a bad note, after being convicted in February 1992 of illegally exporting the money from the sale of her newspaper to G. Koskotas) has left only one other female publisher of a major newspaper in Greece, Aikaterini Vellidis of the Thessaloniki paper *Makedonia*. Males also dominate the top managerial posts of the newspapers. One exception is *Mesimvrini*, whose owners in October 1991 appointed the only female editor of a major daily in Greece today. The growth of the electronic media, however, has been instrumental in attracting a relatively large number of women to the profession.

Since the beginning of the century, when Vlasios Gavriilidis, one of the fathers of modern Greek newspapers, first mentioned the idea, there has been talk about journalism education, the proposed cure-all to the profession's many ills. But either because publishers did not really want better educated, and therefore more demanding, employees, or because the working journalists of the time did not want to face more competition for their jobs, nothing really came of the idea (Paraschos, 1979). Even when the PASOK government discussed in parliament and approved a plan for a university level system, nothing significant happened until the electronic media in the late 1980s showed their public influence and its potential. Since 1990, Panteion University (in Athens), the University of Athens, and the University of Thessaloniki have taken steps to introduce a mass communication or journalism education curriculum. However, while journalists in the past were calling for journalism education at the university level, now they complain that the three schools with departments of journalism and mass communication will produce too many graduates who will end up unemployed (Papachristos, 1991, February). However, Antenna TV and radio stations have promised to hire the top graduates from the nation's journalism schools.

In the meantime, in leafing through Greek newspapers, one cannot fail to notice the advertisements of an active post-secondary education system of private schools, institutes, and free-studies laboratories that aim squarely at those who are interested in studying or getting training in journalism. These programs have multiplied considerably as the electronic media have grown. The advertisements list curriculum instructors who are prominent journalists of the print and electronic media, as well as university professors. The courses offered and the media products students produce seem to be the standard fare found in the mass communications and journalism programs in other Western countries. However, since there is no standardized regulatory authority supervising these programs in Greece, the quality of education offered is unknown. Traditionally these programs have not been taken seriously as post-secondary education and many have been forced to go out of business only to resurface later with new names, different curricula, and new instructors.

ETHICAL ISSUES

In addition to the constraints placed upon them by a relatively press-antagonistic legal system, Greek journalists, like journalists anywhere, have to face the ethical dilemmas of their profession. With the number of media rising, pressures are on the increase on the various political parties, even on those in power, to secure more and loyal voices in the media. Therefore, competition among journalists to satisfy the partisan appetites of publishers and readers, as well as for news and better paying jobs, has made the lives of Greek journalists very tense. Unchecked and unabashed media partisanship is the biggest ethical issue faced by the Greek press today. It is also directly related to the low credibility and general low esteem of the press as an institution of public life.

The partisan expectations of owners and editors present a great challenge to Greek journalists. The *Rizospastis* case referred to in the previous chapter was a good example of this kind of expectation and the turmoil it may cause. Although most Greek journalists will not apply for a job on a newspaper with which they disagree ideologically, many, including some noted editors, have made rather inexplicable professional moves. Alexandros Filippopoulos, for example, who most of his life worked for leftist, anti-American newspapers, also worked in the 1960s for *Ethnikos Kiryx*, an ultrarightist, pro-American newspaper, and again before his death in 1991, he worked for the conservative Antenna radio and television stations.

But the challenges for members of the press are many and go beyond partisan politics to the heart of the profession of information attainment and transmission. Should a journalist work for more than one medium in the same market? In most Western democracies the answer would be no. But because until the last two decades Greek journalists made relatively very little money, this kind of double-dipping has been common. For example, print journalists often work part-time for the electronic media.

A related question is whether a reporter should also work part-time for the press office of a political party or of a government agency. Again, in most Western democracies the answer would be no. But in Greece, government, regardless of party, always has had an irrational appetite for "good press," and has therefore spent considerable amounts of money to promote the hiring of already employed journalists as part-time workers in the government press offices. This is done not only to keep up with the press-office work but to benefit from whatever good-will is spilled over into the news coverage of these journalists once they return to their newsrooms. Notably, in the ESIEA-EIIEA contract that was signed in December 1991, one issue that had been on the top of the agenda but remained unresolved was the contractual treatment of such "multi-positioned" journalists. The publishers wanted to eliminate the practice altogether, but ESIEA did not. In the end, a committee was appointed to study the issue and make recommendations. It is expected that the practice of holding more than one position will not cease. Contractually, however, those journalists holding two jobs will not be regarded as full-time employees of each medium or agency.

Although to many the practice of being on the payroll of both a news medium and a government or a political party branch represents the ultimate prostitution of the journalist's profession, it is no more odious than the well established Greek government practice of spending large amounts of money to sponsor advertisements of government institutions (notably national banks) in newspapers that have been friendly to the government. The same principles are applied in government subsidies to the provincial press and other in other publishing undertakings. This and the practice of facilitating loans for media and publishers have always been some of the darkest and best kept secrets of Greek journalism. With rumors abounding, they also have caused more damage to the profession's credibility than any single malpractice by the journalists themselves.

One good example of government loans to publishers took place in 1983 when state banks gave favorable loans to publisher Thanasis Popotas to publish two pro-PASOK newspapers. Eventually the papers closed and Popotas, who insists that he became involved at the urging of Prime Minister A. Papandreou, ended up in prison convicted of fraud ("Agogi Popota," 1991).

Pontiki ("Chrima me to tsouvali," 1991) revealed that subsidies to "press or cultural organizations" are budgeted in 1992 at $380,000 (compared with $514,000 in 1991 and $400,000 in 1990), and "public relations" expenses are budgeted at $444,000 in 1992 (compared with $315,000 in 1991 and $195,000 in 1990).

ADVERTISING

Until the explosive arrival of television, advertising in Greece had not been a major component in either the economic or the creative life of Greece. Although over the years it has been instrumental in the success of some products, it was utilized only to moderate and varying degrees by businesses, consumers, and media because of the small amount of time available in the government-controlled electronic media and the relatively limited imaginative opportunities offered by the print media. The arrival in the late 1980s of private television and radio, however, along with the accompanying realization of the power of these media in formulating public opinion, signaled the start of a new era in advertising. Advertising very quickly became an indispensable and large part of all sales strategies and budgets.

The money spent on advertising in 1990 (78 billion drachmas, or

$410 million) was 44 percent larger than the money spent in 1989 (53.7 billion drachmas, or $283 million). The 1991 expenditures reached 102 billion drachmas ($551 million) despite the recession and the Persian Gulf war ("Diafimisi '90," 1991; "Diafimisi '91," 1992).

The clear beneficiary of these increases was television. Although in 1989 its share of the advertising drachma was 42.87 percent, in 1990 the share of television was 45.18 percent, and in 1991 it was 54.3 percent. Critics of this sudden and complete domination of the advertising drachma characterized it as a third world-type phenomenon "unmatched in any other country on earth" (Papachristos, 1991, Dec. 15). At the same time, the newspaper share of the advertising drachma dropped from 18.93 percent in 1990 to 15.30 percent in 1991; the magazine share dropped from 28.58 percent in 1990 to 24.60 percent in 1991; and the radio share dropped from 7.31 percent in 1990 to 5.74 percent in 1991.

In 1991, according to Media Services, the largest portion of newspaper advertising money, 45.81 percent, was spent on the Sunday newspapers, led by *To Vima*, with 13.50 percent, followed by the Sunday *Kathimerini* 9.24 percent. The second-largest portion of newspaper advertising expenditures, 40.90 percent, was spent on evening newspapers, led by *Ta Nea*, with 11.85 percent. *Ta Nea* has traditionally had the greatest circulation of any newspaper in the Athens area and by far the most successful classified advertising section. Financial papers received an 9.62 percent share of the newspaper advertising drachma and were led by *Kerdos*, with 3 percent. Morning dailies received only 2.75 percent of the newspaper advertising drachma and were led by *Kathimerini*, with 1.21 percent of total newspaper advertising expenditures. Sports dailies had only .90 percent of the newspaper advertising money and were led by *Athlitiki Echo*, with .24 percent ("Diafimisi '91," 1992).

Despite the increasing popularity of specialized magazines, the magazine advertising drachma in 1991 went primarily (77 percent, down from 81.93 percent in 1990) to general-interest magazines (including television guides) such as *Tachydromos* (11.14 percent), *Eikones* (8.27 percent), and *Kai* (6.2 percent). Specialized magazines earned 18.23 percent share of the magazine advertising money and were led by *4 Trochoi* (2.89 percent) and *Idees & Lysis ya to Spiti* (2 percent), and *Economikos Tachydromos* (1.83 percent).

The service sector of the Greek economy (insurance companies, banks, weight loss clinics, lotteries, political parties, etc.) accounted for most of the advertising expenditures, 25.32 percent in 1989 and 27.5 percent in 1990. Food and drink advertisers represented 24.33 percent of the total expenditures in 1989 and 23.87 percent of the total in 1990. Cosmetics manufacturers represented about 13 percent of the total expenditures for both years, and car and tobacco companies followed, with approximately 6 percent and 3 percent shares respectively ("Syngentrotiki," 1991).

The top television advertisers in 1990 and 1991 were soap, beer, and hard alcoholic drink manufacturers; the top magazine advertisers were weight loss clinics, tobacco companies, and health spas; the top newspaper advertisers were banks, insurance companies, and movie theaters; and the top radio advertisers were insurance companies, political parties, and newspapers and magazines. Generally, however, the Greek advertising market is very dynamic and top advertisers do not remain the same from year to year.

Furthermore, the Greek advertising market has been penetrated by multinational advertising agencies. Of the top 20 advertising agencies (in gross income), all but six are owned, at least partially, by multinationals. At the same time, only two of the top 20 agencies in Greece have no foreign agency affiliation.

The top ten advertising agencies in Greece are: Spot/Thompson Advertising, Adel/SSA, Bold Advertising/Ogilvy & Mather, Lintas: Athens, Olympic DDB Needham, Leo Burnett, BBDO Athens, McCann-Erickson Hellas, Gnomi/Publicis FCB, and Geo/Young & Rubicam ("Foreign agencies," 1991).

6

Radio Today

STATE RADIO

Hellenic Radio (ERA), the state radio broadcasting service, is made up of the following five program services: ERA-1; ERA-2; ERA-3; ERA-4; and ERA-5, or the Voice of Greece. The first four are national services, while ERA-5 is an international short-wave radio service. ERA also has 19 local and regional stations on AM, two AM relay stations, and over 40 FM transmitters throughout the country (see Tables 6.1 and 6.2). In addition, ERA-1 uses two Voice of America (VOA) transmitters for a limited number of hours each day.

The first four program services are also referred to as the First, Second, Third, and Fourth Programs. The First Program, ERA-1, is the oldest and most diverse. It is ERA's news and information program, but also carries popular and traditional music, and occasionally radio plays. The Second Program, ERA-2, is the entertainment service, with more popular music, sports, and a few magazine and public affairs programs. The Third Program, ERA-3, is a fine arts service, while the Fourth Program, ERA-4, is a youth-oriented music and information service. All four services have been greatly influenced by free radio and now carry more hours of live

Table 6.1
ERA AM Radio Stations

Location	Frequency (KHz)	Power (kw)	Affiliation
Athens			
ERA-1	729	150	
ERA-2	1386	50	
ERA-3	666	15	
ERA-4	981	200	
Thessaloniki			
Macedonia 1*	1044	150	
Macedonia 2*	1179	50	
Zakynthos*	927	50	ERA-1 & 2
Kerkyra*	1008	50	ERA-1 & 2
Komotini*	1404	50	ERA-1 & 2
Rhodos*	1494	50	ERA-1 & 2
Chania*	1512	50	ERA-1 & 2
Patras*	1485	1	ERA-1 & 2
Volos*	1485	1	ERA-1 & 2
Ioannina*	765	10	ERA-4
Heraklion*	954	10	ERA-4
Orestiada*	1080	10	ERA-4
Florina*	1278	10	ERA-4
Tripolis*	1314	10	ERA-4
Larisa	945	5	ERA-4
Pyrgos	1350	4	ERA-4
Serres	1584	1	ERA-4
Kavala	1602	1	ERA-4
Kozani	1602	1	ERA-4
Orestiada**	1485	1	ERA-1
Samos**	1602	1	ERA-1
Amaliada	1584	1	private (ERA-1)
Mesologgi	1602	1	private (ERA-1)

*Regional stations   **Relay stations
Source: Radiotileorasi (ERT's weekly program guide).

Table 6.2
ERA FM Radio Transmitters

Location	ERA-1	ERA-2	ERA-3	ERA-4	Power 1-2-3	4
Athens (Parnitha)	91.6	93.6	95.6		10kw	
Athens (Hymetos)				101.8		100
Alexandroupolis	89.8	91.8			3	
Chania	92.9	94.9			3	
Corinthos (Gerania)	97.9	99.9			3	
Heraklion	94.4	96.4			3	
Ioannina	97.8	99.8			3	
Kalamata	92.2	94.2			3	
Kastoria	88.6	90.6			10	
Kavala	89.2	91.2			10	
Kephalonia	96.9	98.9			10	
Kerkyra	91.8	93.8			3	
Mytilini	92.3	94.3		104.4	3	35
Rhodos	88.4	90.4			3	
Thera (Santorini)	96.9	98.9		93.3		35
Thessaloniki	88.0	90.0	92.0		10	
Tripolis	88.3	90.3			10	
Volos (Pelion)	92.8	94.8	96.8		10	

Note: In early 1992 ERA placed two more FM transmitters in Southwestern Greece; in Zakynthos and in Pyrgos.

Thessaloniki 102 FM Stereo is independent of the four Programs.

Aegean Radio broadcasts a limited schedule on Thera (93.3) and Mytilini
(104.4) with 35 kw of power, and originates in Mytilini.

programming, while ERA-1, ERA-2, and ERA-4 also carry advertising. ERA also has two orchestras and a choir.

ERA-1 has the most extensive nationwide network, with a central
AM station in Athens, two AM relay stations, 17 FM transmitters, and
limited short-wave international programming through VOA transmitters. At the same time, ERA-1 is carried for part of each day by

seven regional stations and by two private stations.

ERA-2 also has a central Athens AM station and 17 FM transmitters. The regional station in Kalamata also uses an FM transmitter, built in the aftermath of the 1986 earthquakes. Besides this, ERA-2 is carried part time by seven regional AM stations. ERA-3 has a relatively limited coverage area, with one central AM station in Athens and five FM transmitters, two of which are on Aegean islands and also transmit regional programming.

ERA-4 has one central AM station and broadcasts part time from ten regional stations. It also has a 100-kilowatt FM stereo transmitter in Athens. Its former AM station in Thessaloniki is now the Second Macedonian regional service, which carries the new ERA station FM-102 from Thessaloniki.

ERA-5 broadcasts in 16 languages throughout the day, directed toward different parts of the world. ERA's international broadcasts consist of news, public affairs, and music. The first Macedonian radio station also broadcasts internationally, in Greek, but limits its broadcasts to Europe and the Middle East.

Some of the regional ERA stations were originally established as propaganda stations by the armed forces, and ERA-4 stations in Larissa and Ioannina are still located within army camps. Many of these former YENED/ERT-2 stations still use American equipment given to them during the late 1940s and early 1950s. Regional stations have historically been relay stations for central programs, such as ERA-1, ERA-2, or ERA-3, originating in Athens. They carry locally originated programs, including local news bulletins, for about six hours per day, which amounts to about 30 percent of total programming.

Regional stations have always had a limited infrastructure. Some have very low power, and their signal does not reach their whole province (Lionarakis, 1988, p. 134). Their income is also limited. In 1987 the expenses of the regional station in Crete, located in Heraklion, were five times its income of 2.6 million drachmas ($14,000). At the same time, the regional station of Northwestern Greece had expenses of 20 times its income, and the station in Volos had expenses of 15 times its income (Lionarakis, 1988, p. 172). During one month in 1989, all the regional stations together had programming personnel expenses around 115 million drachmas ($605,000) (Protogyrou and Petroutsou, 1989, Mar. 2).

PRIVATE RADIO

Greek radio broadcasting has been in turmoil since the introduction of free radio in 1987. In 1990 many stations began to specialize their programming, in contrast with previous years, when they had tried to attract everyone. In 1990 there were 276 licensed stations in Greece, besides the state radio stations and the two ERA-affiliated private ones. However, the first 48 licenses granted in 1988 soon expired (Theodorakis, 1991, p. 51). In May 1991, 228 more licenses, granted in 1989, also expired. Today the National Radio-Television Council (NRTVC), which was created in 1989 to license broadcast stations, is facing over 1,300 license and license renewal applications, but it has yet to take action on any of them. Thus, all radio stations today are without a license, and are, therefore, illegal. Although there is a general understanding that the government will not prosecute a station not violating the spirit of the laws, some local prosecutors around the country have taken action against stations not to their liking, on the pretext that the stations are not licensed (Roumeliotis, 1991, Nov. 25). In fact, in 1991 a group of radio amateurs were sentenced to one-month in jail for operating an illegal station (Tiflopontikes ton FM) in 1985 (Roumeliotis, 1991, p. 138).

As the number of radio stations has increased over the last few years, so has the number of problems. The situation is as fluid as ever, reminiscent, as one columnist put it, of "the gold rushers of the far West" (Sotirelis, 1990). Private radio broadcasters, who for years have wanted more freedom from the government, are today calling for government regulation. The Continuous Committee for Local Radio (DETORS) repeatedly calls for more regulation and strict adherence to current laws. At the same time, it calls its members to take individual NRTVC members to court for not performing their duties, in order to force the council to take up license renewal.

There are an estimated 1,525 radio stations operating regularly in Greece. Many of these have applied for a license, others have not. At the same time, an estimated 5,000 amateur stations are also on the air (Roumeliotis, 1991, April). Most of the amateurs have not applied for a license, and either do not broadcast regularly or broadcast only for a few hours each day. The government has reserved space, from 100.7 to 101.4 megahertz on the FM band, for amateur broadcasters to operate legally, without a license, but they are not supposed to use more than 40 watts of power.

Most such stations, however, violate this requirement, while some supposedly amateur broadcasters also carry advertising. At the same time, the space reserved for amateurs has not been respected by other stations, which broadcast on that part of the spectrum and also on frequencies previously licensed.

The frequency situation is a lingering problem. The NRTVC was originally waiting for the Ministry of Transportation and Communications (MTC) to come up with recommendations on radio and television frequencies. Although the MTC has not come up with a comprehensive report, in 1991 it recommended that in addition to those used by the ERA stations, only 57 more frequencies be made available for the Athens area, to allow for the best operations ("Louketo ston aera," 1991). However, in actuality, there are close to 100 stations operating in the area. If only 57 licenses are to be given, it is not clear what criteria the council will use to allocate these licenses.

In addition, myriad other problems or law violations persist. Some stations use more than one frequency; some operate with greater power than allowed; and some have been sold or rented to other interests. Some licensees operate more than one station. All of these practices are clearly illegal. If the laws are to be enforced, someone will have to take the political responsibility of closing down more than 30 radio stations in Athens and many more throughout the country, and of forcing other stations to operate within the legal boundaries. But as newspaper columnist Andreas Roumeliotis (1991, July 26) put it, "Who is going to take it upon himself to enforce the laws?" The biggest violators are powerful business people and publishers, and even the Church of Greece. A former president of DETORS described the situation as "anarchy" (Tasos Papadopoulos, an Athens 98.4 programming consultant; personal communication, July 10, 1991).

OWNERSHIP AND CONTROL

Municipal and Politically Affiliated Stations

Private radio stations in Greece fall into one of seven types of ownership: they are owned by publishers; by shipowners or other industrialists; by municipalities; by political parties; by non-profit organizations; by former amateurs; and by current amateurs.

Municipalities started the wave of free radio and were initially very successful at attracting both audiences and advertising revenues. Today, however, most municipal radio stations have fallen on hard times. Of the 80 or so non-state radio stations regularly operating in the Athens area, in 1991, 10 were municipal stations. Most notable of these were Athens 98.4; Kanali 1 of Pireaus; Diavlos 10, of 10 western suburbs; Tik-Tak, of 9 eastern suburbs; Radio 5, of five suburbs of Pireaus; Radio Kyclos of five northeastern suburbs, and Radio Xenios of Ano Liossia. In the Thessaloniki area, of about 61 radio stations, three are municipal stations operated by the city of Thessaloniki; Radio Kalamaria is operated by the suburb of Kalamaria, and Enato-Kyma is operated by 23 municipalities.

Most municipal stations are operated by city corporations. It is estimated that the average municipal station has operating expenses of 1 million drachmas ($5,265) per month (Vlavianou, 1991). However, the large municipal stations have expenses that surpass 10 million drachmas per month.

Most major municipal stations made profits during their first two years. Stations such as Athens 98.4 and Thessaloniki's FM-100 even made enough to financially support other municipal enterprises. However, there is practically no municipal/provincial station in Greece today that does not lose money. These losses are subsidized primarily by taxpayers or take up money that would otherwise go to other city services.

In Athens, because of the station's huge deficit, a bipartisan city council committee is questioning the need for retaining all of its 254 employees (Nicolopoulos, 1991). Similarly, Kanali 1 loses around 8 million drachmas per year (Dimitris Kapranos, station managing director, personal communication, July 11, 1991). This station is in deep financial trouble in 1992, which has led to talk of its impending closure. Although this is not very likely, there is no doubt that major changes will take place, probably including personnel cuts and programming changes.

Financial problems had forced municipal stations Diavlos 10 and Tik-Tak to initiate discussions about possible simulcasting or sharing of their programs. Nevertheless, in 1992 these stations found themselves unable to continue. As such, municipal stations Tik-Tak, Radio-Kyclos, Radio 5, and Diavlos 10 closed down, while the municipal stations in the Athens area that remain have dropped most of their information programming because of the shortage of funds.

Besides financial problems, the municipal stations continue to have political problems. The first municipal stations took their identities from the size of their particular city, from the political party controlling its administration, and from the personality of the mayor, who was invariably instrumental in the establishment of the station.

In Athens and Pireaus the municipal stations started as large operations with a variety of programs and large production and news staffs, like ERA stations. But unlike ERA stations, they tended to have a relatively more objective approach to news and public affairs. In Thessaloniki the first municipal station was not so objective, but served as the opposition voice to ERA. Similarly, many smaller municipal stations either supported or opposed the government, depending on the political affiliation of the mayor. In towns governed by a Communist Party (KKE) mayor, the station usually took a polemical approach to all mainstream political activities.

The first municipal elections after the birth of the first municipal radio stations were held in 1990. These elections resulted in changes of city administrations, and new political powers now oversaw the municipal radio stations. In the three largest cities, which were also most influential in introducing free radio, all three New Democracy (ND) mayors, the municipal radio pioneers, moved into government cabinet positions when ND won the 1989 parliamentary elections. New Democracy kept the Thessaloniki mayoral seat and supported a successful independent mayoral candidate in Athens, but lost the mayoral race in Pireaus to a candidate of the Coalition of the Left. Before the elections, most candidates did not present any specific plans for the city radio stations, as free radio was no longer an important issue. Most candidates promised that station objectivity would continue, and also pledged no layoffs of staff, even though all but Thessaloniki's FM-100 were losing money (Papachristos, 1990, October).

Despite their promises, once elected, the new mayors had to contend with great financial difficulties. Furthermore, the stations were now facing great competition, as the number of stations had increased dramatically. Although there were no major changes in Thessaloniki, other than attempts at greater objectivity in the municipal stations' news coverage, numerous changes took place in Athens and Pireaus.

The new mayor of Athens, Antonis Tritsis, appointed new management for the station, and he himself took over the presidency of the municipal enterprise that runs the station. The new mayor was very critical of the station's audience losses and directed the station to concentrate more on environmental, cultural, and local matters. This reflected the interests of Mayor Tritsis, who in the past had served as PASOK's Minister of Education, and Minister of Public Works and the Environment (Papadopoulos, personal communication, July 10, 1991). However, the untimely death of mayor Tritsis in early 1992 returned the station in the firm hands of ND, and its future is once again uncertain as it operates in 1992 without a full-time manager.

Naturally, this new direction was also the result of new marketplace conditions, including increased competition, and advertising losses for the station, and of new political conditions. The shift in the focus of municipal stations to more local concerns and more Greek music was inevitable; when the stations were first established they were virtual monopolies, but today they compete with other stations that are becoming more specialized. Athens 98.4 originally had a fifty-fifty mix between Greek and foreign music, but increased the amount of Greek music in 1991 (Papadopoulos, personal communication, July 10, 1991).

In Pireaus, where the new mayor was supported by the Coalition of the Left and PASOK, there was a promise of no major changes. However, changes, did take place, dictated by the new political environment. For example, additional people were hired to reflect the new political orientation of the mayor, although the journalists already on staff were not replaced. Of this station's programming, 40 percent involved news, while 60 percent was music, 70 percent of which was Greek (Kapranos, personal communication, July 11, 1991). In Pireaus, the city council serves as the administrative council of Kanali 1; therefore, the new president of the station's administrative council is the PASOK-affiliated president of the city council. Here too, the emphasis of the station became more local (Kapranos, personal communication, July 11, 1991).

Nevertheless, when changes in Greece's political landscape took place, political problems started affecting this station. The two major parties supporting the mayor of Pireaus, PASOK and the KKE, each soon wanted to exercise more control over the operation of the station. This was partially the result of KKE support for special trials against former PASOK cabinet ministers and former prime minister Andreas Papandreou.

Political party radio stations were also affected by domestic matters and international developments. For example, a schism developed within KKE, between the conservative old guard, which traditionally supported close ties to the USSR, and younger members, who saw developments in the USSR as an omen for the fate of KKE if it did not change. This caused KKE to withdraw from the Coalition of the Left, but some of its members remained in the Coalition and were thus voted out of KKE. This had tremendous implications for KKE-owned media, especially its affiliated radio station 902 Aristera Sta FM. This station had been established in January 1989 by staff members of KKE party organ *Rizospastis*, and it was operated by people aligned with the reformers. Very few of these young people had any experience in radio, but the radio station they started reflected a reforming outlook in Greek society and an openness that was uncharacteristic of political party media. The station's programming included political discussions and Greek and foreign music; it was to a degree influenced by ERA's Third Program. The KKE old guard was cautious at first but eventually began criticizing the station, starting with the complaint that the station did not play traditional folk music (Danikas, 1991). In addition, party people demanded an adherence to the party political line, and the party soon asked for veto power over who could be interviewed on 902 (Thalassinos, 1991).

Nevertheless, the station was very successful and quickly began to reach 10 percent of the Athenian listening audience. In addition, it used relay transmitters to extend its coverage to much of the country. However, this coverage was not enough to allow the station to break even financially. It had about 150 employees and was losing around 15 million drachmas per month, much of it subsidized by KKE (Papachristos, 1990, November).

In the turmoil of the political schism at KKE; the financial losses of the station became a point of contention. Some administrative personnel resigned, but KKE wanted layoffs of additional personnel (who happened to be reformers). When KKE left the Coalition of the Left, 902 covered the issue objectively, which many of the old guard did not like. Later, the party appointed a new station manager, whose censorship of the news resulted in a protest strike by the employees.

In the meantime, the station's listenership had fallen, its deficit had increased, and the station's owner, Radiotileoptiki, a company owned by KKE, declared a lockout (Papachristos, 1991, June). KKE also made a deal with C. Kalogritsas, publisher of the KKE-subsidized newspaper *Proti*, which had closed down in 1990, to operate his radio station Rock FM. This youth-oriented music station, which had started in 1988, did not last long under this arrangement. Soon employee paychecks bounced, and the station was returned to Kalogritsas (Roumeliotis, 1991, July 19). It closed down for a while, but returned to the air in October 1991, after which it was sold again to Athenian entrepreneurs.* It was has since lost much of its political identity

Meanwhile, 902 Aristera sta FM, is once again on the air, as the radio station of KKE and the most visible political party radio station. Most other party-affiliated stations are concealed by their owners, who happen to be publishers (e.g. Radio Athina, Antenna). Other political groups operate such stations in the provinces.

During the numerous elections between 1989 and 1990, the political party candidates in many provincial towns set up radio stations just to promote their candidacy. Others simply paid station owners to broadcast interviews with the candidates, or paid for programs promoting their candidacy (Roumeliotis, 1989, Apr. 17). At the same time, the major political parties packaged whole newscasts and distributed them, free of charge, to stations outside Athens via fax machines. PASOK, for example, distributed such programs to 80 provincial stations (Lakopoulos, 1990).

Private Commercial Stations

Also taking part in the political arena are certain private stations owned by newspaper publishers. These publishers followed the example of mayors and quickly established radio stations, which they saw as a natural continuation of their business. There are some publishers with close political ties, and others whose political orientations are apparent in their newspapers, but who keep a

---

*Since it is illegal to sell a station, it is not clear whether stations are sold, rented, or simply transfered to someone else's control under some secret arrangement. Either way, transfer of control appears to be illegal.

greater distance from political parties.

Avriani's Radio Athina initially went on the air to counter the popularity of municipal stations established by ND mayors. This station plays exclusively Greek music and has a clear pro-PASOK position, as well as a position within opposing PASOK forces. One of its founders, Makis Kouris, is a PASOK deputy in parliament.

The first licensed private, non-municipal radio station on the air was Top FM, operated by the Lambrakis Press Organization. This station kept a relatively objective approach to news and public affairs and tried to be a station for everyone. Following a number of personnel and programming changes, and with increasing competition from newer radio stations, Top FM found itself moving from near the top of the ratings to near the bottom. The station was sold (or rented) to the Alafouzos family in December 1990.

Aristides Alafouzos (see also Chapter 4) is a shipowner who made his entry into the media business during the dark days of Koskotas's departure from Greece in March 1989. Alafouzos bought *Kathimerini* and Sky FM from GRAMMI, the media company owned by Koskotas, after Koskotas fled the country. Koskotas had put Sky FM on the air in September 1988. Although the media purchases by Alafouzos would seem a simple example of an entrepreneur entering the world of media, in Greece, media and politics are inseparable.

The mere buyout of the respected conservative *Kathimerini* was a political act as well. Thus, while Sky FM, operated by Alafouzos's son Yannis, has now become the top station in Athens, its operations cannot be void of politics. In fact, there has been a long feud between the Alafouzos family and Prime Minister Mitsotakis because *Kathimerini* and Sky FM support opposition figures within New Democracy. Taking over Top FM, Y. Alafouzos renamed it Pop FM and brought in foreign programming consultants, who turned the station into an automated continuous foreign music station. However, in 1992 there is political pressure being applied by ND on Alafouzos to return the station to Lambrakis.

Alafouzos is one of many industrialists and shipowners who have entered the media world. Another such businessman is Minos Kyriakou, a shipowner with ties to New Democracy and the owner of Antenna radio and television stations. Antenna FM became a ratings success soon after it came on the air by attracting listeners from party ranks, while others were attracted by its slick programming. This, was one of the causes of the decline of Athens 98.4, which catered to the same listeners. However, when New Democracy took over the government, many of its followers switched their alliances to the now ND-controlled ERA stations, thus causing Antenna to drop to second place in the ratings.

Another businessman who recently entered the media business is Socrates Kokkalis, owner of the telecommunications company Intracom. The world of media is a natural milieu of business people who have major business dealings with the government. Media voices are often a means of exercising influence over public opinion, which in turn gives them some influence in the political arena. Kokkalis started the newspaper *Epikairotita* in the late 1980s, but it closed down in October 1991. Soon after the start of *Epikairotita*, he also established radio station Flash 96.1. The initial success of this station was limited, but the age of specialization saw it become a successful all-news radio station.

Another station owned by a publisher is Klik FM, owned by the publisher of *Klik* and *Gyneka* magazines. This station went on the air in October 1989 as one of the first stations to narrowcast, or target a narrow segment of the listening public. It has been very successful at targeting people between the ages of 20 and 34.

There are also book publishers in the radio business. Galaxy radio station in Athens is owned by a family with publishing interests, while Radio Paratiritis in Thessaloniki is owned by the publishing company Paratiritis.

Former pirates are also well represented on the Greek airwaves. In Athens the most successful such station is Jeronymo Groovy, which caters to teenagers and is usually in the top ten of the ratings charts. Another station with a long history on the airwaves is Epsilon FM. It started as a pirate station on AM in 1972, and after a long absence, it is back on the FM band broadcasting Greek music on a 24-hour basis ("Tria chronia," 1991).

Nonprofit and Amateur Stations

Besides the business use of radio, nonprofit groups also see it as a way to make their voices heard. One such group is the Greek Products Promoters Association, which was one of the first to get a license. Its station, Ellada FM, is exclusively a Greek music station, and is relatively successful.

Another such group is the consumer group, Consumer Federation, which established Radio Katanalotis. Similarly, PAKOE-FM is a station operated by the Greek Center of Ecological Studies. Other nonprofit stations include several church-affiliated stations, such as the successful Radio Station of the Pireaus Metropolis (91.2 FM), which regularly attracts 1 percent of the Athens area listeners, and the less successful station of the Church of Greece (89.4 FM).

Amateur or alternative stations, also nonprofit, are well represented on the Greek airwaves. Among them are the alternative Kokkinoskoufitsa FM (94.6), and amateur efforts like the First Amateur Program (95.1) and Second Amateur Program (104.0) in Athens, and Radio Kivotos and Radio Utopia in Thessaloniki.

Another amateur radio station is Echo FM, which allows its frequency (102.4) to be used by Jazz FM between 10 p.m. and 6 a.m.. Echo FM was formed by some of the members of former pirate station Star Radio, while others from the same group have put a legitimate Star Radio (105 FM) on the air. There are actually a handful of Star FM or Star Radio stations in various parts of Greece, and although they are not affiliated, they are operated mostly by former amateurs. A number of radio stations all over the country are operated by amateur radio enthusiasts, and most of them have never received a license and probably will never request one.

On the other hand, the historic station Kanali 15, which officially went on the air in January 1989, faced financial difficulties early on, and was forced to lay off many of its journalists. Later its founder, Rousos Koundouros, was forced out and the station was sold to industrialists. Eventually this station was sold again, and it is once again facing financial difficulties.

The stations mentioned above are only representative of the types of ownership and by no means exhaust the list of stations. Furthermore, there are a few stations that do not fit into any of the above categories. For example, there are a few foreign-language stations, which retransmit foreign stations or services. Olympic Action Radio (102.1 MHz) is an English-language station that rebroadcasts the BBC World Service, VOA Europe, and CNN radio programs, and also has a few local programs. It is operated by foreign correspondent Paul Anastasiadis, who was involved in the *Ethnos* libel suits. Anastasiadis also established station RFI (106.7 FM) to rebroadcast Radio France International.

Provincial Stations

Over 1,000 radio stations operate outside the two major Greek metropolitan areas. Most of the other 50 provinces have at least one municipal radio station. In addition, each province has five or six private stations and a number of amateur or pirate stations, receives two or three ERA stations, and has one local station that carries, at least on part-time basis, a private Athenian station (Vlavianou, 1991).

Like the municipal stations in the larger cities, their smaller-city counterparts face tremendous financial problems. This is the result of the combination of too many radio stations and an underdeveloped advertising market in the smaller cities. Some private stations operated by former pirates do not worry much about generating revenue, because that is not their primary aim, but the private stations that are intended to become revenue-producing enterprises also face great difficulties. Many of these stations received a license when that became possible, but today are frustrated with the unregulated situation (George Maniatis, advertising manager, Ilis FM, personal communication, July 25, 1991).

Most private provincial stations cater to a younger audience, which is not adequately served by state radio. However, because of its youth, most advertisers do not want to target this audience. In addition, these smaller stations do not have the mechanisms or trained personnel needed to generate advertising revenues. The only radio station personnel who could possibly be characterized as trained in the field are the few former pirates who have built their own radio stations. Even the facilities of these stations are limited; they are usually housed in small apartments, without soundproofing and with minimal equipment. Furthermore, they are caught in a vicious circle because they cannot update their facilities without advertising revenue, and without better facilities they cannot stand out among the competition and thereby attract advertising.

The province of Ilis, in southwestern Greece, is a good example of what has happened in the Greek provinces. Before 1977 this province had only two stations, an ERA-4 regional station and an ERA-affiliated private station. The private station, in Amaliada, is unusual in that it was built in 1953 by a nonprofit group of local residents. In 1959 it became affiliated with ERT, an affiliation that allowed it to operate even when other private stations were closed down and even enabled it to build a relay transmitter in a neighboring province.

Today there are 27 stations in this province, while the people involved admit that the market cannot support more than 6. This includes the 2 stations mentioned previously, a new municipal station, and 24 private stations, some of which initially received a license, while others have not.   This competitive situation has resulted in court battles among some stations, as all broadcast with greater power than allowed, while the Amaliada station is operating on AM and on FM (since 1978).

The Amaliada station has been forced to change its programming and incorporate more live programs, as do the new stations, but the competition in the market has turned it from a prosperous station into a station that is fighting for survival (Antonis Meglis, Amaliada radio station manager, personal communication, July 26, 1991). The station, still a cooperative, put out a call for new members in order to enhance its chances for survival, and its membership rose from 300 to 1,200 (Roumeliotis, 1991, Oct. 18).

Private Stations and the Hertzian Jungle

Athens stations have a variety of ways of extending their signals to reach larger audiences.   One is to use a series of transmitters to broadcast the signal; 902 Aristera sta FM and Radio Athina are the stations with the most national coverage through this clearly illegal method.

Another way is for the Athenian radio station owner to operate another station in another city. For instance, George and Makis Kouris of Radio Athina, are part owners of Radio Thessaloniki. Antenna FM also has a frequency in Thessaloniki. In addition, some Athenian stations pay or arrange with a local station to carry their signal in the provinces on a full- or part-time basis. In Patras, for example, Radio 1 carries Sky FM 24 hours a day. Sky FM also broadcasts in Rhodos, while Rhodes International carries Flash 96.1 part of the day (Roumeliotis, 1991, Oct. 16).

Furthermore, some own more than one station in the same city and have their stations simulcast part of the day. For example, in Thessaloniki, station Radio Anatoliko (92.8) simulcasts news with Radio Paratiritis (Roumeliotis, 1991, Oct. 11). In Athens, Alafouzos'

Melody FM simulcasts news and a few other information programs with its sister station Sky.

An additional way stations can transmit farther is by using greater power or more than one frequency. This is particularly useful in Athens, where the surrounding mountains limit the reach of a single frequency. Thus, some stations use two frequencies by transmitting from different mountaintops. Athens 98.4 uses two frequencies, as do Klik FM, Radio Athina, Antenna FM, and Sky FM. Some of these second frequencies are actually employed by more than one station, making them practically useless (Roumeliotis, 1991, July 23). Furthermore, almost all stations today transmit with greater power than initially assigned. In fact, a handful of Athenian stations can be heard all over the Aegean Islands. It seems that many major radio stations would like eventually to reach a nationwide audiences through a various means. All of these violations have created major problems on the Greek airwaves. Over half of the listeners in the two major Greek metropolitan areas report problems with the reception of their favorite stations ("Enimerotiki erevna," 1991).

One of the pending proposals is for the government to establish "transmission tower parks," where many stations can place their transmitters. As it stands now, stations place their towers anywhere they see fit. In some areas, the public complains about the presence of the towers, which are seen as polluting the environment. A public dispute about transmission towers, involving two amateur, low-power stations in Thessaloniki, resulted in one station being set ablaze, while the police later demolished their towers. In Athens, most stations have illegally placed their towers on the mountaintops, which are government property.

Competition among the stations in this radio jungle has reached new heights. In 1990-1991, there were a series of attacks on radio station facilities, as well as a series of radio transmitter thefts. Meanwhile, a new breed of pirates is proliferating. These new pirates are similar to the pirates of the 1960s and 1970s, except that they are not concerned with being legalized. DETORS is constantly complaining about these pirates because they interfere with private radio stations. Some pirates even purposely transmit on frequencies used by major stations, in an attempt to extort money (Papachristos, 1992, January).

PROGRAMS AND AUDIENCES

ERA's Second Program was the most popular station in Athens until September 1987, when Athens 98.4 went ahead in the ratings. By May 1988 the three municipal stations in the Athens area, 98.4, Kanali 1, and Diavlos 10, were outperforming the four state radio stations in the ratings, while the municipal stations' overall listenership was at 48 percent and going up (Roumeliotis, 1988, July). At this time audience surveys showed that most ERA-2 listeners were PASOK voters, most Athens 98.4 listeners were ND voters, and most Diavlos 10 listeners were KKE voters (Roumeliotis, 1988, May 25).

Seeing the drop in the ERA's audience size, the government panicked and held a major news conference in which it announced that state radio was first in the ratings. They did this by combining audience share for the four Programs and comparing it to individual municipal stations. Even this was not enough in Thessaloniki, however, where FM-100 was attracting 59 percent of the audience. Nationwide, however, ERA-2 was still the most popular ("Proto synolika," 1988).

In April 1989 Antenna FM replaced Athens 98.4 at the top of the ratings. Audiences began to select radio stations according to their musical taste, which is usually directly related to age. For example, even though Antenna was the top station, 44 percent of teenagers listened to Jeronymo Groovy (Roumeliotis, 1989, Apr. 21). Meanwhile, ERA stations were quickly losing more of their audience. ERA-2, the most popular state radio station, was down to 5 percent. At the same time Athens 98.4 fell to third place, replaced in second place by Sky FM (Roumeliotis, 1989, September).

In Thessaloniki, despite the establishment of many new radio stations, the municipal FM-100 was still in first place with 27 percent of the listeners, according to Focus research company. FM-100 was followed by Radio Thessaloniki, with 14 percent; the mayor's other station, youth oriented FM-101 with 8 percent; and Thessaloniki's Antenna, with 7 percent. The new state radio station, FM-102 was far behind, with 6 percent, while collectively the traditional ERA stations were attracting around 2 percent of the listening audience (Roumeliotis, 1990, February).

In Athens in 1991, Sky FM reached first place among listeners, while overall listenership rose to 60 percent. Flash 96.1 also gained audiences, by becoming a strictly news and information station in 1990. It hovers around the top five stations, with about 6 percent of the listening audience. The decline of Athens 98.4, however, has continued (Papachristos, 1991b, Apr. 14) (see Table 6.3). Athens 98.4 attracts older, upper-middle-class listeners, while Pop FM, the continuous foreign music station, Klik, and Jeronymo Groovy attract younger people. Sky FM, on the other hand, attracts listeners of all incomes and ages. Two other stations attracting people from all categories are Antenna and Ellada FM. Radio Athina and ERA-2 attract primarily people over 45 years old (Troupis, 1991). In Thessaloniki, in 1992 FM-100 has dropped to third place behind Antenna and Radio Thessaloniki, while Star FM, a youth-oriented music and sports station, is fourth (see Table 6.4).

As more private stations have come on the air, audience measurements have become important and controversial. Some stations have denounced audience measurement results and have asked not to be included in the ratings. Part of the problem is caused by contradictory results of audience surveys conducted by different companies, which use different research methods.

The main companies involved in audience research on a regular basis are Focus and A. C. Nielsen Hellas. Most of the audience measurements cited here were reported by Focus. This company started its audience surveys in 1988 and today conducts radio audience analyses not only in Athens and Thessaloniki, but also in 38 other provinces year-round. It provides audience reports to ERA, to ERT, to over 65 private or municipal stations, and to 20 advertising agencies. It conducts personal interviews about listening behavior over the preceding 24 hours (Roumeliotis, 1991, July 25). Additional companies in Greece that conduct audience research are AGB Hellas, Alco, Eurodim, Icap Hellas, Matrix, Market Analysis, KEME, MRB Hellas, MPCCJ, Prognosis, Research International Hellas, Stochos, and Strategic Marketing.

Most audience surveys use the day-after recall method. A number of stations in 1991 requested that a listener survey be conducted by a different company besides Focus. This survey, by Alko did not radically change the results, although some stations gained in specific audience demographics. This survey concluded that, on the average, a resident of Athens listen to 1.5 different stations per day. Most people (43 percent), primarily listen to the radio at home, while 10 percent listen primarily in the car, and 10

Table 6.3
Major Athens Radio Stations

Station	Frequency	Ownership	Format	Audience*
Sky	100.4	Alafouzos	variety	39.0**
Antenna	97.1	Kyriakou	variety	17.0
Galaxy	92.1	private	easy listening	7.0
Flash	96.1	Kokkalis	news	6.5
Pop FM	92.4	Alafouzos	foreign	6.4
KLIK	88.0	Terzopoulos	urban	6.3
Melody	100.0	Alafouzos	Greek	4.0
Ellada FM	88.5	nonprofit	Greek	4.0
Radio Athina	99.0	Kouris	Greek variety	3.0
Jeronymo Groovy	88.9	private	youth/music	3.0
ERA-2	93.4	state	music variety	2.6
Athens 98.4	98.4	municipal	variety	2.2
ERA-4	101.8	state	music variety	2.0
ERA-1	91.6	state	variety	1.3
Aristera	90.2	KKE	variety	1.3
Rock FM	96.8	private	youth/music	1.0
ERA-3	95.6	state	fine arts	-***
Kanali 1	90.6	municipal	variety	-
Kanali 15	104.5	private	variety	-
Echo/Jazz	102.4	amateurs	foreign	-
Seven X	98.7	Kouloukountis	sports	-

Source: Focus, as reported in numerous publications, in 1992.
*Averages of audience share over a 6-month period.
**A large portion of the public reports listening to more than one station.
***Less than 1 percent.

percent primarily listen at work (Roumeliotis, 1992, Apr. 19).

Despite the trend toward program specialization, the two most popular stations in Athens, Sky and Antenna, feature variety formats with emphasis on political talk and information. Their programming includes much news and information, Greek and foreign music, talk shows, quizzes, and limited sports programs. In 1989, the Sky FM share of the audience was 8 percent, but over a year it steadily increased, with the help of listener surveys followed by programming changes ("Sky profile," 1991, p. 52). It also carries news and information from the BBC and Deutsche Welle.

Table 6.4
Major Thessaloniki Radio Stations

Station	Frequency	Ownership	Format	Audience*
Antenna Radio	97.5	Kyriakou Kouris/	variety	17.0**
Thessaloniki	94.5	amateurs	variety	16.5
FM-100	100.0	municipal	variety	12.0
Star FM	97.1	private	youth/sports	9.0
Macedonia Kanali 1	98.1	private	Greek	7.2
Radio Paratiritis	93.1	publishers	variety	5.0
Pedia tis Kalamarias	102.6	former pirates	Greek	4.0
FM-101	101.0	municipal	foreign	3.2
A 103	103.0	citizens	variety	3.1
Top FM	104.0	private	foreign	2.5
FM-102	102.0	ERA	variety	2.2
Radio Anatolikos	92.8	private	Greek	1.5
Radio Kalamaria	93.4	municipal	variety	1.1
Ilios Vora	91.4	private	Greek	1.0
Panorama	98.4	private	variety	1.0
Acropolis	106.8	amateur	music	1.0
FM-100.5	100.5	municipal	fine arts	1.0
Mousikes Epiloges	90.8	former pirates	Greek	-***
ERA 2	90.0	ERA	variety	-

Source: Focus, as reported in numerous publications, in 1992.
 *Averages of audience share over a 6-month period.
**A large portion of the public reports listening to more than one station.
***Less than 1 percent.

The other Alafouzos station, Pop FM, reaches about 6 percent of the Athens-area audience. One of the first stations to utilize American music consultants, it plays from a computerized play list of 300 songs per week (Vainakis, 1991, p. 46). The third Alafouzos station is Melody FM, which has an easy-listening format and broadcasts Greek music.

Antenna FM in Athens competes with Sky across all programming categories. However, it is perceived as being too close to New Democracy and thus not objective enough in news coverage.

Flash 96.1 started in May 1989, and Yannis Tzannetakos joined the station as its manager in September. Following his resignation in December 1989, the station made programming changes that eventually turned it into the first Greek all-news station. Perceived as having a left-of-center (PASOK) political orientation, it attempts to be a "listener's newspaper," with six editions per day, lasting four hours each. Its programming consists of news magazines, straight news, interviews, and essays. Each edition has a managing editor, while the whole operation utilizes over 130 journalists. It includes live remote broadcasts, wire service stories, and reports from foreign correspondents. Most of its listeners are men between 25 and 45 years old ("Flash profile," 1991).

Most stations have decreased the size of their news staffs or cut out news entirely, and most have specialized their programming, primarily in terms of music. Initially, free radio stations broadcast much foreign music. Later, however, as specialization increased, stations either broadcast exclusively Greek music or predominantly foreign music. In a survey conducted in 1991, Greek music was found to be very popular in Athens, but even more so in Thessaloniki. A Focus survey in those two cities showed that 74 percent of the listeners in Athens looked for Greek music first in searching for a radio station, while 91 percent did the same in Thessaloniki ("Mousiki erevna," 1991). Stations broadcasting primarily Greek music are Ellada FM, Radio Athina, Melody FM, and Epsilon FM.

According to listener surveys, people over 25 years old, especially, look for Greek music, on their radios while those younger than 25 look for foreign music. In Athens, those interested in foreign music particularly tended to listen to rock music, while in Thessaloniki they listened to dance music (disco, rap, etc.). Other popular foreign music is blues, rock 'n roll, and jazz ("Mousiki erevna," 1991). Athenian stations playing primarily foreign music include, Kiss FM,

Jazz FM, Star FM, Echo FM, Jeronymo Groovy, Pop FM, Klik FM, and Rock FM. Galaxy is one of the most popular all-music stations, and uses easy-listening computerized play lists.

Obviously, radio is not the only means of exposure to foreign music. There is a tremendous music sales market today in Greece, estimated to be a 10-billion drachma ($54 million) business. Of these sales, 25 percent take place around the Christmas season. Unlike other Western nations, however, CDs account only for about 20 percent of all record sales in Greece (Ktenas, 1991a). Of all recorded music sold in Greece in the mid-1980s, 53 percent was foreign and 47 percent was Greek according to an ERT-2 radio broadcast of January 24, 1985. This proportion was exactly the reverse in the 1970s ("Foreign disk," 1979).

The types of foreign music sold in Greece are mainly American and British "pop," rock, disco, jazz, and classical. However, it is estimated that 40 percent of all music sales involve pirated music (Ktenas, 1991b). The emergence of private radio stations has also hurt music sales, as people now have many more listening choices, and many record their favorite artists from radio broadcasts. By 1989 record sales had decreased by 25 percent, while music sales were down by 40 percent (Lacopoulos, 1989, August).

Many people also listen to radio for news and information. According to the Focus survey, 35 percent of the Athenian radio listeners listen to radio mostly for information, while in Thessaloniki that figure is 30 percent. This compares with 26 percent who listen mostly for music in Athens, and 33 percent in Thessaloniki. More people listen exclusively for music—27 percent in Athens and 30 percent in Thessaloniki—than exclusively for information—12 percent in Athens and 9 percent in Thessaloniki ("Enimerotiki erevna," 1991). Nevertheless, the heaviest use of radio to date took place during the Gulf War in 1991, when many Greek radio stations provided up-to-the-minute news (Roumeliotis, 1991, p. 293).

Besides Flash 96.1, other stations carry news. For example, ERA-2 and ERA-4 have daily news magazines, in addition to periodic short newscasts. Other stations with daily news-magazine shows include Sky FM, Antenna, Athens 98.4, 902 Aristera sta FM, and most municipal stations. Tik-Tak was the first municipal station to specialize its programming, targeting a variety of social groups. It used to broadcast many special programs directed at children, young people, and women. On the other hand, music stations have very little news. Klik FM (88 MHz), for example, provides only 88 seconds of sponsored news per hour. Many stations initially also carried programs that relayed the front pages of the day's newspapers. Some simply relayed the top stories in each newspaper, while others read many of the stories verbatim.

There are also stations that carry many hours of sports. Seven X, owned by the Kouloukountis shipowning family, deals exclusively with sports. Style FM, another all-sports station, is closely affiliated with the Olympiakos Football Club. ERA-4 carries sports for 12 hours per week, while other stations, like ERA-2 and Antenna, carry sports primarily on Sundays. Stations such as Sky, 902, Flash, 98.4, and Kanali 1 carry weekly or daily sports news and/or magazine shows ("Athlitikes ekpombes," 1991).

Finally, cultural and fine arts programming is carried not only by ERA-3, but to some degree by many other state, municipal, and nonprofit stations. Various stations broadcast daily or weekly programs on the arts, including programs on theater, literature, and painting, as well as classical, folk, and Byzantine music. Private stations, in particular, have numerous programs about the cinema or about poetry.

Many of the people involved in production or performance for Athens radio stations have moved there from ERA stations or were former pirates, while radio station journalists are usually newspaper trained. Others in a radio are not well trained. Nevertheless, the growth of private radio created a huge demand for qualified personnel, and good on-air personalities, producers, and journalists can make tremendous amounts of money working in radio. Marginal radio personalities and producers also made huge amounts of money during the first two years, but the situation has changed as the increase in the number of stations, and the decrease in advertising revenue has brought salaries down. Radio station personnel in the provinces are marginal, other than the few who have had experience as pirates or happen to have special talent and dedication.

Most provincial radio stations have some relationship with an Athens station or a program syndication company. One of the most important syndicators of news and public affairs programming is the Development Center for Electronic Mass Media (AKHMME). This started as a cooperative effort by the municipal stations Diavlos10 and Tik-Tak, and the Hellenic Corporation for Local Government and Local Development (EETAA). AKHMME came about as a result of the financial difficulties faced by Athens-area municipal stations. As a way to cut costs, five of these stations decided to share their news and information programming in early 1990. However, most of the journalists who would have been affected by the ensuing layoffs went on strike, putting political pressure on the stations not to participate (Roumeliotis, 1990, Jan. 11). In addition there were questions about the legality of the proposed plan, given that Presidential Decree 25/1988, Article 6, does not allow networking of stations or sharing beyond 10 percent of their total programming. The strike and the legal problem forced four of the stations to withdraw. The other two remained and joined with EETAA to create AKHMME, which distributes news and public affairs programs to about 160 stations nationwide. This revenue-producing enterprise also distributes sponsored music-with-information programs, on a barter basis, to 30 provincial stations (Vlavianou, 1991).

Another syndicator of news is Flash 96.1, which sends news via fax machines to 17 stations twice a day, while a few of the 17 stations receive a direct feed of short newscasts from Flash each hour. A similar but more encompassing syndicator is Epikinonia operated by Antenna FM. Epikinonia distributes programs and advertising to 75 stations and also faxes news stories to many of these stations. Roye is another private syndicator, distributing news and programming to 40 provincial stations. Syndicated programs oriented either to music or public affairs usually cost about 20,000 drachmas per hour (Vlavianou, 1991).

One of the more successful syndicators is a private company called Dyktio. Dyktio serves as the advertising representative for 180 stations nationwide, and is also beginning to enter the television field. Dyktio does not produce programs but will occasionally syndicate sponsored programs to stations. Its main activities are in advertising sales; it serves as an agent for advertisers or stations and buys advertising on provincial stations (C. Avramopoulou, Dyktio representative, personal communication, July 10, 1991).

FINANCING

In Greece, as in many other European nations, broadcasting has traditionally been conceptualized as a cultural, not a commercial device. This is clearly stated in the Greek constitution, which directs the state to supervise broadcasting, to guarantee quality, objectivity, cultural growth, and diversity to all the people. Commercialization of the broadcast media, however, both in Greece and in other European nations, according to W. Hoffman-Riem (1987, p. 57), "harbors specific risks to some aspects of this diversity."

Competition among private and municipal stations in Greece, with its accompanying influence over state radio and with an increasing emphasis on ratings, promotes a programming philosophy known in the United States as catering to the "lowest common denominator," and in Greece as "popularismic." Ratings become so important that stations try to attract the largest possible audience by programming only what is popular; thus diversity, indigenous musical traditions, and cultural growth are sacrificed. Radio and television programs become "economic goods to be commercialized in accordance with market conditions" (Hoffman-Riem, 1987, p. 62). This arises out of the American tradition, which is completely new to Greece. Greek free radio came about as a result of the need to fulfill the constitutional intention of encouraging quality broadcasting; however, commercialization and competition do not necessarily allow that constitutional intention to be fulfilled.

Most radio stations in Greece today carry advertising. The exceptions to this are ERA-3, a number of church-affiliated stations, and some amateur stations. However, no station in Greece seems to be making a profit, with the possible exceptions of the very popular Sky FM, Antenna FM, and Flash, and the highly specialized Jeronymo Groovy. Although advertising expenditures since 1980 have been increasing steadily, radio's share of those expenditures has not. In the first seven months of free radio, out of the advertising money that did go to radio, municipal stations took 40 percent. As a result, ERA stations cut their advertising prices by almost 50 percent for some programs ("Triponta kerdi," 1988).

Since the introduction of private television, radio's share of advertising has been decreasing. Radio's share of total advertising expenditures was 6 percent in 1983 ("Diafimisi," 1983), and jumped to 8 percent in 1988 (Roumeliotis, 1990, Jan. 29). However, in 1990 it dropped to 7.31 percent, and in 1991 that share dropped to 5.74 percent ("Diafimisi '91," 1992). During the same period, advertising expenditures have increased 30 percent over the same period the year before, yet radio's advertising revenue only increased by 2.7 percent.

This drop in radio advertising money has jeopardized the survival of Greek radio stations, and, the 7 percent tax imposed on broadcast advertising creates additional problems. The situation in the provinces is even worse. As the number of radio stations increased, competition for the same advertising support became fierce. Many stations, particularly in the provinces, do not follow an advertising rate card, but give tremendous discounts to advertisers. Some stations even provide free advertising to some customers, so as to seem to be demand to other advertisers (Maniatis, personal communication, July 25, 1991). Generally, advertising rates are on a per second basis in larger cities, but many smaller stations sell advertising per spot.

It seems logical, then, that most, if not all, stations turn to other sources for income. The alternative sources of income depend on the type of station ownership. State stations receive a portion of the ERT fee most Greeks pay on their electricity bill, as well as additional government subsidies. Municipal stations generally receive local government funding. Nevertheless, municipal radio seems to have failed, as stations keep closing while others become strictly music stations. Private stations receive substantial funding from other businesses with which their owners are involved. Finally, most provincial stations operate only because their owners have another steady job.

Overall, by 1992 radio advertising expenditures had reached about 5.8 billion drachmas ($31 million) per year. Sky FM received about 44 percent of radio advertising revenues in Athens, while Antenna had dropped to 31 percent. Flash received around 7 percent, while Athens 98.4 around 3 percent, and ERA stations received around 5 percent, collectively, despite their nationwide audiences (Roumeliotis, 1992, July 18).

Most stations face grave financial difficulties. For example, radio stations in 1992 owe more than 10 billion drachmas ($54 million) to the journalists' pension fund ("Selida tou typou," 1991 October), as well as billions of drachmas to other employee pension funds. By law, stations are to pay 21.5 percent of their advertising revenue to this fund but no station had paid it until early 1992 when Sky started doing so (as do television stations Mega and Antenna) (Roumeliotis, 1992, Mar. 2). In addition, hardly any station, pays any music royalty fees except for ERA, which pays 2.4 percent of its gross advertising revenue. At the same time, no private or municipal station except Sky FM pays its share to the national weather service for using weather information (Roumeliotis, 1992, Jan. 7).

THE DIRECTION OF GREEK RADIO

The state monopoly over radio was lifted in Greece because government control over the news could no longer be tolerated. Pluralism was demanded by various public interest groups, including radio pirates, who put pressure on the government to change. Finally, political opportunism dealt the final blow to the state radio monopoly, but as R. J. Simms (1991) indicates, "the groundwork—the dirtywork—was accomplished by the public interest groups and then, when the time was socially correct, the politicians appeared to join the movement" (p. 10).

However, Greek radio today is not satisfying the politicians. Their municipal stations become weaker by the day, and have failed as a form of public radio for the most part, while at the national level, the government is constantly criticized by the new media. Even most amateurs and public interest groups are not satisfied, because they cannot function in an unregulated environment. In the absence of clearly defined laws, and more importantly, with the lack of enforcement of laws that already exist, stations take it upon themselves to sue each other or even face off outside legal boundaries, observing the law of the jungle, where only the strong survive.

Indeed, the future does not look bright for Greek radio stations, as their boom years are now over. Athenian radio experts seem to agree that many stations will eventually close. In Athens, the market apparently cannot support more than about 20 stations. Despite this, few stations have closed down thus far, although many who originally received a license have never gone on the air. At the same time, Mega Channel is preparing its own radio station.

The strong stations now on the air are those owned by publishers and industrialists, who have the financial resources to build the best-equipped stations, attract the best talent, and produce the popular programming needed to attract the huge audiences they need for their financial or political purposes. Real alternative or community radio has not resulted from radio privatization. There are a few exceptions, such as amateur programs that have the beauty of the ideal and the naivete of the innocent, but there is no doubt that they too soon will be corrupted or closed down. Indeed, although some pluralism exists on the Greek radio waves, it exists only because radio is in a state of anarchy.

Ironically, in many respects, it is state radio that is becoming free radio—free from mindless contests, game shows, and sponsored beach parties. This situation has some people wishing for the days of pirate radio (Lacopoulos, 1989, August). Others have simply turned off their radios and have turned to television, a more politically and financially glamorous medium.

ERT's main facilities, located outside Athens, housing ET-1, ERA-1, ERA-2, and ERA-3

7

Television Today

LEGAL FOUNDATION AND CONTROL

Pertinent Broadcast Laws

The current legal structure behind Greek broadcasting is based on Article 15 of the 1975 Constitution, which treats broadcasting as a national resource and places it under the control of the state. Yet the goals and aims of broadcasting as expressed by Article 15 have never been achieved. The successive governments have been unable or unwilling to distinguish between what the Constitution provides, which is broadcasting under "the immediate control of the state" to be used for the common good, and what actually happens, which is broadcasting under the immediate control of the party in power for its own purposes.

Based on Article 15, parliament enacted Broadcast Law 230/ 1975, which created ERT and granted it a monopoly over broadcasting. In 1982 ERT was transformed into ERT-1, as the government took YENED away from the armed forces and transformed it into ERT-2. In 1987 a new broadcast law merged ERT-1 and ERT-2 into a new ERT, putting it in charge of all Greek broadcasting. Law 1730/

1987, as amended, is the legal structure governing Greek broadcasting. It establishes ERT as a public, state-owned, nonprofit corporation intended to provide "information, education, and entertainment to the Greek people." ERT is governed by an 11-member administrative council, the president of which is the chief executive officer, but the corporation is under the jurisdiction of the Minister to the Premiership.

In 1989 a coalition government of the New Democracy Party and the Coalition of the Left enacted law 1866/1989, which allowed the establishment of private television stations. However, according to the constitutional mandate, the state is to exercise direct control over Greek broadcasting. Therefore, this law also created the National Radio-Television Council (NRTVC) as the vehicle through which the state controls broadcasting. Additionally, the council is supposed to facilitate freedom of expression and promote quality broadcasting. The NRTVC replaced the Local Radio Commission and a (political) broadcasting council created by law 1730/1987.

The National Radio-Television Council

The NRTVC was originally composed of 11 members, appointed as follows: three by the party with the highest number of parliament deputies; two by the party with the second-highest number of deputies; one member by the party with the third-highest number of deputies; and one each appointed by the Union of Journalists of Athens Dailies, the Union of Journalists of Macedonia & Thrace (Northern Greece) Dailies, the Central Union of Greek Cities and Municipalities, the Technology (Engineering) Chamber, and the National Audience Federation. All members are to serve six-year terms except initially, when a portion of the members were randomly appointed to two- or four-year terms so that one-third of the council is renewed every two years.

Although the creation of the NRTVC seemed to move Greece closer to similar broadcast regulations of other Western countries, the government was not willing to give the NRTVC complete authority over broadcasting. Because of this, the powers of the council are primarily advisory. For example, although the council can levy penalties on those violating broadcast laws, it can only make recommendations on other important matters. It recommends candidates for the positions of president, vice-president, and members of the ERT administrative council to the Minister to the Premiership, but it must recommend three people per position, from whom the minister chooses one. Similarly, the NRTVC must approve license applications for private radio and television stations, but these licenses are granted by the Ministry to the Premiership.

In a move that further weakened NRTVC independence, in 1990 the New Democracy government decided to change the council's composition. The initial composition of the council aligned most of the members with the leftist parties, PASOK and the Coalition of the Left, by a margin of seven to four. In a Ministerial Decision, 22255/2, (published in the *Government Gazette*, November 5, 1990), by the Minister to the Premiership, the council was enlarged to 19 members. The new additions to the NRTVC included one representative each from the Church of Greece, the Athens Academy, the State Accounting Council, the State Legal Council, the Athens Chamber of Commerce and Industry, the Ministry of Transportation and Communications, the Greek Federation of Labor, and the Union of Owners of Athens Dailies. This new composition tilted the balance of political power toward the conservative government.

However, the decision was controversial, and the other two parties filed suits to have it declared unconstitutional. Finally, on February 29, 1992, the Council of State (constitutional court) declared this ministerial decision unconstitutional (Papachristos, 1992, March). As such, the status of the NRTVC, as well as all its decisions made under this composition, are in limbo. It seems likely that the government will draft a law codifying the decision to enlarge the council.

The first president of the NRTVC was a university law professor with close links to New Democracy, who had a role in drafting law 1866/1989. However, he was out of the country so often that very few meetings of the council took place under his presidency. His term and the terms of three other members expired late in 1991, and the government appointed a new president in early 1992. The new president, Panayotis Ladas, is also a law professor, who served as the lawyer for Kouvelas in the late 1980s, who is now Minister to the Premiership.

The NRTVC lacks the necessary infrastructure and staff to adequately conduct its business. While waiting for new facilities, it is housed in the building of the General Secretariat of Press and

Information, where its offices consist of two rooms, one for secretaries and another for the council's general secretary. This second office is completely empty other than a desk for the general secretary who in 1991 did not have any work to do, insisting that the council could not become fully operational because it did not have any technical or engineering expertise to evaluate license applications or enforce broadcasting laws. In November 1991 the NRTVC decided to create a service composed of engineers, technicians, and lawyers to carry out decisions by the council and to enforce the appropriate laws (Papachristos, 1991, Nov. 17). However, this service has not yet become operational. In addition, the NRTVC requested that the government give it the necessary infrastructure to operate, including a staff and, most important, a report by the MTC clearly identifying the number of radio and television frequencies available in Greece.

The first act of the NRTVC was in 1989, when it drew up political campaign coverage guidelines, but these were ruled invalid by the Council of State, because certain small political parties were completely left out (Kontrarou, 1990). Most of what Broadcast Law 1941/1989 outlined for the NRTVC still has not been established. One exception is the directive that the NRTVC establish (within six months) a code of journalism ethics and programming and advertising standards. This code was introduced two years later, in June 1991, and was very controversial.

The code of ethics applies only to broadcasting, and it deals with the purposes of broadcast programming, crime and terrorism coverage, news coverage of political demonstrations, quiz and game shows, arousal of panic and fear, news objectivity, protection of children, and violence. Article 11 of the code states that those who believe the code has been violated should first complain to station management, but that if they do not get satisfaction, they can complain to the NRTVC ("Kodikas deontologias," 1991).

The council itself was divided about this code, and the vote to adopt it was along ideological lines. Members of the opposition, within the NRTVC, complained that the code is likely to be interpreted differently, depending on which political party happens to be in power. Furthermore, many felt that the code should simply state what stations or journalists should not do, instead of what they should be obligated to do, as it does now (Vgontas, 1991). Journalists also complained because they felt this code was authoritarian even in its style, as many of its clauses were phrased "a journalist is obligated . . . ." (Papachristos, 1991, May 26).

Television Regulation

Broadcast Law 1866/1989, Article 4, allows the establishment of private television stations but does not deal with the important issue of the number of stations that can be accommodated by the frequency spectrum. This law states that the appropriate government ministries, with the consent of the NRTVC, can grant corporations and local governments the right to operate television stations for local coverage. These television signals can be terrestrial, cable, scrambled, or satellite delivered. The law further states that corporate owners of television stations must make public the names of all their shareholders. No one shareholder or family may own more than 25 percent of such a corporation, and each licensee may have only one television station. Finally, television station licenses may not be given to foreign companies, other than from European Community member countries.

According to law 1866/1989, television station licenses are renewable every seven years, and granted only after consideration is given to the applicant's character and experience, and the quality and variety of the proposed programs. Licenses can be revoked by the NRTVC for law violations, and private stations must adhere to limits on advertising and to political campaign guidelines that also apply to ERT. Furthermore, according to this law, a percentage of television stations' profits must be returned to the government. However, this percentage is not defined by the law and as of mid 1992 has not yet been determined by the government. Accordingly, stations have not yet returned any portion of their profits to the government. Similarly, the law requires that a percentage of a television station's revenue be returned to a fund for theatrical film productions. This also has not been done.

Clarifications on licensing of radio and television stations came later, in Presidential Decree 572/1989, which reiterated that private television stations can provide only local coverage. According to this decree, license applications are to be submitted to the NRTVC, but the MTC examines the technical portions. Following approval of the technical standards, the council can recommend approval of a license, which is then granted by the Ministry to the Premiership.

Further clarifications regarding broadcast licenses came in a catch-all 1991 law (1941/1991) that outlines penalties for violation of broadcast laws. For example, those operating without a license may be fined; licensed stations violating the terms of the license may have their licenses revoked; and those interfering with air transport frequencies may have their equipment confiscated and may be fined by the Ministry to the Premiership, following recommendations by the MTC. This law also creates the Center for Frequency Control in the MTC to police frequency use, and it reduces fees for license applicants from a high level set by previous regulations. It also states that NRTVC meetings regarding license applications are closed to all but members of the council and the applicants being considered. Even this law, however, was amended later in 1991, to require NRTVC consent in fines and license revocations. However, all portions of the above laws are constantly violated.

At one of its first meetings, the NRTVC was faced with 102 television license applications, but it did not take any action on them (Protogyrou, 1990). In fact, as of mid 1992, all private and municipal radio stations, as well as all the television stations on the air, are technically illegal.

In 1990 the MTC came up with preliminary recommendations for television frequency allocations, indicating that there are 52 television channels available for the whole country. It recommended 13 stations for the Athens area and 39 for the rest of Greece. This report suggested that, given the geographic profile of Athens, a city surrounded by mountains, complete coverage of the area requires that each station broadcast using three transmitters or three frequencies. This would allow for only 13 television stations in the Athens area. The MTC suggested allowing five private stations and three satellite channels to use these frequencies, reserving one channel for a possible fourth national station. The MTC further suggested the examining the feasibility of cable and other new technologies, to facilitate more stations (Tzalavras, 1991).

In early 1992, the government indicated a willingness to deal with this issue, but first tried to have the NRTVC abdicate its power to decide on the merits of the license applications, because it said it is difficult for the MTC to come up with acceptable engineering standards and adequately enforce them. However, the NRTVC refused. Nevertheless, on July 21, 1992, the NRTVC began the examination of applications for television station licenses. Indicative of the situation is the fact that of the eight applications examined on the first day, six were already on the air. Since there is still no definitive report (as of July 1992) on the frequencies available, it is expected that the NRTVC will not grant any licenses until late 1992 at the earliest.

Furthermore, the NRTVC gave stations until August 31, 1992, to complete their applications, and afterwards it will decide first on licenses for nationwide coverage, and second, on licenses of stations in the Athens area. No mention was made about radio station licenses.

Besides the question of who gets a television license, the government must deal with the issue of which private channels will be allowed nationwide coverage. Although this was not allowed under law 1866/1989, an amendment to this law, taking effect in April 1991, allows "the technical networking of a local television station (to) enable national coverage" under a special license ("Idiotiki tileorasi," 1991). There are two ERT channels being transmitted nationally, and ET-3 to all of Northern Greece and Athens (see Table 7.1). In addition, Mega Channel and Antenna TV cover over 80 percent of the country, while Kanali 29 transmits to Thessaloniki, to a portion of southern Greece, and to the island of Crete. Kanali 29 along with New Channel, are good candidates for a license to extend their coverage nationwide. Other competitors for such a license are Seven X, Nea Tileorasi, Sky TV, and Hellas 62.

However, since the decision on who gets a license for nationwide coverage is clearly a political decision, the government has to walk a tightrope, in that it wants to grant such licenses to its political allies, but at the same time it must not appear to be doing so. For example, if it were to grant such a license to the pro-ND New Channel, it would have to grant one to the pro-PASOK Kanali 29, which it does not want to do. So, the government decided in May 1992 to try to revive the interests of the group of publishers who were initially given a temporary license for Nea Tileorasi. This attempt apparently succeeded and it appears that Nea Tileorasi will go on the air in September 1992. Partners in this group include the Press Foundation, which operates *Eleftheros Typos*; businessman Socrates Kokkalis, who owns radio station Flash 9.61; and Panos Karayannis, who owns *Apoyevmatini* .

Table 7.1
ERT Television Transmitters

Location	ET-1	ET-2	ET-3
Akarnanika	ch. 3	ch. 43	
Alexandroupolis	ch. 6	ch. 27	ch. 32
Athens	ch. 11, 21	ch. 34, 5	ch. 52, 31
Chalkidiki			ch. 21
Chania	ch. 7	ch. 27	
Drama			ch. 35
Florina			ch. 39
Gerania Mt.	ch. 9	ch. 51	
Heraklio	ch. 10	ch. 44	
Ioannina	ch. 10	ch. 25	
Kalamata	ch. 6	ch. 32	
Kastoria	ch. 7	ch. 49	ch. 52
Kavala	ch. 7	ch. 59	ch. 35
Kefalonia	ch. 8	ch. 57	
Kerkyra	ch. 9	ch. 50	
Mytilini	ch. 9	ch. 48	
Pelion Mt.	ch. 6	ch. 41	ch. 44
Rhodos	ch. 9	ch. 42	
Thasos	ch. 39	ch. 23	ch. 26
Thera	ch. 8	ch. 29	
Thessaloniki	ch. 5, 37	ch. 30	ch. 27
Tripolis	ch. 10	ch. 42	

Source: Radiotileorasi, the ERT program guide magazine, 1992.

Television Station Ownership

The introduction of private radio and television to Greece is important not only economically, but politically. Those who built the first major television stations were allowed to do so only because they wielded great political and economic power. For example, the first private television station, Mega Channel, was possible because of the great political and financial might of its shareholders. These shareholders are (1) the Vardinoyannis family, which owns the newspaper *Mesimvrini*, a soccer team, the video distribution company Audiovisual, a number of shipping companies, and Motor Oil Hellas, the company that is first in sales in Greece, with profits of 4.2 billion drachmas; (2) the Lambrakis Press Organization, the largest publishing company in Greece, which is 42nd in sales and has profits of 264.7 million drachmas; (3) Tegopoulos, the publisher of newspaper *Eleftherotypia*, which is 154th in sales; (4) Bobolas, the publisher of *Ethnos*, whose company ranks 141st in sales (Korfiatis, 1992); and (5) the Alafouzos family of shipowners, publishing *Kathimerini* and owners of three radio stations. The Alafouzos family also plans to build its own television station, Sky-TV, in 1992.

The other major private television station, Antenna TV, is principally owned by Kyriakou, who also owns Antenna FM, although his main business is shipping. Other shareholders include Kalogritsas, publisher of the now defunct *Proti*; Pournara, the publisher of the television program guide *Tilerama*; and a group of other shipowners. However, there has always been speculation that Kyriakou owns more than 25 percent of the stock ("Akaliptos," 1990). If this is true, then this station violates the law.

Another major station is Kanali 29, owned by the Kouris brothers, George and Makis, who also own Radio Athina, and the pro-PASOK newspapers *Avriani, Avriani Voriou Elladas* (of Northern Greece), *Niki, Logos*, and the sports daily *Filathlos*. However, in July 1992, there was a falling out between the two brothers and Makis Kouris was in the process of being bought out by his brother George, who is the majority shareholder of G. A. Kouris Inc.

New Channel is also a major Athenian station, owned by a corporation closely tied to the New Democracy Party, and to Kouvelas in particular, who serves as Minister to the Premiership. In 1990 there was much talk that TV-100 employees had actually built this station. At that time Kouvelas was the mayor of Thessaloniki, and was therefore responsible for TV-100.

TV Plus is a private subscription television station that went on the air with the help of the city of Pireaus. It operates about eight hours each evening, but during the day the satellite station Super Channel is transmitted on its frequency, under the terms of an agreement between the two channels. Most of the TV Plus programming is scrambled, and consists of movies. The station had, in 1991, over 2,500 subscribers, who paid about 5,000 drachmas ($27) per month for a special descrambler to access the station ("Tileorasi me syndromi," 1991). TV Plus owners informed the NRTVC that they plan to sell 25 percent interest in the station to Time/Warner, once they get a license.

The first station completely controlled by a political party is 902 TV. This KKE-owned station went on the air in November 1991 and carries mostly news and information, accompanied by cultural programs. It also transmits in the Thessaloniki area.

In addition to the stations mentioned above there are also the three ERT stations and the Cyprus Radio Foundation (RIK) television station operating in Athens. Under a reciprocal agreement, signed in 1990, ET-1 is also being transmitted in Cyprus. In addition, there are at least 20 other channels currently broadcasting in the area. They include: Telecity, TVM, Hi Channel, Kanali 67, Leonidas Channel, Megara Channel, Erini Channel, Leventis Channel, Tsonta Channel (using an ET-2 frequency late at night), Seven-X MCM, Olympos, Hellas 62 (by the Apostolic Church), Cosmos, Super TV, Tileora (by *Eleftheri Ora*), JGTV (Jeronymo Groovy), ITA 8, Hermes TV, Majestic TV, Station X, and Blue Sky, while many more have plans to start operations. Another eight satellite channels are being retransmitted terrestrially in the Athens area.

In the Thessaloniki area, there are a number of private stations broadcasting besides the three ERT channels and RIK. These are the Athenian channels Mega Channel (since March 5, 1990) and Antenna TV, TV Macedonia (since February 1990), Vergina TV, Time TV, Power TV, Hot Channel, Panorama TV, Center Television, Tsender TV, and Ta Pedia tis Kalamarias TV. There are also two municipal stations, Thessaloniki's TV-100 (since December 31, 1988) and Kalamaria's Argo-TV (since October 20, 1989). In addition, there are four satellite channels transmitting on terrestrial frequencies.

Overall, it is estimated that there are over 220 private and municipal television stations operating throughout the country, and that number is increasing steadily. The major stations outside the two largest cities are listed in Table 7.2.

Table 7.2
Major Provincial Television Stations

City or Province	Stations
Alexandroupolis	Alexandroupolis TV
Argolida	Argoliki TV, RTV Electra, Top Channel
Chalkida	Space TV
Chania	Crete TV, Crete 1
Chios	Alithia TV
Corfu	Corfu Channel
Corinthos	Electra TV
Drama	Drama TV
Grevena	Grevena TV
Heraklion	Crete TV, Radiokymata TV
Ioannina	Echo TV, In Channel
Kalamata	Best Channel
Karditsa	Cosmos TV
Lamia	IDM
Larissa	Demotiki TV, TRT-TV (Thessalian Radio-TV)
Lesvos	Lesvos TV
Magnisia	TV Ena
Mesologgi	Star TV
Mytilini	TVA
Patras	Super B, Patra TV
Rhodos	Rhodos TV (TV 4)
Serres	TV Serres
Syros	TV-1
Theva	High Channel, Viotiki TV
Veria	Vergina TV, TV Veria
Volos	TRT-TV
Xanthi	Thraki TV, Xanthi TV

Satellite Channels

As a result of the explosion in the number of private television stations in the country, many of the frequencies used to retransmit satellite channels will have to be used by private domestic stations. This presents a problem for ERT and the Greek government, because they have to decide which satellite channels to drop (see Table 7.3). Already, some private stations have simply taken over frequencies used in their area to transmit satellite channels, or simply replace the foreign station's signal part of the day. In one part of the country, New Channel is broadcasting on a frequency also used by ET-3, thus making it unusable.

ERT has an agreement with two U.S. satellite channels, MTV and CNN, that allows it to retransmit them without remuneration. It seems likely that these two stations will stay on, despite the desire to end up with only one satellite channel per nation of origin, because of the cost saving and because these two stations are so popular and so diverse that, unless the authorities run out of space, they will be kept.

In addition, other channels, whose countries of origin want them retransmitted to Greece for political and cultural reasons, will also stay. For example, TV5 is transmitted on a terrestrial frequency because the French government pressured the Greek government to have at least one French-language channel available. However, this channel may soon go out of business ("France's La Cinq," 1992). Similarly, the German government complained when ERT dropped two German channels. While Germany and France have offered to reimburse ERT for transmitting their channels, the Italian channels scramble their signal part of the day. Nevertheless, the increasing addition of more domestic stations throughout the country not only puts the terrestrial frequencies of satellite stations in jeopardy, but their audiences are also decreasing given that the Greek public now has more domestic programming choices.

Table 7.3
Satellite Channels Broadcasting Terrestrially

Channel	Nation of Origin	Cities Received
RAI Uno	Italy	Athens, Zakynthos, Heraklio, Ioannina, Kefalonia, Mytilini, Rhodos, Florina, Komotini, Nafplio, Patra, Kerkyra, Chania
RAI Due	Italy	Zakynthos, Heraklio, Agrinio, Patra, Florina, Kalamata, Kefalonia, Rhodos, Sparti, Chania
TV-5	France	Athens, Zakynthos, Heraklio, Ioannina, Kerkyra, Larisa, Nafplio, Patra, Chania, Sparti, Florina, Rhodos, Agrinio, Florina Komotini, Kalamata, Mytilini
Super Ch.	Britain	Athens (on TV Plus)
MTV	U.S.	Athens, Thessaloniki, Rhodos, Kerkyra
CNN	U.S.	Athens, Agrinio, Zakynthos, Heraklio, Thessaloniki, Ioannina, Kerkyra, Florina, Komotini, Larisa, Mytilini, Nafplio, Rhodos, Sparti, Florina, Chania
TVE	Spain	Athens, Komotini, Mytilini
Eurosport	Britain	Athens
RIK	Cyprus	Athens, Thessaloniki, Ioannina, Patra, Nafplio, Kerkyra
Horizon	Russia	Athens
SAT1	German	Rhodos
Screensport	Luxembourg	Thessaloniki
RTL	Luxembourg	Thessaloniki

Source: Radiotileorasi, July 13-19, 1991.

PROGRAMMING

Stations and Programs

Greek television has historically offered variety in television programming, much of which is imported. When the socialist government came to power in 1981, however, it attempted to "hellenize" television programming. To do that it started broadcasting alternative programs, such as experimental films, documentaries, and other cultural programs. Even episodes of "Dallas," bought by the previous ERT administration, were followed by a discussion of their ideological messages. It was reported that in 1984 ERT-2 decided not to renew "Dynasty" in order to protect the public. An ERT-2 board referred to "Dynasty's" use of "aesthetic and ideological deception" as the reasons for its success in the ratings (Doulkeri and Dimitras, 1986, p. 144).

This attempt to rapidly and radically change the nature of television did not last long, as the public reacted angrily to many of the new programs. In one case even the prime minister called the station, as did thousands of viewers, to protest the showing of an experimental film that included graphic adult scenes. This caused the panic-stricken ERT employees to take the station completely off the air for the night. Soon the trend toward alternative programming ceased. However, in the 1980s there was a greater variety of television programming, including fewer American programs and more programs from Eastern Europe and the Third World.

In 1987 the government published figures concerning the amount of foreign programming on ERT-1 and ERT-2 from 1981 to 1986, in order to show their decreasing dependence on imported programs. These figures showed that in 1981 foreign programs on Greek television accounted for 42 percent of total programming, excluding educational television. Foreign programming amounted to 51 percent in 1982, 37 percent in 1983, 36 percent in 1984, 33 percent in 1985, and 27 percent in 1986 ("Singrisi," 1987).

It is not known how the government arrived at these figures, as another study of Greek television in 1984 showed greater dependence on imported programming. According to this, during 14 weeks in 1984, foreign programs took up 38 percent of total programming hours on ERT-1 and 47 percent on ERT-2. Most of the imported programs were foreign series and movies. Overall, 61 percent of ERT-1's and 71 percent of ERT-2's entertainment programs were imported. Both channels, were offering the Greek viewer more foreign movies than Greek movies, more foreign series than Greek series, more foreign children's programs than Greek children's programs, and more foreign documentaries than Greek documentaries. The largest percentage of imported programming came from the United States, which accounted for 16 percent of all ERT-1 programs and 21 percent of all ERT-2 programs. Other nations contributing to Greek television were Britain, France, Brazil, Australia, Japan, Canada, and China (Zaharopoulos, 1985, p. 185).

In an attempt to improve its television service, in 1988 ERT decided to expand its programming day, and establish ET-3 as a regional television service for northern Greece ("Archizi," 1988). Before October 1988, the broadcast day of two state television channels lasted 7 to 8 hours on weekdays, and about 12 hours on weekends, for a total of 60 hours per week. Starting in October 1988, however, the broadcast day for both channels expanded to approximately 80 hours per week.

Another study of ERT programming in 1988, before and after the two channels expanded their programming day, showed that the dependence on foreign programming by Greek television had slightly decreased (Zaharopoulos, 1990). Foreign programming on ET-1 averaged about 30 percent in October 1988, as opposed to 38 percent in 1984. American programs continued to take up the bulk of foreign programming on ET-1, contributing 13 percent of the total, as opposed to 16 percent in 1984. ET-2 had also reduced its dependence on foreign programs, which accounted for about 35 percent of the total, as opposed to 47 percent in 1984. The American share of ET-2 total programming hours remained around 19 percent, as compared with 21 percent in 1984. Since the early 1970s ERT-2 (ET-2) has generally been the weaker of the two stations. Often it comes close to running out of programs and resorts to recycling old programs or buying cheap foreign ones.

ERT stations have a different program schedule from the schedule they had in 1988. ET-1 transmits educational television (ETV) programs for a few hours each week, but much less than in 1988. It begins its regular broadcast day at 8 a.m. and ends well after midnight, broadcasting about 18 hours per day, or about 126 hours per week.

ET-2, on the other hand, has given up morning programming and it goes on the air around 2 in the afternoon, except on Sundays, when it starts at 10 a.m. On the average, it broadcasts for 12 hours each day, for a total of 84 hours per week. ET-2 does not transmit educational television programs, but does carry many children's programs. A November 1991 survey of viewers in the two largest Greek metropolitan areas revealed that children watch more adult programs than children's programs. Cartoons attracted 10 to 14 percent of the children watching television, while educational television only attracted about 1 percent (Vidos and Papadopoulou, 1991b).

ET-3 has a more limited program schedule. It starts its day at 4 p.m. and broadcasts until after midnight, averaging about 11 hours. ERT stations do not sign-off at the same time each night. That depends on the length of the last program broadcast, and a late-night discussion program can go on for hours.

ET-1 and ET-2 have changed their programming practices dramatically since the introduction of private television. Their audience is much smaller, and they try to compete with private channels by using more popular programming and a less static schedule. Generally, ET-1 offers a daily morning magazine show, followed by game shows, soap operas, and Greek movies. It runs news, informational, and cultural programs in the early evenings, followed by news, series, and movies. ET-2 starts with series or serials (soaps), followed by children's programs, documentaries or cultural programs, news, movies, and information programs.

The authors conducted a content analysis of television program guides regarding ET-1 and ET-2 programming, using a "constructed" week between October and December 1991, which reveals that these two public stations carry more magazine shows, more movies, and more series than in the past. Game shows also increased on ET-1, because of their high ratings and low production costs (see Table 7.4). ET-1 has become the station with more commercial programming, while ET-2 has increased its percentage of informational, magazine, and cultural programs.

Furthermore, this examination of television programming shows that the foreign portion of ET-1 and ET-2 programming has decreased (see Table 7.5). This is partially due to the expansion of the ET-1 broadcast day, extended to include game shows and a morning magazine program. On ET-2 the change is partially due to repeated broadcasts of older Greek series and Greek movies.

Table 7.4
Types of Television Programs in an Average Week
(in percentages of total)

Program Type	1984		1991	
	ET-1	ET-2	ET-1	ET-2
Movies	17.5	19.0	24.0	18.0
News	14.0	16.0	5.0	9.0
Series/serials	14.0	19.0	23.0	26.0
Children's	12.0	12.0	3.0	7.0
Music/variety	10.5	11.0	1.0	3.0
Sports	8.5	5.0	9.0	8.0
Documentaries	5.5	7.0	1.0	4.0
Informational	5.0	4.0	3.0	9.0
Magazine	3.5	-	18.0	6.5
Public affairs	3.5	4.0	2.0	4.0
Games	2.5	1.5	9.0	-
Arts/cultural	2.5	1.0	1.0	5.5
Religious	1.0	-	1.0	-
Short films	-	0.5	-	-

Nevertheless, Greek television today has much more foreign programming simply because there are many more stations, and the demand for inexpensive programming cannot be satisfied by Greek producers. At the same time there are no limits as to the amount of imported programming that can be broadcast by a station. Accordingly, most major private stations carry an extraordinary amount of foreign programming (see Table 7.6).

The two major private stations broadcast primarily entertainment programs. Over 60 percent of the programming on both channels is in the form of movies and series/serials, and most such programs are imported. Mega Channel broadcasts 24 hours per day and has the largest proportion of foreign programs, due to its great

Table 7.5
Types of Imported Television Programs in an Average Week
(as percentage of total imported)

Program Type	1984		1991	
	ET-1	ET-2	ET-1	ET-2
Movies	63.5	83.0	36.0	51.0
News	-	-	-	-
Series/serials	79.0	70.0	47.0	60.0
Children's	47.5	63.0	60.0	80.0
Musical/variety	40.5	54.0	5.0	35.0
Sports	3.0	3.0	1.0	-
Documentaries	75.0	48.0	20.0	65.0
Informational	26.0	25.0	-	-
Magazine	-	-	-	-
Public affairs	-	-	-	-
Games	-	-	-	-
Arts/cultural	-	-	5.0	45.0
Religious	-	-	-	-
Total imported	38.0	47.0	21.0	41.0
(as a percentage of total programming)				

number of foreign, particularly American, series. Antenna TV, which
broadcasts for about 21 hours per day, also has many American
programs, such as movies, soap operas, and children's programs.
New Channel targets a working class audience with movies, series,
and musical shows.

Most other private stations are smaller, and their programming
depends on their financial resources. They usually carry political
discussion programs, movies, and local cultural and informational
programs. A few such stations also broadcast call-in game shows.
TV Seven-X MCM, carries the Euromusic (MCM) satellite channel, a
European version of MTV, for a number of hours each day, but plans

Table 7.6
Types of TV Programs in an Average Week in 1991, Among Four Major Stations

Programs	ET-1	ET-2	Mega	Ant	ET-1	ET-2	Mega	Ant
	Percentage of Total				Percentage of Total Imported			
Movies	24	18	23	28	36	51	40	37
News	5	9	6	7	-	-	-	40**
Series/serials	23	26	41	35	47	60	59	65
Children's	3	7	9	5	60	80	83	90
Music/Variety	1	3	6	3	5	35	84	100
Sports	9	8	6	3	1	-	-	40
Documentaries	1	4	*	-	2	65	100	-
Informational	3	9	*	2	-	-	-	-
Magazine	18	7	4	13	-	-	-	-
Public Affairs	2	4	1	2	-	-	-	-
Games	9	-	3	2	-	-	-	-
Arts/Cultural	1	5	-	-	5	45	-	-
Religious	1	-	-	-	-	-	-	-
Total imported (as percentage of total programming)	21	41	55	46				

Note: *Less than 1 percent.
**Antenna carries CBS news early in the morning.

to incorporate Greek music programs and music videos, as well as programs targeting young intellectuals.

Most smaller, provincial stations broadcast each day from around 6 p.m. until midnight. They carry mostly information programs, interview shows, news, and movies, and many seem more like the public access stations on U.S. cable systems. Many of the movies shown are low-budget Greek video movies produced in the 1980s and originally distributed through video clubs. The news clips they broadcast are often taken off satellite channels without permission. Some of these stations receive news and information programs from AKHMME. This is a radio program distributor that has moved into television and provides programs to at least 18 provincial TV stations on a barter basis.

Programs and Audiences

Since 1981 the number of television sets in Greece has increased by 40 percent. According to the Greek national statistical service in 1991, 80 percent of the households have a color television set, while 55 percent have a black and white set. Generally it is estimated that over 90 percent of all homes have a television set. At the same time, over 40 percent have a VCR, which is a 25 percent increase since 1981 ("To kalathi," 1991). Nevertheless, the actual figures could be higher, because with the high cost of electronic goods in Greece, thousands of television sets and VCRs are brought into the country illegally, and therefore not reported.

There are several television audience measurement companies in Greece, but the ones that conduct weekly ratings are AGB Hellas, Focus, and Icap Hellas. AGB uses the people meter electronic devide in the Athens and Thessaloniki areas. Focus surveys the whole nation for television viewing by half-hour segments. Icap Hellas uses the Bellview method of computer-assisted telephone interviews.

ET-2 was the most popular television station during the first years of Greek television. As an armed forces station, it had more entertainment programming and was directly competing with ERT. Later, however, it was slowly brought to a more socially responsible, but less profitable, position under civilian administrations, and ERT (ET-1) became the more popular of the two. Viewership for entertainment programming, regardless of channel, fell all through the 1970s and 1980s, however (Protogyrou and Petroutsou, 1989, February).

When Mega Channel came on the air in November 1989, it immediately started at the top of the ratings and has stayed on top since then, with only occasional lapses into second place. In its first week Mega attracted 36 percent of the television audience, as opposed to 26 percent by ET-1 and 11 percent by ET-2 ("Proti mera," 1989). On the other hand, ET-3 has always been at the bottom of the ratings among major channels, since its debut in 1988. These audience measurements are somewhat misleading, because the television audiences in provincial Greece are generally underrepresented; but nevertheless, as more private television stations are introduced, the audience share of ERT stations keeps decreasing.

One advantage ERT had initially was that it had a nationwide audience, which other channels did not have. Because of this, the ERT channels were still very popular overall until the two major private channels, Mega and Antenna, extended their coverage area. In 1991, while the ERT channels reached 100 percent of the Greek cities with over 50,000 population, the two major private channels reached 90 percent of those cities. A survey conducted in the above cities in 1991 found that Mega Channel was the most popular station, ET-1 was second, Antenna TV was third, and ET-2 was fourth. However, Mega and Antenna were first and second, respectively, in the two major metropolitan areas of Athens and Thessaloniki (Papachristos, 1991c, Apr. 14).

The most popular Greek television programs have traditionally been Greek movies, sports, Greek series, the evening news, and one or two foreign (usually American) series or serials per year. In 1990, of the top 50 programs, 34 percent were series/serials, 30 percent were movies, 14 percent were news/information programs, 18 percent were games, and the rest were sports. Of these, one-fourth were Antenna programs; these included "Wheel of Fortune," movies, and information programs. Another one-fourth of the top programs were broadcast by Mega, including movies, Greek situation comedy "Tris Charites," the American series "Matlock," and various information programs. Of the top 50 programs, 22 percent were broadcast on ET-1. These were soccer games and the successful American soap opera "The Bold and the Beautiful" (Alvertos, 1991). In 1991-1992 the most popular television programs were the situation comedies "Tris Charities" and "To Retyre," on Mega; "The Bold and the Beautiful," on ET-1; and "Wheel of Fortune," on Antenna. Following the 1991 season, however, "The Bold and the Beautiful" was bought by Antenna. Other very popular programs include Greek movies, foreign movies, basketball, and soccer.

Old Greek movies and newer foreign ones have always been popular on Greek television. Since the arrival of private television, however, the same old Greek movies are being broadcast every few weeks. There is also competition for recent foreign movies, while Antenna TV sometimes broadcasts Greek and foreign soft-porn films late at night.

Sports programs have also historically been very popular on Greek television, and the emergence of two powerful private channels has created competition for this type of programming. Up until 1990, ERT had a monopoly over televised sporting events. However, the traditional popularity of sports in general, and the emerging popularity of basketball in the 1980s, in particular, made sports a great target for private stations.

The first shot in this battle over sports programming was fired when Mega Channel bought the rights from team owners to televise Greek basketball games in 1991. ERT's loss of this sport became a political issue, one in which even the prime minister became involved (Papachristos, 1991, Sept. 29). To compensate for this loss, the government pressured soccer league officials, and the rights to televise soccer games went to ET-1. A special Saturday game is now played in Greece so that it can be broadcast on ET-1.* For the 1992-1993 season, the bidding war has heated up between the three stations for all sports.

Antenna TV is the channel with more commercial, or lowbrow, programming. It competes seriously with Mega's better-quality programs, and at times overcomes Mega in the weekly ratings. According to AGB audience figures between May 1990 and January 1992, Mega's share of the audience dropped from 35 percent to around 30 percent, while Antenna's went from 21 percent to around 29 percent. During the same period ET-1 remained steady at around 15 percent, while ET-2 continued its decline, from 9 to about 7 percent. At the same time, the share for all other channels combined has been around 12.5 percent (including ET-3's 1 percent), while all the satellite channels together attract about 2.5 percent of the audience, most of which tunes in to CNN. However, the audiences of satellite stations have been steadily decreasing. These same surveys also show that VCRs account for about 3 percent of the viewing audience. During 1992, audience shares for private stations have been increasing, while audience shares for ERT stations and satellite channels have been falling steadily.

---

*When a similar idea was proposed to ET-2 by one of the authors in 1987, he was told that this could not be done.

The introduction of new television channels is a main reason for the drop in VCR use and in the viewership of the satellite channels. Initially many of the new stations showed only slides with their logo or ads, accompanied by music, in order to lay claim on a frequency, but now more of them have regular programming. In the two large Greek metropolitan areas, all such channels together take a good portion of the audience, usually around 15 percent. At the same time, they take up frequencies formerly used by satellite channels; thus viewership of those channels is on the decline.

Despite the huge drop in videotape rentals in 1988 and 1989, first because of the introduction of satellite television and later because of the new private television channels, many people still use their VCRs. Nevertheless, the VCR no longer serves as the programming alternative it once did, when people had to choose between only two television channels. According to a 1991 survey, 13 percent of VCR owners rent one movie a week; about 8 percent rent two movies a week; and 21 percent (mostly teenagers) rent three or more movies a week. The largest number of these movies are action/adventure films; only about 15 percent of them are Greek movies (Stratos, 1991, June).

Program Piracy

The introduction of new media in Greece also brought program piracy. Not only are videotapes pirated, but radio and television stations broadcast programs obtained illegally. Some companies make illegal copies of videotapes for domestic distribution via video clubs, and also for export to Middle Eastearn nations (Papachristos, 1991a, May 19). New television stations sometimes simply rent tapes from their local video clubs and broadcast them. The Motion Picture Association of America (MPAA) has accused some 80 Greek television stations of copyright violations. The only stations not accused are ET-1, ET-2, Mega Channel, and Antenna TV, although ET-3 is accused of 12 violations ("17 minises," 1991). New Channel, alleged to be the biggest violator, was accused of illegally broadcasting 31 foreign films. It has also been sued by a Greek film distributor for violating its licensing agreement, and for nonpayment ("Den plironi," 1991).

American producers estimate their damages are about $23

million from pirated videotape rentals and $12 million for over-the-air piracy. It is estimated that about 45 percent of the videotapes rented in the Athens area and 65 percent in Greek provinces are pirated ("17 minises," 1991). It is also estimated that between January 1990 and September 1991, 180 films were shown illegally on Greek television stations. Even the movie *Batman* was shown on a private television station before it reached the movie theaters ("Helliniki tilepiratia," 1990).

Part of the problem is Greece's antiquated intellectual property laws and the difficulty in getting convictions in Greek courts. For example, MGM representatives in Greece took one station to court five times, but all the cases were dismissed because of technicalities (Papachristos, 1991a, May 19). However, in 1991 the TRT-TV station owner received a four-month jail term for illegal broadcasts. He had been taken to court by local video club owners for broadcasting rented videotapes ("Selida tou typou," 1991, November).

The current Greek copyright and intellectual property laws were enacted in 1920 (2387/1920) and amended in 1929 (4301/1929). Violations of these laws can bring fines of only up to 10,000 drachmas, and a jail sentence of less than two years that can be converted into a fine. On the other hand, the Criminal Code allows for confiscation of equipment involved in piracy, but only if the violators are caught in the act ("17 minises," 1991).

A new intellectual property law is being drafted. This draft was made public in December 1991 and soon became controversial, due to what some see as many gaps in the proposed law (Apergis, 1992). It is expected to be taken up by the parliament sometime in 1992, but it seems unlikely that it will solve the major copyright problems.

FINANCING

Greek private television stations are financed primarily through advertising. Advertising expenditures are increasing parallel to the increase in the number of multinational advertising agencies in the country. Around 60 percent of all advertising expenditures go to these multinational agencies ("Advertising," 1991). Advertising expenditures have increased 30 to 40 percent per year since 1980. At the same time, advertising as a percentage of the gross national product went from .24 in 1971, to .36 in 1983, to .60 in 1990

("Advertising," 1990). This is still low compared with the corresponding figures in other Western nations, but it is rising. As advertising expenditures have increased, so has television's share of these expenditures, while the newspapers' share has steadily decreased.

In 1987 the two Greek television channels accounted for 52 percent of all advertising expenditures in Greece ("Triponta kerdi," 1988). In the following year the excitement over private radio resulted in an increase of radio's share from 6 to 8 percent, and a decrease in television's share to 48 percent. In 1989 television's share dropped again, to around 40 percent. At the same time, total advertising expenditures were increasing much above the rate of inflation, going from 35 billion drachmas ($189 million) in 1988 to 102 billion ($551 million) in 1991 ("Diafimisi '91," 1992).

The establishment of new television stations has caused advertisers to turn to television once again, and television's share of advertising expenditures is rising, while radio's share is falling. In 1990 television's share was 42 percent, compared with 6.75 percent for radio, 26 percent for magazines, 18 percent for newspapers, and 6.7 percent for outdoor advertising ("Mass media," 1991). During 1991, television's share of total advertising expenditures was 54.3 percent. At the same time radio's share has decreased further, and fell to 5.7 percent in 1991. Projections for 1992 indicate that television's share will be around 60 percent, while radio's share will be less than five percent (Papachristos, 1992, Apr. 19).

As the two major private channels make inroads on nationwide audiences, so does their share of television advertising revenue, at the expense of ERT. In 1990 ET-1 received 35.35 percent of television advertising revenue, while Mega received 33.5 percent; Antenna TV, 22.3 percent; ET-2, 8.7 percent; and ET-3, .12 percent ("Mass media," 1991). This was due to ET-1's programming, and more important, to its greater national audience, enabling it to charge more per advertising spot. During the first six months of 1992 private stations took up 90 percent of all advertising expenditures. Specifically, Mega received 40.7 percent; Antenna, 47.3 percent; New Channel, 2.6 percent; ET-1, 7.6 percent; and ET-2 1.4 percent (Papachristoudi, 1992).

An additional reason for the recent increase in television advertising has been changes in the law, once again allowing toy advertising on television. From 1986 to April 1991 toy commercials were banned from Greek television. They were considered unfair and deceptive advertising toward children, and also a threat to the Greek toy manufacturers who saw TV toy advertising as a way for multinational toy manufacturers to drive them out of business. In April 1991, a change in this law (1736/1986) allowed television toy advertising once again, but not before 11 p.m. each evening. However, in December 1991, that regulation was scrapped and all restrictions on television toy advertising have disappeared, although the controversy continues (Vidos & Papadopoulou, 1991a).

The only other items not allowed to be advertised on Greek television are tobacco products. However, beginning in April 1991, law 1943/1991 abolished all restrictions on amounts of advertising on television. Such restrictions had been established by Broadcast Law 1730/1987, which set a maximum of 10 minutes of advertising per hour and a limit on total advertising per day to 8 percent of total programming time. Nevertheless, in July 1992, a Presidential Decree (236) mandated EEC directive 522/89, which puts restrictions on television advertising, such as, a maximum of 15 percent advertising time per daily broadcast; a maximum of 12 minutes of ads per hour; no commercial interruptions sooner than 20 minutes apart; and no commercial interruptions of news, documentaries, and religious programs up to 30 minutes long ("Evropaiko," 1992). It is not certain that in Greece these rules will be obeyed or enforced.

The introduction of private television has drastically changed advertising practices on Greek television, including those of ERT stations. Before the arrival of private stations, ERT rarely interrupted programs to insert commercials and did not accept wholly sponsored programs. But once the major private channels started those practices, ERT stations went along. Recently ERT television stations have even missed the start of sporting events because of commercials; something unthinkable a few years ago. In addition, ERT allows sponsorships of major sporting events, carrying an advertiser's logo throughout the coverage.

At the same time, private channels have refined the art of commercial interruptions and sponsorships. For example, during Mega's evening newscast, the financial news is sponsored by a mutual funds company, and its evening newscasts have two commercial interruptions. On the other hand, Antenna TV has the most commercial interruptions of all major television stations. Furthermore, the 9 to 11 p.m. programming block, which is part of television prime time (8 to 12 p.m.), has such a demand by advertisers that it accounts for close to 90 percent of all television advertising expenditures (Papachristos, 1991, Dec. 29).

Television advertising costs are relatively low compared to costs of other media and to television advertising in other nations. Antenna has eight rate classes, ranging from 700 to 17,500 drachmas ($4 to 94) per second, per spot. At the same time, it sells shorter inserts at a much higher rate. The Mega Channel prices range from 750 to 25,000 drachmas per second, per spot, while ERT's nine rate classes range from 650 to 11,050 drachmas per second, per spot (Bazou, 1991, p. 14). Law 1730/1987 does not allow for inserts, but ERT has started using them, along with the private channels. One difference between ERT and the private channels is that ERT allows advertising only during natural breaks in programming and immediately after the introduction credits or immediately before the closing credits of a program.

Despite increasing advertising revenues, most private stations today are losing money, with the exception of Mega Channel and Antenna TV. Mega Channel, which represents a 1.5 billion drachma ($8 million) initial capital investment, reported 53 million drachmas ($286,000) profit in its first year, and close to 500 million ($2.7 million) in its second year. Antenna reported profits of over 1 billion drachmas ($5.4 million) for 1991 ("Anixan," 1992). Most others, like the newspaper-owned stations, are subsidized by their parent organizations.

ERT stations have also been losing money, not only because of the competition, but also because of the various characteristics and responsibilities they have as public stations. The three ERT television stations do not cooperate in selling advertising; in fact, ET-1 and ET-2 have different bureaucratic mechanisms dealing with advertising. The ERT stations provide free advertising for public welfare campaigns. They mismanage advertising traffic, and there is additional waste and fraud (Anyfanti, 1991). Furthermore, ERT is affected by strikes, as well as changes in programming resulting from ERT's responsibility to the government, such as having to air speeches and parliamentary proceedings.

The financial status of ERT is troublesome to the government. ERT radio and television stations receive most of their revenues from special dues collected from all citizens through their monthly electricity bills. In 1991 these dues were doubled, so the average household in 1992 pays about 500 drachmas ($2.70) per month for

ERT radio and television ("Isfora ya ERT," 1991). This adds to about 27 billion drachmas ($146 million) per year. However, in early 1992 the Greek Consumers Union asked the Council of State (Constitutional Court) to declared this fee unconstitutional.

In 1988 ERT's total budget was 26 billion drachmas. Administrative costs accounted for 21.5 billion, and 4.5 billion went for programming ("Evropaiko boycotaz," 1988). Although in 1986 ERT generated a profit, it has had a budget deficit since 1988. For 1990, a budget of 43.5 billion drachmas included a projected deficit of 14.5 billion (Nicolakopoulos, 1990), and the deficit for 1991 was projected to be at least 23 billion (Stratos, 1991, March). In that budget, of 40 billion drachmas ($216 million), 52 percent was budgeted for administrative and personnel costs, and 48 percent for programming.

Part of ERT's financial problem lies in its responsibility to reach the whole country with a series of television relay transmitters, the operation of which is very expensive. Similarly, the interconnection of its radio networks is very costly. In 1990 ERT paid 1 billion drachmas ($5.4 million) each to the Public Power Company (DEH) and the Greek telephone company (OTE) for interconnection expenses (Koutouzis, 1990, Jan. 29).

ERT today has tremendous debts, despite periodic subsidies from the government. Up to 1987 ERT-2 received 8 billion drachmas in yearly subsidies. But when ERT-1 and ERT-2 were merged into ERT S. A., the regular subsidies ceased (Koutouzis, 1990, Jan. 29). Nevertheless, in 1991 the government subsidized ERT to the amount of 31 billion drachmas (Papachristos, 1991, May 12), but that is expected to drop drastically in 1992 due to the severe economic crisis facing the country. At the same time ERT has a 300 million drachma debt to Eurovision (Papachristos, 1991, May 12), and owes another 2.5 billion drachmas to Greek television program producers (Stratos, 1991, March).

The producers usually play a cat and mouse game with ERT by inflating production costs, knowing that ERT will slash them anyway, and eventually getting the price they want. Generally, Greek hourly series cost about 10 million drachmas per hour ($53,000), and 3 to 6 million per half-hour. On the other hand, imported American programs cost about $1,000 for hourly shows and $600 for half-hour shows, while movies cost around $3,500 ("Global TV," 1992).

As part of the government's attempts to get out of its severe economic difficulties and to privatize the economy, there was talk in

1990 of selling ET-2, but employee pressure and the party's desire to promote itself through state media derailed the plan. Similarly, there was talk of closing ET-3, but reportedly President C. Karamanlis intervened and saved this channel, considered important to Northern Greece for political and national reasons ("Evdomada," 1992). Although ERT has been cutting costs beginning in 1990, this is primarily the result of a decrease in investments. Particularly hurt is investment in equipment, because ERT has been weak in that area for a long time. Generally the ERT infrastructure is weak, especially that of ET-2 and ERA-4, both formerly of ERT-2, which are housed in the former army barracks occupied previously by YENED. These are small buildings, in disrepair, with inadequate equipment. Even such equipment as is bought occasionally stays in storage until it becomes either obsolete or inoperable. Equipment, from microphones to air conditioners, break down often, and cables are sometimes eaten by mice ("Terasties technikes elipses," 1985).

In assessing the television equipment needs for Greece's unsuccessful bid to host the 1996 Olympics, ERT estimated costs in the range of 36 billion drachmas ($190 million) (Gregorakis, 1988). Occasionally, however, ERT receives international assistance, as it did in 1991 from the European Broadcasting Union (EBU), to test HDTV production equipment during its coverage of the 1991 Mediterranean Games. ERT's biggest problem, however, may be political interference and its position in the Greek bureaucracy.

8

Politics in
Greek Broadcasting

NEWS PROGRAMMING AND POLITICAL INTERFERENCE

The Greek Constitution specifically states that broadcasting

> shall aim at the objective transmission, on equal terms,
> of information and news reports as well as works of
> literature and art; the qualitative level of programs shall
> be assured in consideration of their social mission and
> the cultural development of the country.

Although it is debatable whether Greek broadcasting has accomplished these objectives, it is clear that the framers of the Constitution understood the vital role of radio and television in Greek society. They are supposed to objectively inform, educate, and entertain the Greek people for the purpose of moving society forward. Furthermore, the Constitution clearly indicates that the state is to provide adequate supervision and guidance so that the above objectives are met (Alivizatos, 1986). This applies not only to public broadcasting, but through the NRTVC, to private broadcasting as well.

The major political parties in Greece agree with most of the broadcast laws, which state that Greek radio and television ought to be organized in such a way as to serve the informational, educational, and entertainment needs of the people. However, they do not agree on how these goals can best be met. Of these three general purposes of broadcasting, the purpose of education does not receive much attention in Greece although the other two objectives are not being met much better. Political parties only pay attention to the informational objectives of ERT.

Greek radio and television have never been used to transmit objective news and information ("Monomachia," 1984). The Metaxas dictatorship and the colonels' junta established the norms on this matter for radio and television, respectively. Since then, despite constitutional and other changes, each succeeding government has used the broadcast media, particularly television, "as a weapon for propaganda enrichment, as a prestige item, and as a political show-piece to reinforce the leading party" (Kastoras, 1978, p. 4).

Following the return to democracy in 1974, the government asked Sir Hugh Green of the BBC to design a new legal structure for ERT. Most of his recommendations, however, were not incorporated into subsequent laws because they called for greater independence of broadcasting from the government. The government justified this action by stating that Green's recommendations did not reflect Greek reality.

The reality in Greece is that each political party calls for a more "objective" Greek television, but only in terms of giving itself more airtime. Even the New Democracy (ND) Party, which drafted the 1975 Constitution, never gave adequate coverage to other parties while in power. In the post-junta years, ND governments did not allow ERT to broadcast news about other parties because they did not want ERT to deal with politics. Nevertheless, ERT did broadcast news about government political activities insisting that government activities were not politics, but news. However, news of worker strikes, as well as of other sensitive issues, would go unreported. Yet when ND was out of power, it made television a campaign issue, calling it "fascist" because ND felt it did not get fair treatment as the official opposition. Smaller parties have always accused the larger ones of monopolizing television, but these same parties have not convinced the public that if they came to power they would not do the same ("Katagelli," 1988).

During the PASOK tenure, from 1981 to 1989, the party paid

extraordinary attention to news as opposed to entertainment programming, even though many within the party believed there was more to gain by providing better television entertainment (George Stamatelopoulos, former head of ET-2 entertainment, personal communication, Dec. 17, 1987). During the PASOK tenure there were 13 different news division directors and eight different directors-general of ERT-1, while ERT-2 had five different presidents between 1982 and 1987, when it merged with ERT-1. According to S. Papathanassopoulos (1989, p. 33), "the Director General is the scapegoat of the organization, coming under permanent press criticism on one hand, and the wrath of the government . . . on the other."

Top ERT administrators are appointed by the ruling party, not necessarily because of any expertise in the field but because of their position in the party. (The author's personal experience has been that candidates for a position at ERT are questioned about their party affiliation.) In the early 1980s PASOK even appointed a Minister without Portfolio to be in charge of ERT, but he was also dismissed. Such official dismissals were usually because of personality conflicts, for not following party policies, or because the officials mishandled politically sensitive issues.

The news director's position at both ERT television channels has been labeled by many as "the electric chair" ("Afti kathisan," 1988), because those who hold it do not last long. For example, one news director only lasted 13 days, while another was fired over the phone after a short tenure. A news director was dismissed because ERT News relayed a comment from ND without a response from PASOK. Even today, opposition statements are usually relayed on the news only so that a government rebuttal can be made. Generally, newscasts on ERT television seem more like bulletin boards full of statements, primarily by the government, rather than news programs.

In 1985 the PASOK government appointed Costas Laliotis, a member of PASOK's central committee, as Deputy Minister to the Premiership, in effect putting him in charge of ERT. Laliotis, who was determined to create a more democratic ERT, brought in a new secretary-general of press and information, hired a respected university professor as ERT's director-general, and appointed a new ERT-1 news director.

This three-member team attempted to cut the so-called "umbilical cord" running between the Ministry to the Premiership and the news department at ERT. It attempted to allow more objective news coverage, of all political parties, and wanted to create the norms that would be incorporated in the upcoming (1987) broadcast law merging ERT-1 and ERT-2. This experiment, however, only lasted about two months. Several PASOK party members objected to the way ERT was covering various strikes, and they demanded changes. Prime Minister Andreas Papandreou agreed, and the three officials were forced to resign. Papandreou said that ERT's behavior had had a destabilizing character and was reminiscent of the opposition's behavior. He went on to define his concept of how television should function:

> In Greece, we do not have independent private stations.
> We have state television, whose responsibility belongs to
> the elected government. That's why those appointed in
> administration must comply with the policies of the
> government, not their own (Dimitriou, 1985).

Soon Laliotis also left the government, and he resigned his post within the party as well.

In 1988 more dismissals of ERT administrators took place, this time because of the mishandling of a politically sensitive issue in the news. These dismissals were technically illegal, because according to law 1730/1987, the administrative council of ERT must approve them first. This did not deter the government, but its actions resulted in a number of resignations from the administrative council, as well as in the resignation of the first president of the unified ERT, S. A.

It seems that every time a party in power faces political problems, it immediately thinks solutions may be found through improved public relations. The greatest public relations tool belonging to the government is public broadcasting (ERT). This has often been labeled as "the dowry to the administration." As such, when a party is out of power it supports private broadcasting, but not when it is in power. When in power, a party establishes an umbilical cord between its offices in the Ministry to the Premiership and the ERT news departments. This connection goes beyond appointing trusted people to key positions: it often extends to the actual supervision of the daily news operation. Upon Prime Minister Andreas Papandreou's return from London following heart surgery in 1988, and in the midst of the Koskotas scandal, ERT journalists covering the event live were handed a script filled with superlatives about Papandreou. They refused to read the script, not because they were not used to reading prepared scripts, but because this particular script was "ridiculously partisan" (Protogyrou, 1988). The journalists were soon taken off the air, an action that resulted in a journalists' strike against ERT.

Other journalists have relayed similar examples of interference in news operations, but only after they left ERT. As columnist George Votsis (1988) wrote,

> Those who govern treat the journalist employees of state broadcasting not as employees of ERT S. A., but as government employees, because their hiring, promotion, and professional development is exclusively dependent on the government.

The PASOK government, and also the ND governments before it and after it, would sometimes also interfere with entertainment programming. For example, in 1985 a scheduled Mikis Theodorakis concert was preempted because some of his songs satirized the government. After public pressure, the government broadcast the concert very late at night so it would get a limited audience. In many ways this was reminiscent of actions by the ND governments of the 1970s, when ERT would broadcast very popular soccer matches during major strikes. Similarly, the junta would televise soccer on days commemorating events that could bring about anti-junta demonstrations.

In the 1985 election campaign, the government cut short the transmission of a speech by a small party candidate because, it said, the speech's length violated a prior agreement by the parties. Similarly, in 1988 the government cut short the broadcast of a speech by Mitsotakis during a weekly program on events in parliament. When the opposition criticized this action, the government responded that it had the right under law 1730 to "cut things that are not positive contributions to the political dialogue" ("Kyvernisi," 1988).

Nevertheless, once out of power, PASOK members admitted that the handling of television by PASOK had hurt the party in the long run. They saw that their management of ERT, including the numerous personnel changes and the umbilical cord of interference, had resulted in reduced credibility for ERT and the party ("29e kentriki epitropi," 1989; Vagena, 1989, p. 11).

In response, and out of fear of this political interference, political parties have since agreed that ERT radio and television stations will take all their regular information programs, except the news, off the air for the duration of any election campaign. This may seem strange, but the political parties see this as the only assurance that the party in power will not have an excessive media advantage.

However, during election campaigns, parties are usually allocated a certain amount of television time for coverage of campaign speeches, based on their strength in the previous election. During the last elections (in 1990), the parties toned down their huge public gatherings and used television much more. This use was in the form of in-studio discussions of key issues by party representatives, and broadcasting of short portraits of party leaders.

These arrangements did not, however, stop charges of bias or actual interference by the ruling party with regard to news. During the first elections in 1989, the PASOK-controlled ERT news division was unabashedly biased. The day before the second 1989 elections, ND-controlled ERT showed news footage of a New Democracy political rally that had been taken by ND campaign workers, and not by ET-1. This substitution of news footage apparently took place without the knowledge of the station's news director, who had been appointed by the interim coalition government ("Someritis," 1989). This time it was PASOK complaining about biased news coverage. As a result, PASOK had its major political rally broadcast on Channel 29, a brand new channel operating for the first time that evening, built by *Avriani* ("Se kanali," 1989). Nevertheless, as soon as the public had the choice of television channels on which to watch election returns, the majority of them turned to the private stations Mega Channel and Antenna TV ("To Mega," 1990).

In 1989, to reduce government influence over broadcasting, the interim coalition government passed a broadcast law requiring that appointments to the ERT administrative council be made by all parties and that they be approved by the NRTVC. However, in December 1990 ND decided to enlarge the ERT administrative council, from 7 to 11 members. This limited the power of the other parties on ERT's administrative council and resulted in a number of resignations in protest, from both ERT's administrative council and the NRTVC (Papachristos, 1990, Dec. 16).

In addition, since the government has the majority on the NRTVC, and although it must submit three candidates for each administrative council position so the NRTVC can choose one, the government's supporters on the NRTVC elect a predetermined candidate who is favorable to the government. The latest (1992) ERT president is a former naval engineer and member of the New Democracy's finance committee, Vasilis Silyvridis. His appointment was supported only by ND-appointed NRTVC members.

The presence of private channels does not seem to have made a great difference in the political interference with ERT. For example, one television program was ordered off the air because the government said it was too expensive, but according to news reports, the actual reason was that the program's political satire was not favorable to the government (Papachristos, 1990, Dec. 23).

As this is written, once again a government finds itself in political difficulties, this time because of the economy, and turns to its propaganda machine for help. Government ministers have been allowed to appear on ERT programs at will, to explain the government's policies, and have done so a number of times. In addition, the government sponsors television advertising supporting its position on certain issues of national importance, such as the Maastricht Treaty, and major construction projects. Such a use of government funds and media has come under tremendous attack by the opposition. Furthermore, the "umbilical cord" has not been severed—there are reports that it runs directly from the prime minister's office to ERT (Papachristos, 1990, Sep. 30). The ruling party is reported to have a committee that coordinates government media activities, a committee that includes important administrative officers of ERT. Already, under the New Democracy government formed in 1990, there have been two presidents of ERT, and two new directors-general of ET-1 and two of ET-2. When M. Evert was fired as Minister to the Premiership, he was replaced by another former influential mayor, S. Kouvelas, who soon dismissed and replaced the ministry's general secretary for press and information.

The General Secretariat of Press and Information is a department under the Ministry to the Premiership. Its general secretary is a key figure in government propaganda efforts, not only because this position is in charge of ERT, but it is also in charge of other important entities, such as the Athens News Agency (ANA). In addition, it provides subsidies to ERT, ANA, and local press organizations.

These subsidies, which for 1992 amount to 4.75 billion drachmas ($25 million), can go a long way in promoting the party in power ("Chrima me to tsouvali," 1991).

THE BUREAUCRATIC DIMENSIONS OF ERT

The close political proximity of ERT to the government has not only turned ERT into an arm of the government, but has turned ERT employees into civil servants. Most ERT employees serve in non-creative roles, while some technical staff are underemployed. A former ERT-1 director, Nikos Sotiriadis, reported in 1986 that ERT cannot function appropriately because it lacks the necessary know-how, while its employees lack a theoretical and aesthetic knowledge base (Stamatelou, 1986). Most creative or technical personnel, and even journalists, at ERT have learned radio and television on the job.

The ERT bureaucracy involves hundreds of people who have no training in what they are paid to do, but are simply political appointees (Petroutsou, 1988). These can be found throughout the ERT hierarchy ("Nekronoun," 1988). Even the qualified people working for ERT have gotten their positions through a political patronage network, and despite their good intentions, once em-ployed, they simply give up and become part of the bureaucracy in order to survive.

In addition to the regular employees, each successive adminis-tration hires consultants. Some of these consultants are incompe-tent, while others are brought in to do the work of permanent personnel who then become underemployed. Each government also hires temporary personnel to provide employment to party members. Eventually these temporary employees become permanent and slowly make their way into creative positions. It is not uncommon, for example, for someone hired as a typist to suddenly become a radio producer.

Such overstaffing and mismanagement results in burgeoning costs. For example, as the newspaper *Eleftherotypia* pointed out in an editorial, while ET-3, with 600 employees and a 2 billion drachma deficit, attracts about 1 percent of the audience, profit-making Mega Channel, with only 280 employees, attracts over 30 percent ("Apopses," 1989).

The number of employees working for ERT is a subject of

tremendous importance and controversy. A series of reports in *Eleftherotypia* in 1990 outlined some of the problems surrounding ERT and its employees. ERT is reported to have around 5,000 employees throughout the country, although the exact number is hard to know because ERT also hires people to work on short-term projects, usually involving news and information programs, which make up 38 percent of ERT's original programming (Koutouzis, 1990, Jan. 29, p. 24).

Of the 5,000 ERT employees, 3,866 work in Athens, 400 in Thessaloniki, and the rest throughout the country. Of the total number, close to 1,500 are administrative personnel, 1,300 are technical staff, about 800 are programming personnel, and 580 are journalists (Koutouzis, 1990, Jan. 30, p. 15). Among the journalists are a number of actors who work as news presenters. Two former directors-general, Dimitris Korsos and Nikos Syfounakis, both estimate that about one-third of the employees are unnecessary (Vagena, 1989). Another former director-general, George Kontogeorgis, said that the only entity organized in ERT is its employees—the pro-PASOK ERT employee union often governs the direction of the organization (Protogyrou and Petroutsou, 1989, November).

The reported attitude of many employees, as described by former ERT administrators, is that if they are required to produce any work they should be paid overtime. In 1989 overtime pay at ERT amounted to 3 billion drachmas ($16.2 million). There were examples of employees with monthly salaries of 150,000 drachmas ($810), but earning an additional 500,000 drachmas in overtime pay (Koutouzis, 1990, Jan. 30, p. 14). In 1989 a new ERT administration calculated that certain people being paid overtime would have had to work 26 hours per day to have earned the pay they received (Protogyrou and Petroutsou, 1989, October).

There have also been cases of people being paid even though they never showed up for work. This happens because politically appointed employees sometimes face a different administration from the one that appointed them. The new administration then perceives their presence on the job as threatening, so they are simply told not to report for work, even though they continue to be paid.

Law 1730/1987 recommended that ERT employees, especially journalists, work exclusively for ERT. Initially, ERT fired some employees who continued to work for private stations (Roumeliotis, 1989, Apr. 10). But employee strikes and the competition for skilled broadcast personnel from new radio and television stations did not allow for strict enforcement of this desire. The practice of holding two jobs is not new, but was also common in the 1960s, partially as a result of low salaries (McDonald, 1983, p. 144). However, the introduction of new media outlets brought journalists more job opportunities, as well as a lot more money.

In 1990 the new ND government faced ERT's extraordinary budget problem, as well as the large number of ERT employees appointed by PASOK. One way to take care of both was through layoffs. First they fired some consultants, while denying requests by other employees (except journalists) for permission to also work for other stations. However, this did not stop all these employees from doing so; some worked secretly in both places. In 1990 one ET-2 employee took an ET-2 foreign film and gave it to his other employer, Antenna TV, which it broadcast (Protogyrou and Petroutsou, 1990, February). Similarly, there are still journalists who provide news and information to private radio or television stations from their jobs at ERT stations.

The new ERT administration invited BBC experts in 1991 to examine ERT and make further recommendations. One of their recommendations was to reduce employees to 3,000, which is parallel to a recommendation made by Hugh Green in 1975. With this in hand, the government decided to cut more ERT employees by transferring 1,000 of them to other government ministries, in addition to the 760 or so already let go and the 200 retirements ("1,000 tis ERT," 1991). Many of those transferred were sent to the General Secretariat of the Press, which later complained that it had too many employees ("Selida tou typou," 1992, January).

Political pressure and strikes reduced the number of employees to be transferred to 550, but this did not stop periodic strikes. Part of the problem, of course, is the political nature of Greek broadcasting. On one hand, the government transferred PASOK appointees; on the other it replaced them with its own people, despite a hiring freeze ("Prosfiyes," 1991). This time it was PASOK that was asking questions in parliament about ERT employees hired illegally—the same type of questions New Democracy had asked when it was in opposition. In 1992, the government is waiting for a report by the international accunting firm of Ernst & Young on ERT, in order to justify more cost-cutting measures.

The increasing number of ERT employees was primarily due to

political appointments and patronage. In 1982 ERT had only 1,800 employees (Lykiardopoulou, 1991, April). Employees were added by PASOK, to "compensate" for its own supporters not being represented among ERT employees. New people were also hired before every election, to reward patronage or buy voters. Later it was New Democracy's turn to appoint people to ERT, because in the past its followers had not been treated fairly. The financial difficulties facing the nation, however, and the lessening importance of ERT, has given the government the cause for wanting to cut ERT's staff even further, to a reported 2,000 employees or fewer (Papachristos, 1992, May 17). Finally, ERT has given all its employees holding two jobs, including the journalists, until October 1992, to choose one of the two.

In 1991, the public prosecutor's office in Athens was investigating a series of illegal appointments at ERT. It was estimated that from 1987 to 1991 there had been 400 people hired illegally, some without ever applying for a position (Mandrou, 1991, June). Furthermore, the illegal hiring procedures, including fake employment tests, have reportedly not stopped (Lykiardopoulou, 1991, July).

Another area of concern is the way program proposals are approved. Parties in power, without exception, approve program proposals from major political supporters, often people or companies without experience in television production. In some cases, the programs produced by such companies, and purchased by ERT, are not good enough to broadcast (Mandrou, 1991, June). In addition there have been charges that officials have been bribed into approving program proposals, and that ERT employees have created ghost production companies to produce programs for ERT (Lykiardopoulou, 1991, May). Charges against the government indicate that ERT commissioned programs from musicians who had helped ND during its election campaign, and even gave them unusually large down payments ("Spatali," 1991).

The disorganization, unprofessionalism, and lack of funding results in various extraordinary actions on the part of ERT personnel. The epitome of these is the occasional erasing of recorded ERT programs so the tape can be used for new shows. In one case, among other programs erased was a new program that had yet to be broadcast (Theologitou, 1987).

SOURCES OF FEEDBACK FOR PUBLIC BROADCASTING

In addition to political parties, other main sources of feedback for television programming and operational norms are the press, labor unions, and the public. The political orientation of the Greek press results, to some degree, in criticism that is politically motivated, as is most of the criticism by labor unions. Part of the press criticism, however, is justified, in that Greek national newspapers often become channels for feedback from the public to the broadcast stations. Because television is an important issue in the public agenda, newspapers deal extensively with every element of broadcasting. This involves program review and criticism, scholarly criticism, political commentary, and coverage of issues ranging from the most mundane to the most important. As such, the press exercises a great deal of influence over Greek television, as it does over almost all Greek social institutions, and is both a source and a channel for feedback from political groups, scholars, critics, crusading or frustrated journalists, and the general public.

Law 1730/1987, the current legal foundation of Greek state broadcasting, established a built-in mechanism for feedback and social control. It set out to organize a Representative Audience Council for Social Control (Audience Federation) (Article 4). This 50-member council is made up of 6 ruling-party representatives, 10 from all other political parties, 3 representatives of local governments, 6 representing ERT employees, 15 representing other social and scientific organizations, and 10 personalities from the arts and letters. The president of this council is in turn the council's representative on ERT's administrative council. This ambitious plan for channeling social control took a long time to be activated but is currently functioning, although in a limited way.

The feedback that ERT used to receive from the political parties, the press, and the public was mainly negative. People started turning to other sources of home entertainment, first the VCR, later satellite television, and eventually private radio and television, largely as a result of a desire for something different.

Today feedback toward ERT is still negative, which is partially reflected in the drop its audiences. Weekly program ratings have become an important source of feedback for the ERT stations, especially since the introduction of private stations. Because ratings are tied to advertising revenue, they have affected the way ERT attempts to achieve the objectives specified in broadcast laws. ERT has tried to compete with the private stations, but cannot please those who were always critical of it, and now displeases those who want ERT to cater to the objectives specified in the Constitution without regard to the popularity of its programs. In short, Greek state broadcasting in general, and television in particular, has yet to find an identity in the current state of Greek broadcasting.

THE POLITICS OF PRIVATE BROADCASTING

Politics affect private broadcasting as well as public broadcasting. Political orientations play a role in people's viewing and listening behavior, as they do in their newspaper reading behavior. Since, most private radio and television stations are politically oriented, voters of different parties identify more closely with different channels. While ERT channels attract voters from both parties about equally, Mega Channel attracts more PASOK voters, and Antenna attracts more ND voters. Smaller stations are even more strongly identified with political sides. Two channels attracting mostly ND voters are New Channel and Telecity, while strong PASOK voters watch Kanali 29 (Papachristos, 1991b, Apr. 14). In terms of radio, most of Antenna's listeners are ND voters (63 percent), as are most of Athens 9.84 listeners (60 percent), while most of Sky's listeners are PASOK voters (52 percent), as are the plurality of Flash's listeners (47 percent). In addition, 75 percent of Radio Athina listeners are PASOK voters ("Ti vlepoun," 1990).

As has been discussed in previous chapters, politicians and political parties have various relationships with media channels. One case is that of S. Kouvelas, the former mayor of Thessaloniki. As mayor, he illegally established three municipal radio stations in Thessaloniki. In addition, he built television station TV-100, which was managed by Fotis Manousis, Kouvelas's former business partner. Later, Manousis and other people involved in TV-100 built New Channel in Athens, the first president of which was Manousis's wife. Today this television station controls four frequencies throughout the country. Although Kouvelas denies he has ownership interests in New Channel, rumors persist that he does ("Mises alithies," 1991). What makes this case even more interesting is that Kouvelas today is Minister to the Premiership, thus in charge of the mass media. As mentioned in Chapter 7, in 1992 he appointed as the new president of the NRTVC a lawyer who had defended him, while he was mayor of Thessaloniki, when Kouvelas was taken to court by ERT for violating its statutory broadcast monopoly.

As mayor, Kouvelas insisted that he had had to violate certain laws in order to break the government's monopoly over broadcasting. But while he was fighting then against the government's use of police troops that were trying to demolish his transmitters, his own government in early 1992 ordered police troops to arrest Yannis Alafouzos and stop the building of the Alafouzos' transmitter, which is to be used for a new television station, Sky-TV. Kouvelas charged that Alafouzos is trying to illegally build another broadcast station, which would give him too much influence over the airwaves. However, some say that the real problem is that Alafouzos is feuding with Prime Minister Mitsotakis and that the government does not want him to have greater access to media with which to propagate his positions.

This incident brings to public attention the need to finally put some order in the jungle of the airwaves. The government will have to decide what to do about the television frequencies, even though it seems to have given up trying to regulate radio frequencies. Such decisions are supposed to be made by the NRTVC, but the government will probably make these decisions itself and reduce the powers of the Council. One of the reasons for this is that the government does not trust the NRTVC, most of its members of which were appointed by former Minister M. Evert. Already the government has taken the initiative as is evident from the case of the revival of Nea Tileorasi.

In 1989 the interim coalition government put many democratizing controls on the broadcast regulatory process, but that process put in place was just as short lived as the government was. Eventually (possibly sometime late in 1992), decisions will be made about which television stations will be given licenses; decisions that are necessitated by the shortage of spectrum space. These decisions will certainly be made on political grounds, not on the technical or legal grounds, or principles outlined in the Greek Constitution or in related broadcast laws. Therefore, for the foreseeable future, no matter how the details of Greek broadcasting change, the political nature of Greek broadcasting will remain more or less the same.

Conclusion

The Identity of the Greek Media

One of the most intellectually rigorous eras in world history was the period between the fourteenth and eighteenth centuries, when the Renaissance and the Reformation took hold in Europe and eventually nurtured the ideologies that led to the French and American revolutions. It was the time of the "rational man" and his need to fight for his independence from king or bishop. It was also the time to appeal to the "masses" to justify their quest for freedom of thought and action.

The discovery of the meaning and power of the "masses" gave birth to the concept of "public opinion," which in turn necessitated the corollary concept of "mass communication." At the same time, the mass communication process was beginning to take a life of its own. Through the invention of movable type, multi-reproduction typography, and so on, it became technically possible, and soon necessary, to disseminate religious and, later, political ideas.

Europe was fully immersed in this process of cultural transformation, while Greece was still under the rule of the Ottomans. For all practical purposes, therefore, Greece missed all this intellectually fertile period, which shaped the educational, political, and economic development of the continent to which Greece belonged geographi-

cally, historically, and philosophically. The four centuries of Ottoman domination, and the years of guerrilla fighting that ended in the
mid-1820s, left Greece with serious educational and economic
handicaps and with a political scene dominated by larger-than-life
revolutionary heroes and the foreign powers that assisted them.
The first political climate of modern Greece was dominated by
patronage, factionalism, and often murderous acrimony, all in the
pursuit of power. Unfortunately, this set a mood that was to guide
the generations to come.

The absence of a natural evolution of civic behavior and collective
standards and practices, through which other European nations
had gone, brought the Greeks into a nineteenth-century political
climate with which they were not prepared to cope. It should not be
surprising, therefore, that the main role assigned to the new, still
experimental, but exciting instruments of mass communication
was partisan proselytism for political profit, and eventually power.

The resulting first newspaper system, which has been described
in Chapter 2 of this book, set the stage for what is happening among
the Greek media even today. The fate, birth, or death of Greek
newspapers and other media is still being decided not on grounds
of quality of information, presentation, or usefulness to the consumer, but on grounds of partisan appeal, intensity, and loyalty. The
recent total consumer disinterest in a moderate newspaper like
Anagnostis, the notoriously low circulation of a quality newspaper
like *Kathimerini*, and the high popularity of blindly partisan and
loud newspapers on either side of the political spectrum, such as
Avriani and *Eleftheros Typos*, are symptoms of this malaise.

In the era of HDT, DBS, zoned editions, satellite page transmission, transnational publications, magalogs, and desktop publishing,
it is perhaps anachronistic to talk about partisanship as the key to
media success, but in Greece this still seems to be the case.
Illustrations of institutionalized partisan favoritism can easily be
found in the placement of government-sponsored advertising and in
the recent government-inspired prosecutions of Alafouzos's Sky and
Kathimerini.

Publishers and station owners are constantly in bed with politicians, and often media personnel changes, from hiring/firing to
promotion/demotion, seem to be connected more to partisan cre-
dentials and less to work performance. Worse yet, work performance itself at times is synonymous with advancement of party

goals. The recent managerial changes in *Kathimerini*, and the 1991 personnel changes in *Rizospastis* and 902 Aristera sta FM had enough partisan aspects to illustrate this point well.

Obviously Greece is not the only country in the world that has a strongly partisan press. Why then is there so much attention paid to this characteristic of the Greek media? What exactly is it that distinguishes the political or partisan nature of the Greek media from that in other countries? The answers lie in the ubiquitous nature of the practice, in its intensity and tone, and as in its demoralizing impact on the fabric of public life.

With notable exceptions, most of Greece's mainstream media are not only partisan, and proud of it, but seem to advertise their political affiliations in the loudest, crudest, and most cacophonic of voices, in both news and opinion. Tabloid-size newspapers and bulletin-board newscasts are conducive to that kind of news treatment, but of course the cost in credibility loss is inestimable.

This is especially bad for newspapers whose circulations, partially for this reason, have been declining. The electronic media, on the other hand, are in their inescapable initial phase of replacing the print media as the political and partisan agenda setters. Unfortunate though this may sound, it is the natural preoccupation of the electronic media with the widest possible audiences that may serve as their eventual savior, by forcing them to politically detoxify. Such a development would be a welcome change and perhaps might serve as an unexpected safety valve for the constantly pressurized life of Greeks in politics and the media.

Indeed, Greek radio and television are going through a revolutionary period, brought about by a sequence of events characteristic of the country's transition to a more modern European nation. The abolition of the state monopoly over broadcasting has opened up the gates to a flood of new voices, many of which are being heard for the first time. However, the strongest voices are still those of the traditional power interests such as the politicians, publishers, and industrialists or shipowners. The importance of the perpetuation of their media domination can only be measured in terms of social cost, in a country that has perilously large dichotomies in education, income, and political and social participation. In fact, many see this as a clear recipe for a society in crisis—a society consumed by class and government mistrust, and personal as well as collective demoralization.

This crisis may have come about because the traditional ideological foundations of the society are coming loose or becoming outdated, while new foundations necessary for Greece's renewal and transition into the European stage are not yet developed. Structural weaknesses exist in every component of society, including the mass media. People in Greece often refer to their current social environment as rotten, to their political leaders as dinosaurs, and to the media environment as anarchical. The political and media leaders deserve a large measure of the blame for these sentiments.

Despite all this, Greece has some very successful, relatively moderate newspapers, like *Eleftherotypia, Kathimerini, Ta Nea*, and *To Vima*. There is an active, considerably apolitical periodical press. Some of the electronic media have a high potential for playing a constructive role in strengthening the democratic institutions and contributing to the nation's progress.

Furthermore, Greece has a considerable number of well educated, serious, competent, and civic-minded media professionals. Their defense of freedom of expression and of the free marketplace of ideas, and their constant battle against government, secrecy and information manipulation, regardless of party, are as passionate and eloquent as John Milton's *Areopagitica* or the editorial pages of the *New York Times*, the *Guardian*, or *Le Monde*. Paradoxically enough, these professionals can be found at most newspapers, magazines, radio and television stations, they must be the ones responsible for the colorful but questionable media products that adorn Greek kiosks and radio and television sets daily. We have agonized over this incongruity for years. How can so many dynamic, well-meaning, responsible people produce such dissonant products? Do they shed their competence at the entrances of their newsrooms? How can the consumers support these media while they routinely ridicule their credibility?

In a way these may be unfair questions, because they assume that it is possible for the mass media as a social institution to be fully and appropriately functional, while many other institutions in the same society are dysfunctional. Just as there is a form of anarchy on the airwaves and in the press, so does there seem to be one in the rest of the society. As columnist T. Karzis (1987) writes, if we have arbitrary house construction, and arbitrary actions by the church and labor unions, how can we not have arbitrary broadcast stations?

The reasons for this state of affairs are complex and go to the

heart of Greek society and culture. The first reason has its roots in the history of the modern Greek nation. As was discussed before, Greece entered the nineteenth century without the benefit of an evolution of societal values in the areas of human rights, democratic principles, labor rights, pluralism of ideas, class struggle, citizen rights vis-a-vis the government, and so on. Modern Greeks parachuted into the industrial revolution having been deprived of open and constructive discussion of problems and the collective effort to solve them. Democratic debate was not given an adequate chance to dull the sharpness of the tools of open discourse. Hubris became an end in itself, and dialectic compromise became a sign of weakness—self-righteousness and sanctimoniousness followed. Paradoxically, the way to accomplish things was through the leftover Ottoman tradition of baksheesh and patron-client relationships, and not through orderly application of rules or standards.

It should not be surprising, therefore, that when the politicians of modern Greece realized the potential of the media, they tried to "buy" and control them. Through benign as well as questionable means, liaisons were forged between the media (through the publishers, mainly) and the parties in order to guarantee the survival and success of both. The media received an audience and the parties received a vehicle through which they could reach the public. The political immaturity and the low educational level of the audiences of the time were instrumental in making this alliance possible, and perhaps even necessary.

Purchasing partisan loyalty has been part of the Greek media scene for decades, reaching its peak during the political crises of the 1960s, when the legitimately elected Papandreou government was outmaneuvered by the royal couple at the time, the Papandreou party was split, and a minority part of it formed Greece's next government. After several minor government changes, the 1967 colonels' coup ended the political acrimony and uncertainty, but set the country decades backwards.

Following the junta, the democratic governments set Greece in the direction of joining the European Community—a symbolic as well as substantive move into the camp of the West. However, these governments did not manage to alter the structural deficiencies of the society to allow it to make a proper entry. The election of PASOK in 1981, for example, was in many ways a cry by the people for this kind of alterations. Fundamental changes, however, did not take place. Once again, agents of change were incorporated into the existing sociocultural schemes, instead of starting fresh. "Healthy social criticism was labeled anarchist or unrealistic" (Korovelas, 1989), and thus people were traumatized and felt betrayed; many simply gave up.

Furthermore, the combination of low educational status and lack of democratic "training" among the first modern Greeks resulted in Greek society's subconscious fatalism in matters of politics. As the Great Powers settled Greece's government structure, by appointing a foreign king because of the infighting among the Greeks themselves, they also established a precedent that is evident even today—most Greeks feel as though they are not responsible for their condition. By extension, party leaders, as well as partisans, do not believe themselves responsible for the country's problems, which are always supposed to be the fault of others.

This helpless mentality also affects the government's role vis-a-vis its citizens. It seems as though in Greece even democratically elected governments do not serve at the pleasure of the citizens and, therefore, the citizens do not enjoy the respect that an electorate deserves, and that electorates routinely receive in other Western democracies. If citizens are not respected by the government they elect, why should they be respected by the media they only consume?

The way Greek media "behave"—the way they select the news, the angle from which they report it, the language they use, the way entertainment is presented, and so on—points to a lack of respect for the consumer, which does not necessarily emanate from a lack of competence on the part of the media people. This patronizing attitude seems to prevail in both the government and the media.

However, an important change seems to be occurring. Declining newspaper circulations, and the ascendancy of the electronic media as the dominant media in Greece, have brought into the forefront the importance of advertising as the key funder of media, a development that has necessitated a parallel pursuit of more "generic," and larger, audiences. Media marketing has begun to change; the party faithful alone may no longer be adequate for a mass medium's effort to succeed. As a result, in the last three years the media management search for new and larger audiences has focused more than ever on identifying and satisfying the needs of the media consumer.

It is no accident, for example, that the experienced and politically durable Lambrakis chain finds itself controlling more than 25 percent of the total advertising drachma in Greece. Its media marketing strategy is most up to date and Westernized than that of any of its competitors in Greece. Mega Channel, in which Lambrakis is a partner, offers top notch entertainment from Greece and elsewhere, a politically moderate but serious and visually contemporary newscast, and an aggressive pursuit of the advertiser; the chain's evening newspaper, *Ta Nea*, enjoys the highest circulation in Greece by keeping a moderate, left-of-center line very much in tune with the national political mood and running a renowned classified advertising section; its weekly, *To Vima*, a subdued and thoughtful newspaper, is the most respected Greek weekly, with a huge advertising portion; the chain also owns an array of specialized magazines that are extremely successful in both circulation and advertising.

Another example of the evolving marketing strategies is the appearance of newspaper inserts or broadcast programs that deal with the audience's leisure time, health, finances, and the like. This is a trend that, if it continues, will finally bring the Greek media into the same century as their counterparts in other Western.

Nevertheless, the media cannot by themselves make the transition from aggressively partisan reporters of the day's events to fair and utilitarian tools in a citizen's life. Adjustments by other social institutions also will be necessary. First, the political leadership of all colorations must learn to "let go" of the media, give them some breathing room, and allow them to freely woo the marketplace and deal with its dangers. At the same time, these leaders must learn to respect the independence of the press and the value of public assessment and criticism, even seemingly unfair criticism. In a strong and tested democracy, such media "excesses" are routinely tolerated in order to safeguard open debate, a democratic system's lifeblood.

Media owners, on the other hand, should to perform a self-examination to decide whether they are in the media business to make money while serving the audience by ever-improving products, or to promote a partisan agenda in the pursuit of personal power. The money-for-service model has proven successful in most developed Western democracies; if the partisan-power model continues to dominate the Greek media, partisan contamination of information will continue to undermine media credibility. In either case, letting professionals run the daily media operations without partisan prerequisites would go a long way toward cleansing the system from the malaise that has troubled it and Greek civic life for decades.

Furthermore, media professionals themselves must learn to respect the information process and its consumers. The information process consists of the identification, collection, and presentation of news. These phases are governed by the media professionals' human selectivity limitations and by the filtration system of biases this selectivity implies. It is essential that the news "processors" understand their shortcomings and the value and rights of the competing voices in the marketplace of ideas.

It is also essential that media professionals appreciate the intelligence, sensibilities, needs, and wishes of their audiences. The extreme partisan lens, through which reality and truth have been seen for years, is becoming outdated. There is no doubt that it served a purpose, and a moderate version of it still has a role to perform in the era of political pluralism, but it can no longer be seen as the only criterion of newsworthiness. Although polyphony can play a constructive role in a developing society like that in Greece, malicious cacophony can be retrogressive or even disastrous. Extreme partisanship in the media has exacted too high a price of Greek society. The perpetual, crude, and intense ridicule of public figures and societal institutions has so undermined the political and moral fabric that the country's development, as measured by most socioeconomic or cultural yardsticks, has come to an almost complete halt. The dynamism of the value system that empowered Greeks to survive the adversities of their history seems to have been numbed, anesthetized by the continuing inability of the power elite to solve national problems. The media, as part of this elite, bear a large responsibility for this current institutional paralysis, although perhaps it is utopian to expect the media to initiate any positive change in Greece. As John C. Merrill (1974, p. 24) said, "A media system reflects the political philosophy in which it functions. . . . A nation's journalism cannot exceed the limits permitted by the society; on the other hand, it cannot lag very far behind."

Leading or following, however, there is no doubt that Greece's future will be significantly affected by the road its media take. Because relatively few of them are educated as journalists, possess the required independence of mind, and command enough of the owners' respect to be "left alone" to do their job, Greek journalists have seemed content to follow casually the wishes of the media owners and those in power. They have not been able to declare a "war" for their independence; the partisan divisions within the journalists' groups themselves have made it impossible for them to play an important role in that front. The arrival and promise of the electronic media, however, seem to offer a unique opportunity for them to do so. This opportunity should not be missed, lest Greece play catch up to its European partners for yet another century.

Finally, some attention must be paid to the media consumer. Although normally it is considered an "easy way out," and unfair to blame "the people" for a nation's problems, in this instance the status of the media should not be reviewed without considering the identity of their audience. The Greeks are a society of dichotomies and antagonisms; perhaps because of temperament, because of history, because of the limited educational level, and because of low national self-respect. In a self-destructive way, partisanship has become a safe harbor of ideological equilibrium and the press system seems to be a natural extension of this mentality. This has brought few benefits, while the rest of the world has moved forward at a faster pace. Perhaps a more self-critical attitude on the part of the public; a more ambitious, self-confident personal agenda; and a more demanding and critical attitude toward the media might develop an impetus among media professionals for an attempt to create a truly competitive marketplace of ideas. Perhaps only then will respect given to self as well as to others, will flourish and societal institutions, media and government included, will have a chance to flourish with it.

Greece without a doubt is at a critical crossroads. Philosophically and systematically all its institutions ranging from the power elite and the intelligentsia, to the media and the common citizens are faced with the difficult dilemmas of change. The fundamental choice they must make is between the old, known, but tired and anachronistic way of civic life, and the bold, unknown, risky but promising course that challenges tradition and demands a new approach to making democratic decisions. If the latter course is chosen, it is only natural that it create a new "contract" between mass media and mass audiences based on the public's new informational needs. It is also natural, that such a new relationship require a new set of principles and competencies on the part of the media, so the contemplated changes will have to reach to the very "raison d'etre" of Greece's mass media.

Are today's Hellenes determined to enter the twenty-first century with a new covenant between themselves and their mass media? Perhaps, a preliminary answer to those questions might be found in some media's recent steps toward more audience-sensitive policies. Perhaps, this signals the beginning of an effort on the part of the media to transform themselves from dysfunctional paragons of public life to catalysts for progress. It could not have come at a better time.

References

Advertising. (1990, September). *Media, 4*, p. 18.

Advertising. (1991, January). *Media, 8*, p. 5.

Afti kathisan stin "electriki karekla" [These sat on the "electric chair"]. (1988, July 4). *Eleftherotypia*, p. 26.

Afxanonte i mikres monades me hamilo kostos [On the increase are small units with low cost]. (1991, November 1). *Pontiki*, p. 28.

Agogi Popota kata tou A. Papandreou [Suit (by) Popota against A. Papandreou]. (1991, July 25). *Eleftherotypia*, p. 5.

Agria epithesi kata tou typou [Wild offensive against the press]. (1991, June 7). *Pontiki*, p. 25.

Akaliptos o Themelis ya ton Antenna [Themelis unprotected as to Antenna]. (1990, January 3). *Eleftherotypia*, p. 4.

Alivizatos, N. K. (1986). *Kratos ke radiotileorasi* [State and broadcasting]. Athens: Sakkoulas.

Alvertos, P. (1991, January). Tileoptikes protimises [Television preferences]. *Media, 8*, p. 18.

Anagnosimotita periodikon [Readership of periodicals]. (1990, July). *Media, 3*, pp. 17-18.

Anagnostopoulos, N. (1960). Paranomos typos, katohi: 1941-44 [The illegal press, occupation: 1941-44]. Athens: Nikolopoulos-Papakyriakopoulos-Leonnatos.

Androulakis, N. (1978). *Afthentia kai periivrisi* [Authority and insult]. Athens: Sakkoulas.

Anixan e fakeli 8 kanalion [Files of 8 stations opened]. (1992, July 22).
    Eleftherotypia, p. 7.
Anyfanti, G. (1991, March 20). ERT—peran tin kato volta e diafimises
    [ERT—advertising on a downturn]. *Eleftheros Typos*, p. 3.
Apergis, F. (1992, February 17). Pnevmatiki idioktisia [Intellectual
    property]. *Eleftherotypia*, p. 32.
Apopses [Opinions]. (1989, December 14). *Eleftherotypia*, p. 8.
Apostolou, G. (1988, March 25). E doryforiki ktypa to video [Satellite
    hits video]. *24 Ores*, p. 1.
Archizi to trito kanali [The third channel is starting]. (1988, September
    1). *Eleftherotypia*, p. 26.
Arios Pagos ekrine [The supreme court decided]. (1992, April 5). *To Vima*,
    p. 60.
Athinaiko Praktoreio Eidiseon [Athens News Agency]. (1990, July).
    Media, 3, p. 16.
Athlitikes ekpombes [Sports programs]. (1991, June 1-7). *Diplo-
    Tilerama*, p. 82.
Bakoyannopoulou, S. (1988, April 30). E pirates ton video [Video
    pirates]. *To Vima*, p. 53.
Balis, Y., and Kapsis, M. (1986, December 7). Radio ke TV, efodos sta
    salonia mas [Radio and TV, charge into our living rooms]. *Ethnos*,
    pp. 11-13.
Bays, K. (1988, October 12). 50 chronia hellinikis radiofonias [50 years
    of Greek radio]. *Eleftherotypia*, p. 33.
Bazou, V. (1991, June 1-7). E chrisy star ton media [The golden stars of
    (mass) media]. *Diplo-Tilerama*, pp. 14-16.
Boyd, D. A. (1986). Pirate radio in Britain: A programming alternative.
    Journal of Communication, 36 (2), pp. 83-94.
Campbell, J. K. (1964). *Honour, family and patronage: A study of
    institutions and moral values in a Greek mountain community*. Oxford:
    Clorendon.
Chakos, D. (1987). Pirate radio stations. Unpublished manuscript
    (personal copy).
Chalkou, M. (1990, January 21). Diafimisi to 1989 [Advertising in
    1989]. *Kathimerini*, p. 36.
Chrima me to tsouvali ya propaganda [Money by the sackful for propa-
    ganda]. (1991, December 5). *Pontiki*, p. 38.
Clogg, R. (1979). *A short history of modern Greece*. Cambridge,
    England: Cambridge University Press.
Color TV arrives. (1979, August-September). *Greece: A monthly record*,
    p. 7.
Cowell, A. (1987, October 11). Greeks loosen curb (and tongues) on
    radio. *New York Times*, p. 19.

Anyfanti, G. (1991, March 20). ERT—peran tin kato volta e diafimises [ERT—advertising on a downturn]. *Eleftheros Typos*, p. 3.

Apergis, F. (1992, February 17). Pnevmatiki idioktisia [Intellectual property]. *Eleftherotypia*, p. 32.

Apopses [Opinions]. (1989, December 14). *Eleftherotypia*, p. 8.

Apostolou, G. (1988, March 25). E doryforiki ktypa to video [Satellite hits video]. *24 Ores*, p. 1.

Archizi to trito kanali [The third channel is starting]. (1988, September 1). *Eleftherotypia*, p. 26.

Arios Pagos ekrine [The supreme court decided]. (1992, April 5). *To Vima*, p. 60.

Athinaiko Praktoreio Eidiseon [Athens News Agency]. (1990, July). *Media, 3*, p. 16.

Athlitikes ekpombes [Sports programs]. (1991, June 1-7). *Diplo-Tilerama*, p. 82.

Bakoyannopoulou, S. (1988, April 30). E pirates ton video [Video pirates]. *To Vima*, p. 53.

Balis, Y., and Kapsis, M. (1986, December 7). Radio ke TV, efodos sta salonia mas [Radio and TV, charge into our living rooms]. *Ethnos*, pp. 11-13.

Bays, K. (1988, October 12). 50 chronia hellinikis radiofonias [50 years of Greek radio]. *Eleftherotypia*, p. 33.

Bazou, V. (1991, June 1-7). E chrisy star ton media [The golden stars of (mass) media]. *Diplo-Tilerama*, pp. 14-16.

Boyd, D. A. (1986). Pirate radio in Britain: A programming alternative. *Journal of Communication, 36* (2), pp. 83-94.

Campbell, J. K. (1964). *Honour, family and patronage: A study of institutions and moral values in a Greek mountain community.* Oxford: Clorendon.

Chakos, D. (1987). Pirate radio stations. Unpublished manuscript (personal copy).

Chalkou, M. (1990, January 21). Diafimisi to 1989 [Advertising in 1989]. *Kathimerini*, p. 36.

Chrima me to tsouvali ya propaganda [Money by the sackful for propaganda]. (1991, December 5). *Pontiki*, p. 38.

Clogg, R. (1979). *A short history of modern Greece.* Cambridge, England: Cambridge University Press.

Color TV arrives. (1979, August-September). *Greece: A monthly record,* p. 7.

Cowell, A. (1987, October 11). Greeks loosen curb (and tongues) on radio. *New York Times*, p. 19.

Danikas, D. (1991, May 5). Etsi ftiaxame ton 902 [That's how we made 902]. *To Vima*, p. 77.

Den plironi drachmi [It does not pay a drachma]. (1990, October). *Media*, 5, p. 7.

Diafimisi [Advertising]. (1983, January 27). *Economikos Tachydromos*, p. 56.

Diafimisi '90 [Advertising '90]. (1991, February). *Epikinonia*, 3, pp. 6-7.

Diafimisi '91 [Advertising '91]. (1992, April). *Epikinonia*, 8, pp. 4-13.

Dimitriou, M. (1985, November 24). To paraskinio tis paretisis [The resignation's background]. *To Vima*, p. 2.

Dimosiografika [Of journalism]. (1991, December 12). *Pontiki*, p. 4.

Dimotiko kanali anakinose o Kouvelas [Municipal channel announced by Kouvelas]. (1987, November 14). *Eleftherotypia*, p. 16.

Dinopoulos, A. (1987, July 18-25). 21 chronia hellinikis tileorasis [21 years of Greek television]. *Tilerama*, pp. 16-19.

Diokete dimosiografos ya ypothalpsi eglimatia [Journalist is prosecuted for protecting a criminal]. (1992, 21 July). *Pontiki*, p. 15.

Dizard, W. P. (1966). *Television: A world view*. Syracuse, N.Y.: Syracuse University Press.

Doulkeri, T. (1990). *Mesa mazikis epikinonias kai isotita ton dyo fylon* [Media of mass communication and the equality of the two genders]. Athens: Papazisis.

Doulkeri, T., and Dimitras, P. (1986). Greece. In H. J. Kleinsteuber, D. McQuail, and K. Sione (eds.), *Electronic media and politics in Western Europe* (pp. 135-147). Frankfurt: Campus Verlag.

Efthimiou, P. (1987, June 21). E proklisi tis eleftheris radiofonias [The challenge of free radio]. *To Vima*, p. 7.

Ekviasmos Evert [Blackmail by Evert]. (1987, February 19). *Ta Nea*, p. 5.

Emery, W. B. (1969). *National and international systems of broadcasting*. East Lansing: Michigan State University.

Enimerotiki erevna [Information survey]. (1991, April). *Epikinonia*, 5, pp. 18-20.

ERT: O Kouvelas mas kovi theates ke diafimises [ERT: Kouvelas is cutting our viewers and advertising]. (1989, January 12). *Eleftherotypia*, p. 19.

ESIEA. (1969, August 23). Enosis Syntakton Imerision Efimeridon Athinon [Union of Journalists of Athens Dailies]. Urgent Announcement. Mimeographed circular.

Esis ke e "E" [You and "E"]. (1992, July 21). *Eleftherotypia*, pp. 12-13.

Ethniki epityhia sto Davos [National success at Davos]. (1992, February 2). *Eleftheros Typos*, p. 1.

Evdomada pou perase [The past week]. (1992, May 15). *To Vima*, p. 69.

Evropaikes Ekdoses [European Pushishing]. (1992, May 24). *To Vima*,

p. 77.

Evropaiko boycotaz stin ERT [European boycott of ERT]. (1988, November 10). *Eleftherotypia*, p. 26.

Evropaiko "Savoir Vivre" ya ta kanalia [European "know how to live" for the channels]. (1992, July 23). *Eleftheros Typos*, p. 37.

Fate matia diafimisi [Feast your eyes on advertising]. (1991, July 9). *Ethnos*, p. 21.

Fatsis, I. (1986, December 2). Eleftheri radiofonia [Free radio]. *Ta Nea*, p. 2.

First Greek TV started in Athens. (1965, July 12). *Broadcasting*, p. 79.

Fitras, Y. (1988, December 3). Tileorasi Pirea ston aera [Pireaus television on the air]. *Eleftherotypia*, p. 11.

Flash profile. (1991, April). *Epikinonia*, 5, pp. 50-51.

Foreign agencies (1991, March 25). *Advertising Age*, p. S-34.

Foreign disk biz booming as European sound grows louder. (1979, October 10). *Variety*, p. 72.

France's La Cinq to file for bankruptcy. (1992, January 6). *Electronic Media*, p. 104.

Frazee, C. (1977). Church and state in Greece. In J. A. Koumoulides and D. Visvizi-Dontas (eds.), *Greece in transition: Essays in the history of modern Greece 1821-1974* (pp. 128-152). London: Zero.

Garoufali, M. (1982, December). The Greek press under fire. *Press Topic*, 4, p. 2.

Gemelos, D. M. (1972). The Greek character and television in Greece. Unpublished master's thesis, Brooklyn College, New York.

General Secretariat for the Press and Information. (1988). *The Greek press: Past and present*. Athens, Greece: Ethniko Typographio.

Global TV programming prices. (1992, April 6). *Variety*, p. 42.

Greece's disinformation daily. (November/December 1983). *Columbia Journalism Review*, pp. 5-7.

Greek armed forces TV accepting ads. (1967, October 30). *Advertising Age*, pp. 60-61.

Greek radio-TV law. (1976, February). *New Greece*, pp. 10-15.

Gregorakis, M. (1988, May 5). E yaya mas e ERT [Our grandmother ERT]. *Eleftherotypia*, p. 43.

Hasapopoulos, N. (1986, Dec. 7). Kleftes ke astinomy sta hertziana kymata [Cops and robbers on hertzian waves]. *To Vima*, p. 27.

Hatzidoulis, C. (1988, May 21). Embros, edo radiofonikos stathmos Athinon [Over, this is Athens radio station]. *Eleftherotypia*, pp. 32-33.

———. (1988, May 23). E proti zontani ekpombi [The first live broadcast]. *Eleftherotypia*, pp. 22-23.

———. (1988, May 27). E protes apopires ya idrysi radiostathmou [The first attempts to establish a radio station]. *Eleftherotypia*, p. 31.

————. (1988, June 1). E proti zontani ekpombi apo to Parnaso. *Eleftherotypia*, p. 10.

Helleniki Eteria Topikis Anaptixis ke Aftodyikisis [Hellenic Corporation for Local Development and Local Government. (1988). *Radiofono ke topiki aftodyikisi*. Athens: EETAA.

Helliniki tilepiratia stin proti selida [Greek television piracy on the front page]. (1990, October). *Media*, 5, p. 7.

Hoffman-Riem, W. (1987). National identity and cultural values: Broadcasting safeguards. *Journal of Broadcasting and Electronic Media*, 31 (1), pp. 57-72.

Holden, D. (1972). *Greece without columns: The making of modern Greece*. Philadelphia: Lippincott.

Iatrides, J. O. (1977). Greece and the origins of the cold war. In J. A. Koumoulides and D. Visvizi-Dontas (eds.), *Greece in transition: Essays in the history of modern Greece 1821-1974* (pp. 236-251). London: Zero.

Idiotiki tileorasi panelladikis emvelias [Private television with natiowide coverage]. (1991, March 27). *Thessaloniki*, p. 44.

International Press Institute. (1955). Government pressures on the press. *IPI Survey No. IV*.

Ipourgion Proedrias Kyverniseos, Geniki Diefthinsis Typou [Ministry of the Premiership, General Secretariat of the Press]. (1968). *Epitiris tou Ellinikou typou* [Anniversary of the Greek press]. Athens: Ethniko Typographio.

Isfora ya ERT [Dues for ERT]. (1991, March 10). *To Vima*, p. 67.

Kanelli, L. (1987, May 31). Kalimera Athina [Good morning Athens]. *To Vima*, p. 36.

————. (1988, February 28). Crach sti videoagora [Crash in the video market]. *To Vima*, p. 51.

Karzis, T. (1987). O Don Quixotis sto vasilio tis aftheresias [Don Quixotis in the kingdom of arbitrary]. *Eleftherotypia*, p. 9.

Kastoras, S. (1978). Greek television: A descriptive study of its programming and production as an approach to human communication. Unpublished doctoral dissertation, University of Southern California, Los Angeles.

Katagelli tin ERT e diakommatiki [Charges against ERT by the multi-party committee]. (1988, November 23). *Eleftherotypia*, p. 26.

Katastrofi gia tin Ellada to Davos [A catastrophe for Greece at Davos]. (1992, February 2). *Avriani*, p. 7.

Kayos, P. (1987, August 1). Video nea [Video news]. *Ta Nea*, p. 30.

Kazakopoulos, K. (1987, October 5). E Plaka kalodiaki [Plaka wired]. *Eleftherotypia*, p. 18.

Keshishoglou, J. E. (1962). The development of broadcasting in Greece. Master's thesis. University of Iowa, Iowa City.

Kodikas deontologias [Code of ethics]. (1991, July 6). *Eleftherotypia*, pp. 22-23.

Kokkalis ehi filous pantou [Mr. Kokkalis has friends everywhere]. (1991, July 12). *Anti*, p. 31.

Kominis, L. (1985). *E krisis tou Ellinikou typou* [The crisis of the Greek press]. Athens: Kaktos.

———. (1990). *Ta mystika tis dimosiografias* [The secrets of journalism]. Athens: Kastaniotis.

———. (1991, February). E krisis to kathimerinou typou [The crisis of the daily press]. *Epikinonia, 3*, pp. 40-41.

Kontoyannis, G. (1992, July 12). E Avghi plisiazi sti dysi tis [Avghi nears its dusk]. *Kathimerini*, p. 7.

Kontrarou, G. (1990, April 29). Ethniko symvoulio radiotileorasis [National radio-television council]. *To Vima*, p. 32.

Koray, C. (1988, October 27). Doriforiko [Satellite]. *Eleftherotypia*, p.18.

Korfiatis, C. (1992, June 14). E 200 megaliteres tou 1991 [The 200 largest of 1991]. *To Vima*, pp. D26-D28.

Korovelas, A. (1989, May 4). E etia tis simerinis vathias politikis crisis [The cause of today's deep political crisis]. *Eleftherotypia*, pp. 6-7.

Kotsaki, D. (1988, July 9). To Elliniko radiofono egine 50 chronon [Greek radio turns 50 years old]. *Diplo-Tilerama*, pp. 82-84.

Koumarianou, A. (1991, January 6). E gennisi tou Ellinikou typou [The birth of the Greek press]. *To Vima*, pp. B8-B9.

Koundouros, R. (1987, December 11). Eleftheri radiofonia [free radio]. *Eleftherotypia*, p. 9.

Koutouzis, V. (1990, January 29). Akrivi mas ERT [Our dear (expensive) ERT]. *Eleftherotypia*, pp. 24-25.

———. (1990, January 30). Akrivi mas ERT, #2 [Our dear (expensive) ERT]. *Eleftherotypia*, pp. 14-15.

Ktenas, S. (1991a, December 29). Disekatomiria meta mousikis [Billions with music]. *To Vima*, p. D14.

———. (1991b, December 29). Diplasiasmos poliseon ke kasetopiratias [Doubling of sales and cassette piracy]. *To Vima*, p. D14.

Kyklofories tou protou examinou [The circulations of the first six months]. (1991, September 5). *Pontiki*, p. 28.

Kyriazidis, N. (1990, July 28). E chronies ton megalon kerdon [The years of big profits]. *Anti*, pp. 28-31.

Kyrtsos, G. (1992, February 2). Mystirio Alafouzou [The Alafouzo's mystery]. *Eleftheros Typos*, pp. 14-15.

Kyvernisi: Mona-zyga dika mas stin TV [Government: All ours on TV]. (1988, November 22). *Eleftherotypia*, p. 31.

Lacopoulos, G. (1989, August 6). O magicos cosmos ton hertzianon [The magical world of hertzian waves]. *To Vima*, pp. 31-33.

———. (1990, March 4). Ta kommata ston aera [The parties on the air]. *To Vima*, p. 4.

Legg, K. R. (1969). *Politics in modern Greece*. Stanford, Calif.: Stanford University Press.

———. (1977). The nature of the modern Greek state. In J. A. Koumoulides and D. Visvizi-Dontas (eds.), *Greece in transition: Essays in the history of modern Greece 1821-1974* (pp. 283-296). London: Zero.

Lionarakis, N. (1988). E symvoli tis T.A. stin anaptixy topikis radiofonias [The contribution of local government in the development of local radio]. In Hellenic Corporation for Local Development and Local Government [Helliniki Eteria Topikis Anaptixis ke Aftokyikisis] (eds.), *Radiofono ke topiki aftodyikisis* (pp. 131-174). Athens: EETAA.

Louketo ston aera [Lock on the air]. (1991, July 25). *Eleftheros Typos*, p. 3.

Lykiardopoulou, C. (1991, April 20-26). Apetite xekatharisma [Clean up is demanded]. *Tiletheatis*, p. 30.

———. (1991, May 28-31). Ya tis metataxes stin kratiki TV [About the transfers at state TV]. *Tiletheatis*, p. 34.

———. (1991, July 22-28). ERT: Ke omos oli ta yxeran [ERT: And yet they all knew it]. *Tiletheatis*, p. 38.

Macridis, A. (1987). Presenting "Selides." Unpublished manuscript (personal copy).

Makris, P. (1988, May 21). Kerees doryforikis se kathe spiti ke gytonia. [Satellite antennas in every home and neighborhood]. *Eleftherotypia*, p. 20.

Mandrou, I. (1991, June 9). To megalo fagopoti [The huge feast]. *To Vima*, p. 59.

———. (1991, July 21). Katargite e aftepaggelti dioxi gia periivrisi archis [The automatic prosecution for insulting the authorities is canceled]. *To Vima*, p. A25.

Margiori, D. (1987). Star radio. Unpublished manuscript (personal copy).

Mass media. (1991, February). *Epikinonia, 3*, p. 4.

Mayer, K. (1957). *Istoria tou Ellinikou typou* [The history of the Greek press]. Athens: Dimopoulos.

McCain, T. A., and Lowe, G. F. (1990). Localism in Western European radio broadcasting: Untangling the wireless. *Journal of Communication, 40* (1), pp. 86-101.

McDonald, R. (1983). *The pillar and the tinderbox: The Greek press and the dictatorship*. New York: Marion Boyars.

McNeil, W. H. (1978). *The metamorphosis of Greece since WWII.* Chicago: The University of Chicago Press.

Merrill, J. C. (1974). *The imperative of freedom: A philosophy of journalistic autonomy.* New York: Hastings House.

Mises alithies ke ta psemata tou Kouvela [The half-truths and lies of Kouvela]. (1991, November 14). *Pontiki,* p. 34.

Monomachia ya tin TV [Battle for TV]. (1984, October 16). *Ta Nea,* p. 1.

Mousiki erevna [Musical survey]. (1991, April). *Epikinonia,* 5, pp. 14-15.

Mouzelis, N. (1978). *Modern Greece: Facets of underdevelopment.* New York: Holmes & Meier.

Na grafete oti "pame kala" [You should write that "we are doing well"]. (1991, July 5). *Pontiki,* p. 34.

Nea dianomi rolon ston Rizospasti [New roles in Rizospastis]. (1991, April 21). *To Vima,* p. 76.

Nekronoun ta kanalia [The channels are going dead]. (1988, November 29). *Eleftherotypia,* p. 26.

Neofotistos, M. (1988, March 18). Programma TV se cassettes apo to demo [TV programming on cassettes from the city]. *Eleftherotypia,* p. 12.

New radio TV network to reach all Greece. (1971, December 31). *New York Times,* p. 13.

New U.S. radio in Greece. (1949, November 21). *New York Times,* p. 5.

Nicolakopoulos, D. (1990, November 25). Epigontos montaz [Emergency editing]. *To Vima,* p. 68.

Nicolopoulos, D. (1991, October 13). Tripes e apothikes tou demou [Holes in the city warehouses]. *To Vima,* p. 61.

Nomoi [Laws]. (1988, September 12). *Ephimeris tis kyverniseos,* p. 1.

Olson, K. F. (1966). *The history makers: The press of Europe from its beginnings through 1965.* Baton Rouge, LA: Louisiana State University.

Olympus ke e ERT-1 [Olympus and ERT-1]. (1984, December 23). *Ta Nea,* p. 10.

132 kathimerines efimerides, 115 evdomadiees [132 dailies, 115 weeklies]. (1991, August 9). *Pontiki,* pp. 26-27.

1000 tis ERT ypo metataxi [1000 of ERT (employees) to be transfered]. (1991, May 7). *Eleftheros Typos,* p. 3.

Papachristos, G. (1987, June 28). O radiostathmos tis dichonias [The radio station of divisiveness]. *To Vima,* p. 26.

———. (1990, September 30). Pios elengchi ta kanalia [Who controls the channels]. *To Vima,* p. 78.

———. (1990, October 7). Ypopsifiy dimarchy choris programma ya ta hertziana [Mayoral candidates without programs for the hertzian waves]. *To Vima,* p. 70.

————. (1990, November 18). O emphilios polemos sto KKE epektinete ke sta hertziana [The civil war in the KKE expands to the airwaves]. *To Vima*, p. 76.

————. (1990, December 16). Pros trito gyro paremvaseon sta radiotileoptika [Toward a third round of interference in broadcasting]. *To Vima*, p. 68.

————. (1990, December 23). Endokyvernitikes syngrouses ya tis diefthinses sta kanalia [Intragovernmental collisions about the administration of the channels]. *To Vima*, p. 78.

————. (1991, February 24). Yperparagogi dimosiografon [Over-production of journalists]. *To Vima*, p. A45.

————. (1991, March 3). Ti symvaini me tin Kathimerini [What's happening with Kathimerini]. *To Vima*, p. 76.

————. (1991, March 17). To chroniko enos kavga [The account of a fight]. *To Vima*, p. 76.

————. (1991, March 31). Pedio machis o Rizospastis [Battlefield Rizospastis]. *To Vima* p. 76.

————. (1991, April 7). Rizos kata Tegopoulou [Rizos vs. Tegopoulos]. *To Vima*, p. 68.

————. (1991a, April 14). Symvivastiki lysi ston Rizospasti [Compromise solution at Rizospastis]. *To Vima*, p. A45.

————. (1991b, April 14). Ke peious stathmous akoune [And which stations they listen to]. *To Vima*, p. 77.

————. (1991c, April 14). Pia kanalia vlepoun e Hellines [Which channels Greeks watch]. *To Vima*, p. 76.

————. (1991, May 12). Ta kratika kanalia se ptohefsi [State channels in bankruptcy]. *To Vima*, p. 77.

————. (1991, May 19). Chora opou anthizy piratia [A country where piracy blooms]. *To Vima*, p. 77.

————. (1991, May 26). O demosiografos ophily [The journalist is obligated]. *To Vima*, p. 76.

————. (1991, June 23). Diaspasi ke sta hertziana [Split also on the airwaves]. *To Vima*, p. 76.

————. (1991, September 29). Pos to Mega pire to rebound [How Mega got the rebound]. *To Vima*, p. 76.

————. (1991, November 3). E fthinousa poria ton efimeridon [The deteriorating course of newspapers]. *To Vima*, p. A48.

————. (1991, November 11). Ti symvaini me ti Nea Vradyni? [What's happening with New Vradyni?]. *To Vima*, p. A50.

————. (1991, November 17). Se pia kanalia tha dothi e adia ya panneladiki emvelia [Which stations will be given a license for nationwide coverage]. *To Vima*, p. 76.

————. (1991, December 15). Ta entypa tou DOL kyriarha kai stin agora ton diafimiseon [DOL publications dominate the advertising market]. *To Vima*, p. A60.

———. (1991, December 29). Serial tou paralogou sta idiotika kanalia [Serial of the absurd at the private stations]. *To Vima*, p. 76.

———. (1992, January 12). Ta hertziana sto eleos ton piraton [The hertzian waves at the mercy the pirates]. *To Vima*, p. 76.

———. (1992, February 2). Pia kanalia tha paroun adia [Which channels will get a license]. *To Vima*, p. 68.

———. (1992, March 1). Meta to Pascha e adies [The licenses after Easter]. *To Vima*, p. 68.

———. (1992, April 12). O tzogos anevazi tis kyclofories ton tileoptikon periodikon [Lotteries are lifting circulations of television magazines]. *To Vima*, p. 76.

———. (1992, April 19). O polemos tis diafimisis chtipay to radiofono [The advertising war is hurting radio]. *To Vima*, p. 76.

———. (1992, May 17). ERT, prika tis exousias [ERT, dowry to the administration]. *To Vima*, p. 76.

———. (1992, May 24). Ta polla prosopa tis krisis [The many faces of the crisis]. *To Vima*, p. 76.

Papachristoudi, M. (1992, July, 18). Psachnonte ya diafimises [Searching for advertisements]. *Eleftheros Typos*, p. 37.

Papacosma, V. S. (1979). Post-junta Greece in historical perspective. *Indiana Social Studies Quarterly*, *32*, pp. 122-141.

Papadopoulos, G. (1968). *To pistevo mas* [Our creed]. Athens: Geniki Diefthinsis Typou.

Papaioannou, A. (1988, June 8). Perimenoun pos ke pos ta idiotika [Waiting for private (TV)]. *48 Ores*, p. 10.

Papandonakou, A. (1987). Kanali 1. Unpublished manuscript (personal copy).

Papandreou, A. (1970). *Democracy at gunpoint*. Garden City, N.Y.: Doubleday.

Papaspyrou, I. (1987, October). Radio-eleftheri [Radio-free]. *To Tetarto*, pp. 67-70.

Papathanassopoulos, S. (1989, June-July). Greece: Nothing is more permanent than the provisional. *Intermedia*, *17*, 29-35.

Paraschos, M. (1979, January). Numerous obstacles hinder formal training in Greece. *Journalism Educator*, *34* (1), pp.114-115.

———. (1983). Legal constraints on the press in post junta Greece: 1974-77. *Journalism Quarterly*, *60* (1), pp. 48-53.

Parte thesi [Take a stand]. (1991, October 6). *Ethnos*, pp. 18-19.

Pavlopoulos, P. (1991, October 6). Nomikes apopses tis pliroforisis [The legal views of information]. *Kathimerini*, p. 12.

Pelorio thema [A huge issue]. (1991, September 29). *Ethnos*, p. 1.

Periodikos typos: pou pai; [Where is the periodical press going?]. (1991, July 18). *Pontiki*, p. 25.

Petropoulou, K. (1986, December 16). Radiofoniko dimotiko chroniko [Municipal radio chronicle]. *Ta Nea*, p. 5.

Petroutsou, M. (1988, August 24). Kaftes mazes vlakias [Hot masses of stupidity]. *Ta Nea*, p. 27.

Polemos petrelaion [Oil wars]. (1991, July 6). *Eleftherotypia*, p. 45.

Politiki grammi dikaioma tis idioktisias [Political direction is the right of ownership]. (1991, October 3). *Pontiki*, p. 33.

Pou ofilete e crisi ston typo [what is the source of the crisis of the press]. (1992, July 9). *Pontiki*, p. 17.

Pretenteris, I. (1986, December 7). Pos fthasame sti radiofoniki anixi [How we arrived at radio spring]. *To Vima*, p. 24.

———. (1989, July 30). Pos fthasame stin eleftheri TV [How we arrived at free TV]. *To Vima*, p. 8.

Prosfiyes kata Evert apo tous pros metataxi [Grievences towards Evert from those to be transferred]. (1991, October 3). *Pontiki*, p. 34.

Proti mera, proto to Mega channel [First day, first is Mega Channel]. (1989, November 22). *Eleftherotypia*, p. 22.

Proto synolika to kratiko radiofono [Collectively state radio is first]. (1988, July 27). *Eleftherotypia*, p. 26.

Protogyrou, M. (1988, October 31). Timorisan tous tris [They punished the three]. *Eleftherotypia*, p. 26.

———. (1989, July 26). Tarazi ta thola kanalia e adia ya idiotiki TV [The license for private TV is disturbing the muddy channels]. *Eleftherotypia*, p. 26.

———. (1990, January 13). 102 kanalia ekanan etisi ya sychnotites [102 channels filed applications for frequencies]. *Eleftherotypia*, p. 11.

Protogyrou, M., and Petroutsou, M. (1989, January 12). Heri synergasias ERT pros Pirea [Hand of cooperation by ERT towards Pireaus]. *Eleftherotypia*, p. 26.

———. (1989, February 13). Epistratevete o "Agnostos Polemos" ["Agnostos Polemos" is being drafted]. *Eleftherotypia*, p. 26.

———. (1989, March 2). Pluralismos ke laikismos [Pluralism and populism]. *Eleftherotypia*, p. 26.

———. (1989, September 1). O rolos tis radiofonias [The role of radio broadcasting]. *Eleftherotypia*, p. 26.

———. (1989, October 20). 26 ores to 24oro [26 hours a day]. *Eleftherotypia*, p. 26.

———. (1989, November 15). Kontogeorgis: Elima ke to '90 [Kontogeorgis: Budget deficit also in 1990]. *Eleftherotypia*, p. 26.

———. (1990, February 1). Ston isagelea ipalilos tis ERT [ERT employee to the prosecutor]. *Eleftherotypia*, p. 26.

Radio apo ta idia [Radio of the same]. (1987, June 1). *Ta Nea*, p. 18.

Radiofonia en Elladi [Radio in Greece]. (1956). *Neoteron engyclopedico lexicon helios.* Athens: Helios.

Radiofonikos stathmos Thessalonikis [Thessaloniki radio station]. (1945, April). *Radiofonia-Tileorasis*, p. 14.

Roumeliotis, A. (1988, May 10). E protes adies [The first licenses]. *Eleftherotypia*, p. 27.

———. (1988, May 25). Proti se akroamatikotita [First in listenership]. *Eleftherotypia*, p. 27.

———. (1988, July 14). Proti e choris anasa ekpombi [First, the 'choris anasa' program]. *Eleftherotypia*, p. 27.

———. (1988, October 17). Syntonistiki epitropi idioton [Coordinating committee of private (broadcasters)]. *Eleftherotypia*, p. 27.

———. (1988, October 31). Eikosi dyo stathmi ston ourano tis Thessalonikis [Twenty-two stations in the skies of Thessaloniki]. *Eleftherotypia*, p. 27.

———. (1988, November 8). Yorgos: yme apogoitevmenos apo tin eleftheri radiofonia [George: I'm disappointed by free radio]. *Eleftherotypia*, p. 2.

———. (1989, January 20). E proti apergia [The first strike]. *Eleftherotypia*, p. 27.

———. (1989, February 9). 172 Adies se 45 lepta [172 licenses in 45 minutes]. *Eleftherotypia*, p. 27.

———. (1989, March 7). Apo chtes ston aera to radio Amvrakia [Since yesterday radio Amvrakia is on the air]. *Eleftherotypia*, p. 27.

———. (1989, April 10). Eklogikes fourtounes sta radiokymata [Election tidal waves on the airwaves]. *Eleftherotypia*, pp. 24-25.

———. (1989, April 17). Radio chaos enopsi ton eklogon [Radio chaos facing the elections]. *Eleftherotypia*, p. 27.

———. (1989, April 21). Allous akoune e mikri ke allous e megali [Youths listen to different (stations) than the elders]. *Eleftherotypia*, p. 27.

———. (1989, May 2). Sychnotites se alexiptotistes, ochi sto Anti [Frequencies to parachutists, not to Anti]. *Eleftherotypia*, p. 27.

———. (1989, September 25). Fthinoporini sfygmometrisi [Autumn survey]. *Eleftherotypia*, p. 27.

———. (1990, January 11). Crisi apo to pantrema ton pente [Crisis from the marriage of the five]. *Eleftherotypia*, p. 27.

———. (1990, January 29). Pyei pyran ta chrimata apo tis diafimises [Who received the money from advertising]. *Eleftherotypia*, p. 27.

———. (1990, February 6). Analytika e akroamatikotites [Listenership analytically]. *Eleftherotypia*, p. 27.

————. (1990, July 9). Enas neos stathmos sto Agrinio [A new station in Agrinio]. *Eleftherotypia*, p. 27.

————. (1991). *Eimaste ston aera* [We are on the air]. Thessaloniki: Paratiritis.

————. (1991, April 23). Afinoun tous paranomous, eklisan ton nomino [They do not close the illegal (stations), they closed the legal one]. *Eleftherotypia*, p. 27.

————. (1991, July 19). Rock FM: Eminan me tis kokkines epitayes sto heri [Rock FM: They were left holding the red checks]. *Eleftherotypia*, p. 27.

————. (1991, July 23). Pos allaxe o radiochartis tis Attikis [How the radio map changed in Attiki]. *Eleftherotypia*, p. 27.

————. (1991, July 25). Ke to potiri xechilise [The glass runneth over]. *Eleftherotypia*, p. 27.

————. (1991, July 26). Pios, pios, pios moro mou, pios? [Who, who, who baby, who?] *Eleftherotypia*, p. 27.

————. (1991, October 11). Enas stathmos "anatolikos" [An "eastern" station]. *Eleftherotypia*, p. 27.

————. (1991, October 16). Idou e Rhodos [Here is Rhodos]. *Eleftherotypia*, p. 27.

————. (1991, October 18). Edo Amaliada [This is Amaliada]. *Eleftherotypia*, p. 27.

————. (1991, November 25). O nomos yparchi mono ya tous microus [The law exists only for the little ones]. *Eleftherotypia*, p. 35.

————. (1991, December 9). Ti krivy sto panteloni tou to kratos [What the state is hiding in its pants]. *Eleftherotypia*, p. 35.

————. (1992, January 7). Kegome [I'm in flames]. *Eleftherotypia*, p. 41.

————. (1992, March 2). Den theloun na plirosoun ageliosimo [They do not want to pay the tax]. *Eleftherotypia*, p. 31.

————. (1992, July 18). Mia pita ya to kalokairi [A pie for the summer]. *Eleftherotypia*, p. 26.

Rousseas, S. (1967). *The death of a democracy.* New York: Grove.

Roussis, N. (1987, February 16). Mati ston cosmo [Eye to the world]. *Ta Nea*, p. 21.

Sadgwick, A. C. (1953, June 7). Greece's villages get world's news. *New York Times*, p. 12.

Schwab, P., and Frangos, G. D. (eds.). (1973). *Greece under the junta.* New York: Facts on File.

Se kanali fantasma katefyge o Andreas [Andreas went on a ghost channel]. (1989, October 31). *Eleftherotypia*, p. 6.

Selida tou typou [Press page]. (1991, October 17). *Pontiki*, p. 2.

Selida tou typou [Press page]. (1991, November 14). *Pontiki*, p. 2.

Selida tou typou [Press page]. (1992, January 18). *Pontiki*, p. 2.

Selida tou typou [Press page]. (1992, March 5). *Pontiki,* p. 2.

17 minises ekanan Americani paragogi [17 suits filed by by American producers]. (1991, October 17). *Pontiki,* p. 15.

Sims, R. J. (1991, April). Pluralism in transition: Cultural implications of the legalization of private and municipal radio broadcasting in Greece. Paper presented at the Broadcast Education Association Convention, Las Vegas, Nev.

Singrisi hellenikou-xenou programmatos [Comparison of Greek-foreign programming]. (1987, July 17). *Pontiki,* p. 30.

Sky profile. (1991, February). *Epikinonia, 3,* pp. 52-53.

Someritis: Den antexa tis juntes [Someritis: I couldn't take the juntas]. (1989, November 4). *Eleftherotypia,* p. 23.

Sotirelis, G. (1990, July 20). Radiotileorasi ke nomimotita [Broadcasting and the law]. *Ta Nea,* p. 4.

Spatali ekatomyrion [Waste of millions]. (1991, October 3). *Pontiki,* p. 34.

Stafyla, L. (1987, December 7). Yati diafonite? [Why do you disagree?]. *Ta Nea,* pp. 10-11.

Stamatelou, C. (1986, December 8). Interview with ERT-1 director general N. Soteriadis. *Ta Nea,* p. 21.

Stern, L. (1977). *The wrong horse.* New York: Times Books.

Stratos, C. (1991, March 3). E anavathmisi tis . . . ERT [The renewal of ERT]. *To Vima,* p. 77.

———.(1991, June 2). To video stin Hellada [Video in Greece]. *To Vima,* p. 77.

Syngentrotiki diafimistiki dapani 1990 [Total advertising expenditures 1990]. (1991, January). *Media, 8,* p. 21.

Terasties technikes elipses [Tremendous technical shortages]. (1985, January 16). *Ta Nea,* p. 27.

Thalassinos, G. (1991, April). Istoria misous ke erota [Story of hate and love]. *Epikinonia, 5,* pp. 14-15.

Theodorakis, S. (1991, February). Ena prochirographima ya radio-TV [A rough draft about radio-TV]. *Epikinonia, 3,* pp. 49-51.

Theologitou, R. (1987, March 17). Svistike kata lathos [Erased by mistake]. *Ta Nea,* p. 21.

Ti tha giny me ta kanalia [What is going to be done with the channels]. (1986, December 14). *To Vima,* pp. 31-34.

Ti vlepoun, ti akoun, ti diavazoun [What they see, what they hear, what they read]. (1990, December 2). *To Vima,* p. 78.

Tileorasi me syndromi [Television by subscription]. (1991, February). *Epikinonia, 3,* p. 47.

To kalathi tis nikokyras yemizi me video [The house wife's basket is filling with video]. (1991, October 19-25). *Tiletheatis,* pp. 14-15.

To Mega sarose stis ekloges [Mega swept in the elections]. (1990, October 28). *To Vima*, p. 78.

To proto kai to telefteo [The first and the last]. (1991, July 12). *Pontiki*, p. 36.

To syntagma tis Elladas [The constitution of Greece]. (1990). Athens: Pontiki.

Tolios, A. (1986, November 12). Ne sto elefthero radiofono [Yes to free radio]. *Ta Nea*, p. 25.

Tria chronia Epsilon FM [Three years of Epsilon FM]. (1991, August 3-9). *Tiletheatis*, p. 33.

Triantafillopoulos, M. (1987, March 5). Genithike eleftheri [It was born free]. *Ta Nea*, p. 23.

Triponta kerdi ya ta kratika [Three-point profits for the state (stations)]. (1988, June 8). *24 Ores*, p. 10.

Tromokratia kai chrima [Terrorism and money]. (1991, October 3). *Pontiki*, pp. 18-19, 23.

Troupis, K. (1991, June 29-July 5). Peous radiostathmous protimoun e Athineoi [Which stations Athenians prefer]. *Diplo-Tilerama*, p. 36.

Tsampras, Y. (1985, April 6). Deftero programma [Second program]. *Tilerama*, p. 21.

———. (1985, April 27). ERT-2. *Tilerama*, p. 16.

Tsoucalas, C. (1969). *The Greek tragedy.* Baltimore: Penguin.

29e kentriki epitropi PASOK [29th Central Committee of PASOK]. (1989, August 7). *Eleftherotypia*, p. 21.

Tzalavras, T. (1991, February). Apostolos Kratsas [Interview with the Minister of Transportation and Communications]. *Epikinonia, 3*, pp. 8-9.

UNESCO. (1947). *Report of the commission on technical needs in press-radio-television.* Paris: UNESCO.

Vagena, N. (1989, September 2). [Interview with] Nikos Syfounakis. *Eleftherotypia*, pp. 10-11.

Vainakis, V. (1991, April). Mousiko kouti [Music box]. *Epikinonia, 5*, pp. 45-49.

Vatikiotis, P. J. (1974). *Greece: A political essay. The Washington Papers, Vol. 22.* London: Sage.

Venizelos, E. (1989). *E raditileoptiki ekrixi* [The radio-television explosion]. Thessaloniki: Paratiritis.

Vgikan ta "megala mahairia" [The long knives are out]. (1991, July 12). *Pontiki*, pp. 36-37.

Vgontas, A. (1991, July 14). Tris enstases ya tous kodikes deontologias [Three objections about the codes of ethics]. *To Vima*, p. 68.

Vidos, K., and Papadopoulou, M. (1991a, December 22). Ne e ochi stis diafimises pechnidion [Yes or no to toy advertising]. *To Vima*, p. B2.

————.(1991b, December 22). Ta pedia anisycha stin epithesi tis TV [Children unruly in the TV attack]. *To Vima*, p. B2.

Vlachos, H. (1972). The colonels and the press. In R. Clogg and G. Yannopoulos (eds), *Greece under military rule* (pp. 59-74). New York: Basic Books.

Vlastari, G. (1991, February). E krisis tou periodikou typou [The crisis of the periodical press]. *Epikinonia, 3*, pp. 39-40.

Vlavianos A. (1987). A few words in the night. Unpublished manuscript (personal copy).

Vlavianou, A. (1991, October 13). Kathe nomos radiofono [Each province a radio station]. *To Vima*, p. 24.

Voros, F. K. (1978). Current educational reforms: An overview. *Comparative Education Review, 22*, pp. 7-10.

Votsis, G. (1988, October 31). Kakotechni ke entechni propaganda [The fine art and bad art of propaganda]. *Eleftherotypia*, p. 9.

Wittner, L. S. (1982). *American intervention in Greece: 1943-1947.* New York: Columbia University.

Yobazolias, M. (1987, November 16). Den allaxame [We did not change]. *Eleftherotypia*, p. 19.

Zaharopoulos, T. (1985). Foreign mass communication in Greece: Its impact on Greek culture and influence on Greek society. Doctoral dissertation, Southern Illinois University at Carbondale. *Dissertation Abstracts International, 47*, p. 03-A.

————. (1990, March). The dimensions of Greek television. Paper presented at the Broadcast Education Association Convention, Las Vegas, Nev.

Index

About the Authors

THIMIOS ZAHAROPOULOS is Associate Professor and Director of graduate studies in Communication at Pittsburg State University in Kansas. He also taught for two years at the American College of Greece in Athens, and worked briefly in Greek television production. Zaharopoulos' research includes press-related national images, intercultural communication, and the press and foreign policy.

MANNY E. PARASCHOS is Professor of Journalism and the first Dean of Emerson College's European Institute for International Communication in Maastricht, the Netherlands. He has taught at the University of Missouri and the University of Arkansas at Little Rock, where he chaired the Department of Journalism and founded the *Journal for Arkansas Journalism Studies* and the state's Urban Journalism Workshop for minority high school students. He is the editor of *Greece and the American Press*.